DEVELOPMENTS IN TOURISM RESEARCH

ADVANCES IN TOURISM RESEARCH

Series Editor: **Professor Stephen J. Page**
University of Stirling, UK
s.j.page@stir.ac.uk

Advances in Tourism Research series publishes monographs and edited volumes that comprise state-of-the-art research findings, written and edited by leading researchers working in the wider field of tourism studies. The series has been designed to provide a cutting edge focus, for researchers interested, in tourism, particularly the management issues now facing decision-makers, policy analysts and the public sector. The audience is much wider than just academics and each book seeks to make a significant contribution to the literature in the field of study by not only reviewing the state of knowledge relating to each topic but also questioning some of the prevailing assumptions and research paradigms which currently exist in tourism research. The series also aims to provide a platform for further studies in each area by highlighting key research agendas, which will stimulate further debate and interest in the expanding area of tourism research. The series is always willing to consider new ideas for innovative and scholarly books, inquiries should be made directly to the Series Editor.

Published:

For other titles in the series visit: www.elsevier.com/locate/series/aitr

Related Elsevier Journals — sample copies available on request
Annals of Tourism Research
International Journal of Hospitality Management
Tourism Management

DEVELOPMENTS IN TOURISM RESEARCH

EDITED BY

JOHN TRIBE

University of Surrey, Guildford, UK

DAVID AIREY

University of Surrey, Guildford, UK

ELSEVIER

Amsterdam • Boston • Heidelberg • London • New York • Oxford
Paris • San Diego • San Francisco • Singapore • Sydney • Tokyo

Elsevier
Linacre House, Jordan Hill, Oxford OX2 8DP, UK
Radarweg 29, PO Box 211, 1000 AE Amsterdam, The Netherlands

First edition 2007

British Library Cataloguing in Publication Data
A catalogue record for this book is available from the British Library

Library of Congress Cataloging-in-Publication Data
A catalog record for this book is available from the Library of Congress

ISBN: 978-0-080-45328-6

Cover photo "Discovering Tourism" by John Tribe.

For information on all Elsevier publications
visit our website at books.elsevier.com

Printed and bound in The Netherlands

07 08 09 10 11 10 9 8 7 6 5 4 3 2 1

Contents

Foreword

As part of its celebrations in 2006, to mark 40 years of tourism and hospitality studies, the School of Management at the University of Surrey held an international conference with the title *Cutting Edge Research in Tourism*. This attracted in the region of 200 participants from around the world who presented 150 or so papers and who over 4 days learned about and debated developments, themes and challenges in tourism studies. It was clear from the presentations and discussions that tourism research is thriving and is progressing in a range of new and exciting directions. The idea for this book came from these new directions with the idea of capturing what is happening in tourism research by making a selection from the papers at the conference.

The introductory chapter and the introductions to Sections 2 and 3 of the book provide an overview and commentary on the directions. The papers were then selected to illustrate the kind of work that is being taken forward by researchers in the field with the final chapter pointing to some of the new challenges. Obviously the selection of 15 from the 150 papers that were presented at the conference was a difficult task. Equally challenging was the attempt to reflect the many different faces of tourism research. Inevitably there are omissions. The authors take full responsibility for omissions but hope that the papers that were selected amply demonstrate what was obvious at the conference that tourism research is thriving.

David Airey and John Tribe
Guildford, UK
April 2007

Acknowledgments

The 15 papers in this volume were selected from the 150 or so papers presented at the Conference held at the University of Surrey in June 2006. These 150 papers were all initially refereed and edited by colleagues at the University of Surrey and we are grateful for their support, particularly to Dr. George Papageorgiou and Dr. Edit Szivas who undertook the editing for the CD of the conference proceedings.

The Conference at Surrey could not have taken place without the generous support of the British Academy and Guildford Borough Council as well as the recognition of AIEST, the Association for Tourism in Higher Education, PATA, The Tourism Society, TTRA, and the UN World Tourism Organization. We are grateful for their support and indeed for the support of the School of Management at the University.

Contributors

DAVID AIREY
  University of Surrey, Guildford, UK.
David Airey is Professor of Tourism Management and Pro Vice-Chancellor at the University of Surrey. He has been involved in tourism since 1975. In 2005 he co-edited with John Tribe the *International Handbook of Tourism Education* published by Elsevier. He received the EuroCHRIE President's Award in 2005 and the United Nations World Tourism Organization Ulysses Award in 2006.

ALISTAIR ANDERSON
  The Robert Gordon University, Aberdeen, Scotland.
Alistair Anderson is Professor of Entrepreneurship and Director of the Centre for Entrepreneurship at Aberdeen Business School. He is particularly interested in the social aspects of interaction and entrepreneurship. Current themes being explored are rural entrepreneurship, social capital, social constructions and associated topic areas.

SUSANNE BECKEN
  Lincoln University, Canterbury and Ministry of Tourism, Wellington, New Zealand.
Susanne Becken is a Principal Research Officer at Lincoln University and is seconded to the New Zealand Ministry of Tourism. She has completed a range of consultancy projects in tourism, energy use and climate change. She is on the editorial board of the *Journal of Sustainable Tourism*, acted as a contributing author to the fourth IPCC report on climate change and is an invited member of the Climate Change and Tourism Expert Team of the World Meteorological Organisation.

SCOTT CAMPBELL
  Eagle Technology, Wellington, New Zealand.
Scott Campbell is a GIS Analyst for Eagle Technology Ltd., Wellington, NZ. He has worked in the field of GIS for over 12 years in both the UK and for the last 3 years in New Zealand. While in the UK he led a team within ESRI (UK), which was responsible for the creation of the *MapObjects* embeddable GIS technology for ESRI Inc. as well as contributing to the *Exploring ArcObjects* series of books. He is currently working on projects involving the application of GIS technology to the Postal Industry.

DONNA CHAMBERS

Napier University, Edinburgh, Scotland.

Donna Chambers has a background in the tourism public sector in her native Jamaica and in tourism education and research in the UK. Her research interests include tourism and politics, heritage representation, discourse theory and post colonial perspectives. She is currently a lecturer in tourism and programme leader for postgraduate tourism programmes at Napier University.

CHRIS COOPER

University of Queensland, Ipswich, Queensland, Australia.

Chris Cooper is Foundation Professor and Head of the School of Tourism, the University of Queensland, Australia. He is the co-editor of the journal *Current Issues in Tourism* and the author of numerous leading tourism texts and research volumes. He currently Chairs the Education Council of the UN World Tourism Organization.

ROSS CULLEN

Lincoln University, Canterbury, New Zealand.

Ross Cullen is Professor of Resource Economics at Lincoln University. His research spans several areas in environmental and resource economics. His research in tourism has focused on its environmental effects, infrastructure to manage those effects and the yield from public sector services for tourism.

MARIALAURA DI DOMENICO

Unviersity of Cambridge, Cambridge, UK.

Marialaura Di Domenico's research includes analyses of tourism enterprises and social entrepreneurship in terms of issues of regional development, regeneration and community-led initiatives.

LARRY DWYER

University of New South Wales, Sydney, NSW, Australia.

Larry Dwyer is Qantas Professor of Travel and Tourism Economics at the University of New South Wales, Australia. He publishes widely in the areas of tourism economics, management and policy. Larry is a member of the International Academy for the Study of Tourism and the International Advisory Board of the Business Enterprises for Sustainable Tourism Education Network (BESTEN).

PETER FORSYTH

Monash University, Clayton, Victoria, Australia.

Peter Forsyth has been Professor of Economics at Monash University, Australia since 1997. Most of his research has been on applied microeconomics, with particular reference to the economics of air transport, tourism economics and the economics of regulation.

HAROLD GOODWIN

Leeds Metropolitan University, Leeds, UK.

Harold Goodwin is Director of the International Centre for Responsible Tourism, and is a partner in the Pro-Poor Tourism Partnership. He wrote the initial paper on 'Sustainable

Tourism and Poverty Elimination' for the British government in 1998, and drafted 'Tourism and Poverty Alleviation' for the UN World Tourism Organization in 2002.

TONY GRIFFIN
University of Technology, Sydney, NSW, Australia.
Tony Griffin is in the School of Leisure, Sport and Tourism at the University of Technology, Sydney. With a professional background in environmental planning, he has published extensively on subjects ranging from hotel development to sustainable tourism. Much of his recent research has focused on understanding the nature and quality of visitor experiences in a variety of contexts, including urban tourism precincts, national parks and wine tourism.

CATHY GUTHRIE
The Robert Gordon University, Aberdeen, Scotland.
Cathy Guthrie is Hon. Secretary of the Tourism Management Institute. After 14 years in public sector destination management, she researched the impact of ICT on the role of TICs in destination marketing to gain her MSc at Robert Gordon University. Her PhD research focuses on destination interactions, and she retains an interest in all aspects of destination management, in particular, training, tourism policy and destination ICT.

C. MICHAEL HALL
University of Canterbury, Christchurch, New Zealand.
C. Michael Hall is Professor of Marketing in the College of Business and Economics, University of Canterbury, New Zealand and Docent, Department of Geography, University of Oulu, Finland. Co-editor of the journal *Current Issues in Tourism* he has published widely on a range of tourism related topics. Current research and teaching interests focus on human mobility and regional development, gastronomy, place branding and tourism and global environmental change.

BRUCE HAYLLAR
University of Technology, Sydney, NSW, Australia.
Bruce Hayllar is an Associate Professor and Head of the School of Leisure, Sport and Tourism. Bruce has an extensive portfolio of applied research projects for both the public and private sectors with a particular interest in the experience of people in learning and leisure environments. Bruce's research interests are in urban tourism, tourism precincts and phenomenological approaches to understanding the experience of tourists.

PETER JONES
University of Surrey, Guildford, UK.
Peter Jones is the ITCA Professor of Production and Operations Management, and Director of the Travel Catering Research Centre at the University of Surrey. He is an author or editor of twelve textbooks and over 40 refereed journal articles and has presented at conferences in fourteen countries on five continents. He has a doctorate from the University of Surrey and an MBA from London Business School.

GRAHAM MILLER

University of Surrey, Guildford, UK.

Graham Miller's research focuses on the corporate responsibility of the industry and the contribution tourism can make towards a sustainable transition. With Louise Twinning-Ward he is co-author of *Monitoring for a Sustainable Tourism Transition* published by OUP. He is involved in teaching undergraduate and postgraduate students in tourism, sustainability and ethics.

NOEL SCOTT

University of Queensland, Ipswich, Queensland, Australia.

Noel Scott is a Lecturer of the School of Tourism, the University of Queensland, Australia. His research interests involve destination management and marketing.

RICHARD SHARPLEY

University of Lincoln, Lincoln, UK.

Richard Sharpley is Professor of Tourism and Head of the Department of Tourism and Recreation at the University of Lincoln, UK. The author of a number of books and journal articles, his principal teaching and research interests include the sociology of tourism, rural tourism, island tourism and, in particular, the relationship between tourism and sustainable development.

DAVID G. SIMMONS

Lincoln University, Canterbury, New Zealand.

David Simmons is Professor of Tourism and Director of the Tourism, Recreation Research and Education Centre (TRREC) at Lincoln University, New Zealand. His research interests have traditionally focussed on tourism planning and more recently embraced the question of bringing public and private sector perspectives into a framework of sustainable tourism yield.

STEPHEN L. J. SMITH

University of Waterloo, Waterloo, Ontario, Canada.

Stephen L. J. Smith is a Professor of Tourism at the University of Waterloo. He specializes in tourism economics and statistics, with a particular interest in the definitions and measurement of tourism phenomena.

RAY SPURR

University of New South Wales, Sydney, NSW, Australia.

Ray Spurr is Director of the Sustainable Tourism CRC Centre for Tourism Economics and Policy Research and a Senior Research Fellow at the University of New South Wales, Australia.

MARCUS L. STEPHENSON

Middlesex University Dubai, Dubai, United Arab Emirates.

Marcus L. Stephenson is Head of Tourism and Chair of Research at Middlesex University Dubai, United Arab Emirates (UAE). He has published extensively in the field of tourism, race and ethnicity, and has conducted ethnographic research in the UK and the Caribbean. He is currently researching sociological-based impacts of the tourism industry in Dubai (UAE).

NANCY STEVENSON

University of Westminster, London, UK.

Nancy Stevenson is the Campus Senior Tutor and the undergraduate Tourism Programme Leader at the University of Westminster. She originally qualified as a town planner and worked for a decade in Australia and in three London Boroughs, developing and delivering land use and regeneration policies and projects. Her main academic interests are public policy, planning, urban regeneration and development.

JOHN TRIBE

University of Surrey, Guildford, UK.

John Tribe is a Professor of Tourism at the University of Surrey, UK. He has authored books on strategy, economics, education and environmental management and his research concentrates on sustainability, epistemology and education. He edits the *Journal of Hospitality, Leisure Sport and Tourism Education*. He has led two major EU projects on tourism and forests and on curriculum development in Moldova and is currently director of a project to develop a digital image library for tourism.

SHANE VULETICH

Covec Limited, Auckland, New Zealand.

Shane Vuletich is a Director of Covec Limited, an independent New Zealand-based economics consultancy. He has managed the New Zealand Ministry of Tourism's forecasting programme for the past 6 years, and has consulted widely within the tourism industry. He is a trusted advisor to the Ministry of Tourism and the private sector on issues relating to primary data collection, data validation, spatial analysis, forecasting and strategy. Shane is responsible for the design and development of the New Zealand Tourism Flows Model.

YEVVON YI-CHI CHANG

Kainan University, Luzhu, Taiwan.

Yevvon Chang's research has focused on investigating the implementation of modern manufacturing concepts in the flight catering industry. Prior to taking up a post as an Assistant Professor in the Business School of Kainan University in Taiwan, she worked as the International Travel Catering Association Research Officer at Surrey. In 2005, her research was recognised with the Award of Student Best Paper at the 23rd EuroCHRIE conference.

SECTION 1:

A REVIEW OF TOURISM RESEARCH

Chapter 1

A Review of Tourism Research

John Tribe and David Airey

The Context of Change

Tourism research has come a long way since the first developments in the identification and delineation of a tourism subject area in the mid-1960s. It has moved in interesting new directions, both generated and responded to different challenges and applied itself to novel situations. So at the outset it is worth reviewing some key changes in the short history of tourism studies. At the early stage, as noted by Airey (2005), knowledge about tourism, reflected in the very comprehensive reference list for one of the early textbooks about tourism (Burkart & Medlik, 1974), was dominated by government and other official reports and studies. In other words, tourism was drawing very much on what Tribe (1997) has referred to as *extradisciplinarity*. By this Tribe was referring to knowledge that did not originate from academic study and hence from the disciplines but rather that was generated largely from the context of practice, management and government. This therefore largely consisted of knowledge from 'industry, government, think tanks, interest groups, research institutes and consultancies' (Tribe, 1999, p. 103). Another indication of the type of early knowledge about tourism can be seen in the policy of one of the major academic validating bodies in the UK, the Council for National Academic Awards, which as late as the 1990s interpreted research in this field in a very wide sense to include consultancy and professional practice (Glew, 1991).

The first substantial body of 'academic' research, for which, according to Tribe (1999, p. 103), 'disciplinary-based methodology and peer review are the hall-marks of quality control', came mainly from the economists. Indeed by the time Archer (1977) came to write his state of the art book on tourism multipliers, there was already a fairly full body of academic literature on this aspect of tourism economics. At this stage in its development, tourism was to some extent dominated by business and economics approaches so that research and teaching came under the threat of the tyranny (Aronowitz & Giroux, 1991) of this particular discipline. The influence of economics in the development of tourist studies is triangulated by other writers. For example, an analysis of doctoral dissertations completed in the USA found the largest contributions from the field of economics (Jafari & Aaser, 1988). It was found that anthropology, geography and recreation were next in the order of importance. Recently Tribe (2006b, p. 366) searched the CABABS abstract database for 2002 and found a 'predominance of economics appearing in 38% of the titles, keywords or abstracts, followed by sociology with 7%, geography with 6%, psychology with 3% and philosophy and anthropology each with 1%'. The predominance of economics in tourism has also been commented upon by Rojek and Urry (1997) and Franklin and Crang (2001).

This is not to say that that there was no other serious research and writing about tourism but by and large the contributions from other discipline areas were far more fragmentary. For example, Butler (1980), from a geographic perspective, published his work on tourism area life cycles based on research from the late 1970s, Cohen (1972) and MacCannell (1973) were contributing to an understanding of the sociology and social dimensions of tourism even earlier, and as early as the 1940s scholars such as Brunner (1945) and Pimlott (1947) were writing about the development of tourism from an historical and social perspective. However, these were very much the beginnings of research in tourism, marked notably by relatively isolated contributions leaving plenty of gaps in the knowledge base. And although the first journal (*Tourist Review*) specifically devoted to tourism was established in 1945, it was not joined by others until 1962 (*Journal of Travel Research*), 1973 (*Annals of Tourism Research*) and 1980 (*Tourism Management*). An investigation of these journals tells an interesting story. Kim (1998) conducted a content analysis of titles, abstracts, keywords and authors/affiliations of articles from the *Journal of Travel Research* (1972–1997) and *Annals of Tourism Research* (1973–1997). The top subject areas in terms of total citations were found to be Economics, Tourism Product, Tourism Development, Research Methodology, Geography, Anthropology, Psychology, Tourism Hardware, Political Science, Sociology, Tourism, Tourism Attraction, Marketing, Tourism Impact, Art, Environment, Multidiscipline, History, Evolution of Tourism and Tourism Planning. This fairly fragmentary pattern of development, including the rather more advanced development of business and economic aspects, is captured by Tribe (1997) in his depiction of the study area of tourism as two separate fields – a field related to the business of tourism (TF1) which by the mid-1990s was fairly well developed and comprehensive or in Tribe's words (1997, pp. 653–4) 'has some coherence and structure and a framework of theories and concepts' and the non-business area (TF2) which he describes as having no unifying element but rather 'bits of atomized knowledge [emanating] from the disciplines themselves'.

The process of development since the mid-1990s has seen a marked change and Jafari's (2001) charting of the development of tourism helps us to understand these changes. Jafari plotted the journey of tourism studies across four platform phases. The first, 1960s phase, – the advocacy platform – was dominated by economists. The cautionary platform evolved in the 1970s and emphasised the negative as well as positive impacts of tourism – particularly on the environmental front. The adaptancy platform which became popular in the 1980s turned its attention to alternatives to mass tourism. The fourth platform – the knowledge platform – identified by Jafari, sees tourism as a more mature study and offers a more comprehensive understanding of tourism than the more partial earlier platforms. The study of tourism now fits better with the view of Graburn and Jafari (1991, p. 7) who commented that 'no single discipline alone can accommodate, treat or understand tourism; it can be studied only if disciplinary boundaries are crossed and if multidisciplinary perspectives are sought and formed'.

Over the period, the number of tourism scholars and the volume of research have expanded enormously. As a simple illustration, for example, there are now an estimated 40 specialist tourism academic journals published in English (Morrison, 2006) and PhD completions in the UK related to tourism increased more than 8-fold between 1990 and 2002 (Botterill & Gale, 2005). But simple growth does not provide the full sense of the change. For, at the same time many of the gaps in knowledge have been completed and the methodological approaches and research techniques have extended. Tribe's 'bits of atomized knowledge' on the non-business side of tourism have become far more joined to represent a more coherent domain of study. Aitchison (2006, p. 417) has described this as a 'cultural turn' suggesting that 'tourism studies [Tribe's non-business field], with its social and cultural underpinning, has emerged as a distinct field from tourism management [Tribe's business field], with its primarily economic underpinning'. The boundaries of this can of course be redrawn to represent tourism *tout court* as a field combining both business and non-business elements. Indeed most tourism programmes attempt exactly this and the developed knowledge now allows it to be achieved. But the important thing is that the knowledge base is now far more complete. Xiao and Smith (2006a, p. 495) conducted a content analysis of the 30-year comprehensive subject index of *Annals of Tourism Research* with a view to analysing the making and changing of the field of tourism. In terms of changes they report the following:

> Over the years, citation frequencies of headwords have been changing in the index to reflect the shift of focus in subject areas … Fifty-two headwords were found to represent rising patterns in terms of periodic citation frequency. They are grouped into eight broad subject areas, encompassing typology of tourists, community and development, alternative experience/ product, socio-cultural aspects and change, geopolitical regions/focus, literature/research/methods, marketing and management, and environment. In contrast, twenty-seven headwords, grouped into nine broad subject areas – including economics, industry and transportation, hospitality, recreation, impacts, North America, tourism (in conventional/narrow sense), Third World, and sociology, were reported with declining frequency.

Similarly, the methodological approaches and research techniques are now far more complete. Given the early predominance of the disciplinary approach of economics it is hardly surprising that positivist research methods took hold in tourism. Some ten years back, in 1997, Ryan asked questions about the balance of methods being used and suggested the possibility that tourism researchers are 'entrenched in a positivist tradition that was blinding us to developments in other social sciences' (1997, p. 3).

Echtner and Jamal writing in the same year concluded that 'the evolution of tourism studies might be seen to be plagued by the same phobia that dominates all of the social sciences, namely the need to become more "scientific" and the resulting attachment to more traditional positivist methods' (1997, p. 877). For Echtner and Jamal then positivism represented a means by which tourism scholars operating in a young field of studies could be taken seriously by their peers operating in older established disciplines. The bias towards positivism was also noted by Riley and Love (2000). They carried out an investigation into the number of quantitative versus qualitative articles appearing in four tourism journals. They covered the period from the inception of the journals up to 1996 and found the dominant method in tourism journals to be positivism.

But just as the hegemony of economics has given way to a much more eclectic muti-disciplinarity in tourism, so positivism has relinquished its grip in terms of methods. Dann and Phillips (2001) have identified and commented on a recent trend where tourism research is moving towards a more qualitative approach and away from pure quantification. The increasing presence of qualitative studies is also noted in Botterill, Gale and Haven's (2003) analysis of UK dissertations where they found that 'quantitative ... and qualitative ... methods were reported in roughly equal proportions' (p. 288). More recently, introducing a special issue of the journal *Tourism Recreation Research*, Tribe (2006a) commented that

> the totality of tourism studies has now developed beyond the narrow boundaries of an applied business field and has the characteristics of a fledgling post-modern field of research. A sign of increasing maturity is the emergence of more reflexivity and there is evidence of an increasing range of tourism research which offers a counter-balance to tourism as a business practice and which encourages researchers to follow innovative and radical lines of enquiry. We may even point to it the establishment of 'new tourism research'.

Aitchison (2006) has illustrated these methodological changes with examples from geography where 'theoretical perspectives, such as post structuralism and postmodernism, with their emphasis on the symbolic and cultural nature of space, place and identity, have formed new uses of discourse analysis, in-depth interviewing and diary keeping, observational analysis and the role of the actor network theory'. In this volume Chambers reports on research informed by a post-colonial approach which concludes that 'recent attempts by the UK to bring Jamaica in line with developed world thinking on homosexuality can be perceived as a form of colonial discourse in which the [former] colonised are constructed as primitive and barbaric with the aim of the imperial project being to ensure cultural and moral improvement'. She thereby invokes a strong challenge to the liberal consensus in this area. These approaches are a long step from input–output analysis long pursued by the economists or factor analysis by the social scientist, but the key point is that they now belong among the methodological approaches of the body of tourism scholars and tourism as an area of scholarly endeavour is all the stronger for it. One worry in this changing landscape of tourism research has been the extent to which it has relied on case studies. This has long been characterised as a weak approach among social science methods (Franklin & Crang, 2001; Oppermann, 2000). However, recent work by Xiao and Smith (2006b, p. 738) counters this view concluding that the 'prevalent arguments of case studies as conceptually and analytically weak is not justified'.

Understanding Change

As has been shown, changes in tourism research can be mapped along a number of different lines broadly tracking how we research and what we research. In terms of how research is conducted, changes in approaches may be analysed by dividing the question into two further subsections. First, we have witnessed the changing influences of different disciplines. It has been observed that the rising swell of interest by cultural geographers in tourism now competes strongly with the once dominant discipline of economics. Second, whilst positivism is still important in tourism research, a noticeable use of a more diverse repertoire of methodologies has been described. For example, the chapters in this text by Stevenson (grounded theory), Hayllar and Griffin (phenomenology) and Scott and Cooper (network analysis) each draw on new methodological approaches.

The interesting changes in what is being researched have also been commented on. Of course, one would expect that management issues retain a significant interest for researchers. Tourism is after all a significant industry. But we can witness a strong interest in consumption and performance issues that now complement questions surrounding aspects of production. Issues of tourism embodiment are also gaining greater exposure in the literature.

But we also need some analytical framework by which to try to understand the changing patterns of tourism research. A robust framework would also allow reflection and critique about the state of play of tourism research. Recently Tribe (2006b) has offered some insight in this area. In his quest to understand what factors influence *The Truth About Tourism* he has invoked the concepts of the knowledge force field and the researcher's gaze. By doing this he underlines the fact that tourism research is of course a human activity that is socially constructed within a world of existing structures. He therefore wishes to understand the location and operation of power in the construction of tourism knowledge and the following paragraphs recount some of his main arguments.

One finding is that tourism (like research in other areas) is subject to a double selectivity. This occurs at two points which relate to the *what* and the *how* factors alluded to above. When a researcher turns his or her gaze upon the world of tourism the first selection occurs. To adapt the usage of Bernstein's (1971) term, the framing of an area of interest or a problem takes place. This necessarily selects things to go in the frame and things which are excluded. But a second selection subsequently occurs as the research process continues. For the researcher selects how the problem is to be approached. What methods are to be utilised and what disciplines are to be used to interrogate the problem? The researcher's gaze and its double selectivity is therefore at the root of understanding the outcomes and patterns of tourism research.

The knowledge force field offers a theoretical basis for understanding the influences on the researcher's gaze. This recognises that academics are not of course independent truth seekers but rather that they are subject to a number of guiding forces. Five significant forces have been identified. These are person, position, rules, ends and ideology.

The force of person recognises that like tourists, researchers are also embodied. That is to say they have gender, colour, age, ability, interests and a complex psychology of likes and dislikes. It is precisely because of this individual variability that positivist research likes to stress its objectivity and therefore discount any researcher subjectivity. But this is difficult to achieve. These things affect our gaze and subtly influence our framings. For example in considering the gender aspect of person, several authors have noted the exercise of patriarchal power in tourism research. Aitchison (2001) found that males outnumbered female authors by four to one in her gender analysis of authors in journals in leisure and tourism studies. It is interesting to note the predominance of white, able-bodied males in the membership of the panels of the 2008 UK Research Assessment Exercise where, of panel members who responded, 82.4 per cent reported their ethnicity as White British, 73.0 per cent of the respondents identified themselves as male and only 1 per cent of the total respondents indicated that they considered themselves disabled. (www.rae.ac.uk/panels/members/equalops.doc). Similarly with regard to colour and ethnicity, Marcus Stephenson raises the *socio-political implications of rural racism and tourism experiences* in his chapter in this volume. Stephenson argues that popular representations of the countryside result from the shared viewpoints of a particularly situated and embodied group of people and that this expression of Englishness excludes black minorities from appreciating rural environments. Such issues tend to be overlooked and underreported by the current body of tourism researchers.

Rules are important in the exercise of power in the creation of tourism knowledge since they provide either explicit or implicit guidelines about how things should be done as well as providing the criteria for distinguishing between what is permissible and what is non-permissible. Disciplines and methodologies indeed can be conceptualised as sets of explicit, coherent rules and moves that are shared by and abided by their membership. Each of these therefore contributes to the double selectivity of the researcher's gaze. Disciplines have both helped and hindered tourism research. The major disciplines of economics (tourism multipliers), sociology (the tourist gaze), anthropology (host/guest relations) and geography (tourism area life cycle) have contributed strongly to the knowledge base of tourism. Tourism is above all a multidisciplinary field of study. But those in traditional disciplines have sometimes sought to undermine tourism for its alleged 'Mickey Mousiness'. More significantly tourism is often faced with the unyielding, inappropriate and unsympathetic structures which established disciplines have constructed in the Academy. A good example of this is the Economic and Social Research Council (ESRC), which funds much of University research in these fields in the UK. Any tourism submission to this funding body must be made under a disciplinary heading so that it can be sent for 'appropriate' expert evaluation. Disciplines include Management and Business studies, Economics, Area and Development Studies, Social Anthropology and Sociology. Many tourism research projects fall foul of this classificatory system which is not sensitive to the epistemology of the field.

Whilst disciplines and methodologies present explicit rules, the concepts of paradigms, discourses and traditions offer insights into other subtle, implicit, forces that have a less visible but no less significant impact on the directions of tourism research. The notion of paradigms has been considered in tourism research but any idea of an overarching paradigm is rejected. There is no orthodoxy apparent in tourism research indeed the number of journals in publication, their eclectic titles and the fact that new titles are able to appear demonstrates that there is no effective enforcement of a particular research line. Discourses operate in a different way to paradigms. They show how social practices are constructed, marked out and perpetuated in language. It might be argued that a discourse of business and management did at one stage saturate much of the territory of tourism research. Indeed this discourse still governs those who occupy this particular territory. But there is evidence of resistance to any monopolising tendency of a business and management discourse. Critical, cultural and sustainability discourses, amongst others, may be discerned within the field.

Traditions are less rigid than paradigms since different traditions often coexist within a field of study and unlike paradigms they are more flexible and adaptable. However, they do develop and become entrenched as researchers build on the emerging core values and routines attracting new supporters and dropping dissidents. They are therefore prone to create infrastructures based around people, publications, research agendas and departments. There is certainly evidence of a strong management tradition in tourism.

Positionality is another important element in the knowledge force field. For example, the geographical situatedness (in terms of country of origin and/or work, language and cultural community) of a researcher as well as the location of tourism studies within a particular university department each influence the practice of tourism research. In terms of the first of these, the concentration of contemporary tourism research within a few mainly developed countries and the dominance of English language in the rhetoric of tourism research each lead to certain world views being privileged over others which become peripheralised. In terms of the latter, it is possible to discern departmentalism at work in the forging and forming of tourism research. The popularity of Management and Business Schools as homes for tourism research mean that management agendas can inhibit the full possibilities of tourism development.

The purposes or the ends of knowledge also exert an important influence on what truths researchers seek. This idea incorporates questions about the funding of research and therefore introduces issues of performativity (Lyotard, 1984) and commoditization. A naïve view of universities might be that they relentlessly and independently pursue 'the truth' without fear or favour. In this view it is the importance of the discovery or insight that drives the research agenda. Against this view it may be countered that researchers' time is ever more accountable in the modern university. Research, like everything else must therefore secure a clear funding stream. Where research is led by funding it is clearly the agenda of the funding agencies which determines the direction of enquiries. Examples of this include the ESRC in the UK and the Sustainable Tourism Co-operative Research Centre (STCRC) in Australia. However a number of points of caution should be noted here. First, as previously mentioned tourism does not in fact capture much mainstream research funding (the exception to this being Australia). Second, much tourism research (unlike physics or medical research) does not require major funding. Third, many tourism researchers seem to be able to manage their sponsoring departments in a way which creates some individual research time and space. All of these factors explain perhaps why there is an abundance of esoteric tourism research that seems to be led by interest rather than to satisfy externally imposed agendas.

Finally, ideology and culture are identified as important elements in the tourism knowledge force field. The term 'ideology' has become somewhat imprecise in modern usage and is often taken to mean a guiding set of principles that operate at a micro level (such as the ideology of a political party). But here it is taken at its macro level to stand for the common set of beliefs and values that permeate a particular society in a particular epoch. It clearly shows that it has similarities and differences with culture. But we might discern its special meaning by reference to the UK, where we can witness a number of different cultures coexisting all of which are dominated by a free market, capitalist bourgeois ideology. Interestingly, where cultures are generally identifiable (e.g. by clothes or by customs), ideologies are often deeply embedded and less clearly visible. Additionally, Gramsci (1971) introduced the term hegemony to describe how the cultural beliefs, values and practices of a dominant group became entrenched and caused the suppression and partial exclusion of those of others.

The interesting thing about ideologies is that they are difficult to see when we are so deeply immersed in them and saturated by them. For example it could be said that two particular aspects of ideology have an impact on tourism research. First, a generally shared belonging to a free market system with much consumer choice. Here the way things are become so taken-for-granted (rich West, cheap overseas tourism, poorly paid labour, etc.) that they become part of the eternal background rather than important issues to be researched. In this text, Harold Goodwin's chapter titled 'Measuring and Reporting the Impact of Tourism on Poverty' represents a counter-example of this tendency. Similarly, Michael Hall's chapter 'Tourism and Regional Competitiveness' holds up for scrutinising the taken-for-granted ideology within which tourism development takes place tracing the drive for competitiveness to the power of the neoliberal project.

Second, there seems to be a widely shared adherence within the Academy to liberal values. But liberalism is not a universal value. Of late, of course, Islamic values have come into sharp conflict with those of liberalism/the West. Tourism research does not yet offer much insight into tourism that would exist under radically different value systems to a liberal one. (Indeed, Chambers' chapter in this volume illustrates this issue very graphically in the case of homosexuality and tourism in Jamaica.)

Current Research Themes

Against this background of change and development, the University of Surrey, which was one of the pioneering centres for tourism studies, organised a conference in June 2006 to celebrate 40 years of tourism studies at Surrey. With the title, *Cutting Edge Research in Tourism: New Directions, Challenges and Applications*, the conference was designed to explore, with colleagues from around the world, the ways in which the research picture of tourism is now being drawn, both in subject coverage and methodological approaches. A key aspect of this conference was that it was pitched to attract scholars from a wide range of disciplines in contrast to the recent trend in conferences where specialisation has become the hallmark (e.g. cultural tourism, tourism and photography, lake tourism, etc.). Thus the conference should offer a view of the bigger picture of the state of tourism research. The 15 chapters in this book have been selected from the 150 papers presented at the conference to capture the current stage of tourism research. They also include the papers from three keynote speakers.

Set against the broad background of Tribe's (1997) depiction of the study area of tourism as two separate fields, it is interesting that 10 years later, it is still possible to group research into that which has an economic/business orientation and that which is more concerned with cultural/social and other non-business issues, with the former set substantially in the positivist tradition and the latter providing more qualitative analysis. This division gives a starting point to group the chapters in this book. The first group, *Researching Tourism Business*, provides examples of work exploring aspects of particular tourism sectors through to macro-economic perspectives. The second group, *Researching Tourism Experiences and*

Challenges, includes chapters dealing with the experiences of tourists themselves as well as the ways in which tourism brings challenges that need to be addressed. Still, as Tribe described, it is more difficult to identify a unifying theme for the 'non-business' than for the 'business' field of tourism. But what has changed is that the non-business field is now much more populated with researchers. The chapters here reflect some of the range of work in this field and in both fields the chapters give examples of new research areas and approaches.

However, although the book still reflects Tribe's two fields, it is perhaps evidence of the growing maturity of tourism research, that it is just as interesting to observe how the boundaries between the two groups are also often blurred. There is recognition by many of these authors of the multi-dimensional nature of tourism and by a breadth in their engagement with different research traditions. Michael Hall chapter gives an illustration of the importance of this overlap in understanding tourism. But perhaps stronger evidence of maturity is the extent to which the challenge to existing understandings is coming from within the tourism academy itself. The tourism academy has matured to a point where it has the knowledge and tools to test and retest what we take for truths about the subject area, a point that is picked up in the final chapter of the book.

This final chapter is authored by Donna Chambers who directly and comprehensively offers 'An Agenda for Cutting Edge Research in Tourism'. In this chapter, Chambers first marshals those key ideas that have emerged within the discourse of tourism and then considers subsequent challenges to them. In the first section of her chapter, Chambers considers authenticity (McCannell), the tourist gaze (Urry), the host and guest (Smith), the Tourism Area Life Cycle model (Butler) and old tourist/new tourist dichotomy (Poon).

According to Chambers, 'objectivist approaches to authenticity (like that of McCannell) which dominated the thinking on authenticity within tourism studies have been displaced and it is now generally accepted that authenticity means different things to different people and indeed, is historically, culturally, politically and even personally determined'. There has therefore been a paradigmatic shift in approaches to authenticity and a plethora of journal articles have been written based on new understandings of authenticity which reflect its plural meanings. Turning her sights to Urry, Chambers recalls that a key critique of the gaze is that it is ocularcentric. This leads her to note that the concept of embodiment has destabilised the 'tyranny of the visual' and this challenge has led to a renewed interest in the role of the body and performance within tourism studies. With regard to the host/guest dichotomy Chambers notes that in its early usage it emphasised tourism as a way in which the West exploited the rest but she continues that 'by the time Smith published a third edition of the book in 2001, it was evident that there was some departure from this host/guest dichotomy'. Regarding Butler's 'Tourism Area Life Cycle Model' Chambers invokes challenges to it including the fact that it does not address endogenous or exogenous factors that might affect the development of a destination. Finally with regard to Poon, Chambers notes that 'new tourism has not totally displaced old tourism but both are coexisting. Indeed, there has emerged also a kind of hybrid tourist who displays some characteristics of the new tourist and some of the old tourist. Further old tourism is still flourishing (in the form of the packaged tour) more than ten years after Poon predicted its demise'.

Chambers concludes her chapter, and the book with some thoughts on a possible agenda for cutting edge research. She rightly notes that it is impossible to propose a universal agenda for cutting edge research and therefore cautions that these are her own thoughts. They are

> First ... cutting edge research in tourism should embrace novel methodologies, methods, practices and pedagogies in and of tourism which will inspire new ways of seeing, being, and knowing.
>
> Second, cutting edge research should be about embracing difference, not for its own sake, but in so far as difference can open up our understanding to the multifarious discourses and practices of tourism.
>
> Finally an agenda for cutting edge research in tourism should be self reflective in declaring and indeed in critiquing its own paradigmatic assumptions.

Postscript

Finally, it would be useful to comment beyond the *Cutting Edge* conference and this selection of chapters to consider in general how well tourism research is moving in new directions in 2007 and is offering practical applications to the world of which it is now such a major part. Alongside these papers, we should therefore briefly consider books, journal articles and conferences that illustrate contemporary trends. In terms of journals there seem to be two interesting recent additions that demonstrate the full breadth of tourism studies and its changing directions. First, in *Tourist Studies* the editors (Franklin & Crang, 2001) encourage contributors to 'provide an alternative to the existing positivist, managerially oriented material which predominates in the current literature on tourism. These approaches may include qualitative, humanistic and ethnographic methodologies, and feminist and ethnic perspectives on tourism'. Second, the new journal *Mobilities* perhaps seeks to undermine somewhat tourism studies by moving us to the concept of mobilities. This concept, according to the editors Hannam, Sheller and Urry (2006, p. 1), 'encompasses both the large-scale movements of people, objects, capital and information across the world, as well as the more local processes of daily transportation, movement through public space and the travel of material things within everyday life'. So *Tourist Studies* seems to illustrate a naming, framing, consolidation and point of crystallisation for research that is TF2 – the non-business of tourism – oriented. *Mobilities* on the other hand seems to offer a potential challenge to the very concept of tourism studies.

A brief look at some current conference and book titles illustrates the rich diversity of academic interest in tourism. For example conference titles include: *Cultural Tourism: Negotiating Identities*; *Perspectives of Rural Tourism in the New Europe*; *Tourism in Transition*; *Visions of Transmodern Tourism*; *Fusion Cuisine and Placemaking*; *Tourism after Oil and beyond Nature*; *Tourism, Mobility, and Technology*; *Enhancing Destinations and the Visitor Economy*; *Gazing, Glancing, Glimpsing: Tourists and Tourism in a Visual World*; *Dark Tourism: Current Themes, Issues* and *Consequences and Promoting an Academy of Hope?* Book titles encompass *Tea and Tourism*; *Tourism in the Middle East*; *Cultural Tourism in a Changing World*; *Lake Tourism*; *Tourism Crises: Causes, Consequences and Management*; *Micro-Clusters and Networks: The Growth of Tourism*; *Consumer*

Behaviour in Tourism; *Moving Through Nets: The Physical and Social Dimensions of Travel* and *The Critical Turn in Tourism Studies*. This eclectic mix of titles surely demonstrates the vibrancy and sweep of tourism studies. Tourism studies have indeed developed a long way since its narrow business beginnings.

But perhaps five small notes of caution will serve as a coda to this optimistic conclusion. First, there does appear to be some Balkanisation of tourism studies which is generating ever more smaller units of analysis – we seem to be further than ever from broad tourism theories. Second and perhaps ironically, the business of tourism does seem currently to be overrun by more social and cultural studies. Third, although the two fields of tourism TF1 (business) and TF2 (non-business) both now show signs of comprehensive coverage with coherence and infrastructure – these do seem to be splitting into separate camps. This is surely a cause for concern as in practice most tourism puzzles are multi and interdisciplinary ones. Fourth, sustainability research has become obfuscated by micro issues of conserving hotel towels. The big issue of climate change and air travel has been largely side-stepped. And fifth, as Tribe (2006b) has cautioned, the truth about tourism is still mainly told by similarly situated researchers. Despite our interesting conference titles and research papers – many significant truths remain under- and untold.

References

Airey, D. (2005). Growth and change. In: D. Airey, & J. Tribe (Eds), *An international handbook of tourism education* (pp. 13–24). Oxford: Elsevier.

Aitchison, C. (2001). Gender and leisure research: The "codification of knowledge". *Leisure Sciences*, *23*(1), 1–19.

Aitchison, C. (2006). The critical and the cultural: Explaining the divergent paths of leisure studies. *Leisure Studies*, *25*, 417–422.

Archer, B. H. (1977). *Tourism multipliers: The state of the art*. Cardiff: University of Wales Press.

Aronowitz, S., & Giroux, H. (1991). *Postmodern education: Politics, culture and social criticism*. Minneapolis: University of Minnesota Press.

Bernstein, B. (1971). On the classification and framing of educational knowledge. In: M. Young (Ed.), *Knowledge and control: New directions for the sociology of education* (pp. 47–69). London: Collier-MacMillan.

Botterill, D., & Gale, T. (2005). Postgraduate and PhD education. In: D. Airey, & J. Tribe (Eds), *An international handbook of tourism education* (pp. 469–480). Oxford: Elsevier.

Botterill, D., Gale, T., & Haven, C. (2003). A survey of doctoral theses accepted by universities in the UK and Ireland for studies related to tourism 1990–1999. *Tourist Studies*, *2*, 283–311.

Brunner, E. (1945). *Holiday making and the holiday trades*. London: Oxford University Press.

Burkart, A. J., & Medlik, S. (1974). *Tourism past present and future*. London: Heinemann.

Butler, R. W. (1980). The concept of a tourist area life cycle of evolution: Implications for management and resources. *Canadian Geographer*, *24*, 5–12.

Cohen, E. (1972). Toward a sociology of international tourism. *Social Research*, *39*, 164–182.

Dann, G., & Phillips, J. G. (2001). Qualitatitive tourism research in the late twentieth century and beyond. In: B. Faulkner, G. Moscardo, & E. Laws (Eds), *Tourism in the twenty-first century: Reflections on experience* (pp. 247–265). London: Continuum.

Echtner, C. M., & Jamal, T. B. (1997). The disciplinary dilemma of tourism studies. *Annals of Tourism Research*, *24*, 868–883.

Franklin, A., & Crang, M. (2001). The trouble with tourism and travel theory. *Tourist Studies*, *1*, 5–22.

Glew, G. (1991). *Research and scholarly activities in support of honours degree teaching* (with special reference to consumer and leisure studies courses). London: CNAA.

Graburn, N., & Jafari, J. (1991). Introduction: Tourism and the social sciences. *Annals of Tourism Research*, *18*, 1–11.

Gramsci, A. (1971). *Selections from the Prison notebooks*. New York: International Publishers.

Hannam, K., Sheller, M., & Urry, J. (2006). Editorial: Mobilities, immobilities and moorings. *Mobilities*, *1*, 1–22.

Jafari, J., & Aaser, D. (1988). Tourism as the subject of doctoral dissertations. *Annals of Tourism Research*, *15*, 407–429.

Jafari, J. (2001). The scientification of tourism. In: V. L. Smith, & M. Brent (Eds), *Hosts and guests revisited: Tourism issues of the 21st Century* (pp. 28–41). New York: Cognizant Communications Corporation.

Kim, S. (1998). Content analysis: Annals of Tourism Research and Journal of Travel Research, Unpublished MS Thesis, PhD University of Wisconsin-Stout, Wisconsin, USA.

Lyotard, J. (1984). *The postmodern condition: A report on knowledge*. Manchester: Manchester University Press.

MacCannell, D. (1973). Staged authenticity: Arrangements of social place in tourist settings. *American Journal of Sociology*, *79*, 586–603.

Morrison, A. M. (2006). Tourism, hospitality and leisure journals. Available at http://www.alastairmmorrison.com/journal_02.htm#list. Accessed on 3 March 2006.

Oppermann, M. (2000). Triangulation: A methodological discussion. *International Journal of Tourism Research*, *2*, 141–146.

Pimlott, J. A. R. (1947). *The Englishman's holiday*. London: Faber and Faber.

Riley, R., & Love, L. (2000). The state of qualitative tourism research. *Annals of Tourism Research*, *27*, 164–187.

Rojek, C., & Urry, J. (1997). *Touring cultures*. London: Routledge.

Ryan, C. (1997). Tourism: A mature discipline? *Pacific Tourism Review*, *1*, 3–5.

Tribe, J. (1997). The indiscipline of tourism. *Annals of Tourism Research*, *24*, 628–657.

Tribe, J. (1999). *The Philosophic Practitioner*. PhD Thesis, University of London, London.

Tribe, J. (2006b). The truth about tourism. *Annals of Tourism Research*, *33*, 360–381.

Tribe, J. (2006a). Towards new tourism research. *Tourism Recreation Research*, *30*, 1–3.

Xiao, H., & Smith, S. L. J. (2006a). The making of tourism research: Insights from a social sciences journal. *Annals of Tourism Research*, *33*, 490–507.

Xiao, H., & Smith, S.L.J. (2006b) Case studies in tourism research: A state of the art analysis. *Tourism Management*, *27*(5), 738–749.

SECTION 2:

RESEARCHING TOURISM BUSINESS

Introduction

The eight chapters in this section of the book deal with various aspects of tourism as a business both at the level of the individual firm or sector as well as in the context of the whole economy. Between them the chapters explore three different broad themes which together represent three of the main strands which have been pursued in tourism research since its early beginnings: namely the study of operations; economic impacts; and measurement. The two chapters dealing with operations focus on maintaining competitiveness in particular sectors and businesses in tourism by, in one case, diversification and in the other by new systems and processes. The chapters dealing with impacts provide examples of work which is being carried out to understand better the role of tourism in helping some of the world's poorer countries. This is in the same stream of research that started with economic impact studies in the 1960s (International Union of Official Travel Organizations, 1966), but now takes a much broader multi-dimensional and critical approach that embraces far more than economics. The final theme is about understanding more precisely and accurately the economic dimensions of tourism. This involves both improving the measurement as well as exploring the definitions of tourism, both of which have echoes in some of the earliest work in tourism (United Nations, 1963). Together these chapters provide examples of the ways in which researchers, primarily in the business field, are developing their work and it is clear from this body of work that, although they have a "business" perspective, the researchers here are very conscious that tourism is not solely an economic or business activity and that positivist approaches are not the only ways to solve tourism puzzles.

The chapter by Marialaura Di Domenico and Graham Miller titled *Are Plastic Cows the Future for Farming? Implications of an Alternative Diversification Model* makes a fitting opening for this section on tourism business. It applies contemporary academic thinking in tourism to areas of possible business practice but it also presents a challenge in that it pitches tourism as a development and growth route against traditional and powerfully entrenched and defended interests such as farming. The problem which is addressed is that of the economic difficulties facing many farmers particularly those in the developed world. The chapter provides an overview of the relationship between farming and tourism activities and notes that most academic studies on farming and tourism have focused on the provision of tourism accommodation as a key method of farm diversification. It therefore sets a new direction for research in its examination of farm-based tourism attractions as an alternative method of diversification for farmers. Di Domenico and Miller offer an empirically grounded framework for analysis, a typology of farm attraction diversification strategies and suggest reasons why attractions might be part of such strategies. They also consider to what extent the development of farm attractions can encourage or diminish the commitment of farmers to traditional farming practices.

From plastic cows to plastic trays, Yvvon Chang and Peter Jones focus on another sector of tourism and bring us up to date with advances in airline catering in their chapter — *Implementation of Mass Customised Manufacturing in the Flight Catering Industry*. This is an important paper in tourism since operations management is crucial to the provision of many of its services but perhaps somewhat overlooked in terms of research. Chang and Jones initially remind us of some of the factors in the external environment which have affected the flight catering industry. These include significant changes to the nature of the airline business, changes in industry concentration and an intensely competitive environment. All of these create a dilemma for flight caterers who on the one hand are driven by competition and business customer power to lower their product prices, but the same business customer power does not wish to see any compromise to the quality of the products. At the same time the flight catering industry is faced with another dilemma which is that of operating at high volume whilst dealing with high variety of products. It is in the light of these factors that the authors investigate and evaluate mass customisation as a possible strategy. Of course, the term appears to be a contradiction but the authors explain how it represents a synthesis of two existing approaches to production, namely job shop and assembly line. Chang and Jones investigate the policies and practices of mass customisation and the extent to which it has been applied in current flight catering operations. They find that whilst the flight catering industry exhibits many traits of mass customisation, the approach has not yet been fully implemented.

From operations, the next two chapters move to work considering the impacts of tourism and its position as a route to development. Richard Sharpley, in his chapter titled *Tourism in The Gambia: 10 years On*, rehearses for us the reasons why tourism is often seen as an effective strategy for development — not just because of its potential economic impacts on incomes and jobs but also because of the relentless growth in tourism where global international arrivals and receipts continue to increase annually. But Sharpley counsels that the introduction of tourism does not invariably set a nation on the path to development not only because of the recurrent shocks that impinge on it but also because of power asymmetries between developing and developed countries. In the light of this, Sharpley evaluates the contribution of tourism to development in The Gambia. He notes that in the 1993–1994 season around 90,000 arrivals were recorded so that tourism's contribution to GDP was about 10%. He also notes that since then international tourist arrivals to both Africa as a whole and West Africa in particular have increased steadily. But not so for The Gambia where arrivals have remained stagnant so that in 2004 tourist arrivals were virtually unchanged from the 1993 to 1994 total. In the light of this, Sharpley considers the reasons for the arrested development of the sector and suggests ways in which tourism may be planned in the future so as to contribute more sustainably to the country's development.

On a similar theme, Harold Goodwin in the chapter titled *Measuring and Reporting the Impact of Tourism on Poverty*, examines the measurement not just of tourism's economic impact but its wider impact on poverty. This takes as a starting point that poverty is multi-dimensional and that the impact needs to be understood in a multi-dimensional way. In Goodwin's words "The challenge is to develop 'simple indicators and systems to measure the impact of tourism on poverty,' and to develop and use 'reasonably robust yet simple indicators of poverty alleviation.' " Goodwin helps us to understand the detail of this challenge through the three examples of "reasonably robust yet simple indicators of poverty alleviation," which he presents in the chapter. On a practical note he adds that these methods are significant because they can realistically be used in the field to assess defined impacts of tourism on poverty. In the first case, Goodwin focuses on Egypt where secondary data are analysed to estimate the contribution of tourism to household incomes in the Nile Valley. In the second case, monitoring data from Tanzania is presented that relates to a coffee plantation project. In the third case, pre- and post-intervention incomes and employment are reported from a specific intervention in The Gambia. Underlining the importance of evidence, Goodwin concludes that "practitioners owe it to the funders and those they encourage to commit time and resources to their initiatives, including the poor themselves, to demonstrate significant beneficiary impact."

The third theme in this section relates to measures and definitions. The growth of tourism and its recognition as an increasingly important economic activity has brought with it the need to assess its contribution more rigorously and more broadly. Two chapters consider this from the perspective of tourism yield. In the first of these, Larry Dwyer, Peter Forsyth and Ray Spurr investigate *Productivity and Yield Measurement in Australian Inbound Tourism using Tourism Satellite Accounts [TSA] and General Equilibrium Modelling [CGE].* This chapter is essentially about the application of measurement and forecasting techniques to the tourism sector of the economy. Initially, the differences and relationships between the two techniques are described and then their uses are evaluated. The authors note that the choice of model depends on the task at hand. For example, TSA can be used to ascertain how variables such as value added in the tourism industry or tourism-related employment, are impacted on by a change in demand. On the other hand, a CGE model must be used to investigate how economy-wide variables are impacted on. In this case, TSA cannot be used since they do not include information on anything other than the tourism industry. Finally, two examples illustrate the uses of the models. First, the Australian TSA was used to provide a source of data for the analysis of the performance of the industry. Second, the authors demonstrate how the yield of tourists from different origins can be measured to the tourism industry (using the TSA) and to the economy as a whole (using the CGE).

In their chapter *Assessing Tourism Yield: An Analysis of Public Sector Costs and Benefits*, David Simmons, Susanne Becken and Ross Cullen also investigate the concept of yield but broaden out to consider issues beyond economics. Their aim is to offer concepts and tools to support the notion of sustainable development which as they point out is at the core of New Zealand's Tourism Strategy. With this in mind they make the important point that tourism yield can be applied to three different contexts and levels. These are the financial yield, economic yield and sustainable yield. This wider conceptualisation of tourism yield has resulted as the authors have "seen the need to reach out from 'profit and loss' and 'residual income' metrics at the firm level (financial yield), to examine the costs and benefits (revenues) of public sector entities (economic yield), and, when sustainability is added as a goal, to a consideration of measurements of 'ecological and social services' (sustainable yield) engendered by tourism production and consumption." One of the findings of their study is that whilst measurement of the financial costs and benefits of tourism is relatively straightforward, those relating to social costs and benefits are often still problematic. So the application of cost benefit analysis to economic and sustainable scenarios remains hampered by the challenge of measuring externalities.

The chapter by Susanne Becken and Shane Vuletich (*Developing a GIS-Supported Tourist Flow Model for New Zealand*) provides an example of work that exploits technological advances to understand more fully and accurately the dimensions of tourism. This brings together the wealth of data that exist on tourism movements in New Zealand into a tourist flow model to estimate the volumes of tourists travelling down the main transport corridors by season and with forecasts that extend to 7 years. Using a GIS interface this can then be accessed and visualised. The important thing about this work is that the results, which show the flows, provide key information for a range of users that can inform decisions about market development, planning, impact assessment and carrying capacity, all in a form that is readily accessible.

Finally in this section is a chapter that seeks to challenge some of the bases on which the business of tourism is measured. In his chapter *Duelling Definitions: Challenges and Implications of Conflicting International Concepts of Tourism*, Stephen Smith opens with a review of the nature of tourism and its significance as an area of economic activity. He next considers the World Trade Organization's conception of tourism in the context of the General Agreement on Trade in Services (GATS) followed by that of the International Monetary Fund in the Balance of Payments methodology (BPM5). Noting the progress made in developing Tourism Satellite Accounts, Smith concludes by noting that "researchers have a significant role to play in helping to refine and apply methods and concepts associated with measuring tourism as an internationally traded commodity … Tourism is too important to be left on the margins of international trade negotiations whether through ignorance of tourism researchers or misunderstandings of trade negotiators."

Of course, these eight chapters only cover a part of the territory of the tourism business. Forecasting, marketing and performance are just a few of the other areas in which significant advances have been made by researchers over the past forty or so years. But to return to one of the themes of this book, what they, with other work, represent is both a more sophisticated and broader coverage of the territory, such that we are now far better informed about tourism as a business, as well as an awareness that economics and business perspectives and methodologies alone are not always sufficient. This represents a part of the maturity of tourism research.

References

International Union of Official Travel Organizations. (1966). *Study on the economic impact of tourism on national economies and international trade*. Geneva: IUOTO.

United Nations. (1963). *Recommendations on international travel and tourism*. Rome: United Nations Conference on International Travel and Tourism.

Chapter 2

Are Plastic Cows the Future for Farming? Implications of an Alternative Diversification Model

Marialaura Di Domenico and Graham Miller

Introduction

This research concentrates on the relationship between tourism and farming within the operational dynamics of the diversified enterprises studied. The purpose of the research is to establish the extent to which the tourism attraction either facilitates as a supportive, secondary activity, or effectively erodes and replaces the need or desire for traditional agricultural practices, using the owner-manager's definitions to frame the research. In addressing this purpose, the farmers' tourism-based business goals and orientations in terms of starting up or continuing to operate a tourism venture are considered. Interaction between the farm owners and the tourists is evaluated from the perspective of the former and the use of any defence mechanisms in ensuring privacy or distance from tourists is discussed. Future plans for the tourism enterprise from the case studies analysed are also outlined in terms of whether there are further growth and development objectives such as succession plans or whether it is essentially lifestyle oriented in nature. The chapter contributes to the knowledge on farm tourism by addressing farm attractions rather than farm accommodation and then mapping the specific needs and orientations of the farmer/farming family using a typology of farmers seeking to diversify specifically by embracing the farm attraction as an enterprise model. This chapter outlines the components of this typology, devised as a result of the fieldwork and analysis conducted.

Farm Diversification in the UK

Total income from farming in the UK is estimated to have fallen 5.4% in 2003/4 to US$5.7 billion, the same level earned in real terms as during the late 1980s and early 1990s

Developments in Tourism Research
Copyright © 2007 by Elsevier Ltd.
All rights of reproduction in any form reserved.
ISBN: 978-0-080-45328-6

(DEFRA, 2005). Subsidies received as a consequence of engaging in agricultural production have fallen by 10%, so that average net farm income is expected to fall by 29% between 2003/4 and 2004/5. The Countryside Alliance (2001) believes farm incomes have dropped 90% since 1995 . These income figures conceal large variations as smaller farms have been particularly, badly affected by the changes leading to the subsequent decrease in the number of privately owned family farms and their increasing marginalisation (Chaplin, Davidova, & Gorton, 2004; Whatmore, Munton, & Marsden, 1990). This decline has created the pressure for farms to diversify. Yet, in some respects diversification is not new. Farmers have constantly sought to identify new crops and new agricultural activities that would enable them to produce an improved rate of return and to continue farming. However, as options to diversify within farming have reduced, so farmers have had to look over agriculture's fence to other industrial sectors for alternative strategies (Peachey, 2003). Opportunities to do so have been plentiful. The Rural Enterprise Scheme will distribute more than $287 million to UK farmers to assist with diversification between April 2001 and 2006 (BBC, 2003).

McInerney, Turner and Hollingham (1989) estimated that 42% of farm holdings in England and Wales were involved in diversified activities, while University of Exeter (2003) estimate this has now increased to 58% of farms in 2002 being engaged in diversification. The National Farmer's Union (NFU) (1999) estimate that 62% of farms receive non-farming income, although this includes money earned from taking additional employment away from the farm. Bateman and Ray (1994, p. 2) refer to this broadest view of diversification as 'pluriactivity'. The need to take employment away from the farm may strike the smaller farm disproportionately hard as they lack the access to capital required to make the structural changes to the farm necessary for typical diversification options.

Among farms that have diversified, University of Exeter (2003) report a mean profitability of $17,883, but acknowledge the effect of very successful, large businesses in skewing the mean figure as four out of five farms did not achieve this level. Indeed, the report cites two-thirds of the diversified enterprises generated output of less than $9437. Such figures show that despite falling earnings non-agricultural diversification represents a small part of total farm income. However, what this fails to acknowledge is the importance to individual farms of this financial contribution. Further, concentrating on earnings risks the deracination of the diversification enterprise from the lifestyle approach taken to the running of the farming enterprise. Indeed, a survey by the NFU (1999) showed that while 45% of farmers cited the raising of income as their reason to diversify, 13% claimed 'personal interest'. Investigating the reasons for quitting a diversified business 52% of the respondents to the University of Exeter (2003) survey cited 'too much hassle' and only 25% because of 'insufficient financial returns', demonstrating the importance of non-financial considerations.

Yet, while the majority of diversification enterprises do involve farm accommodation, this trend is more prevalent in large farms, possibly reflecting the initial resources and large capital investment required to convert farm buildings to holiday accommodation. As economies of scale are not available to small farms the economic pressure to diversify is significant and farm attractions may represent an alternative with lower capital barriers to entry. Furthermore, farm attractions have been able to create indoor facilities, partially overcoming the problem of seasonal demand that affects accommodation and so dramatically improving the potential rate of return on investment. Attractions can be easily copied, which combined with low barriers to entry and strong rates of return can create a problem. However, many attractions are borne out of personal interests and where they create an attitudinal and knowledge barrier that competitors who seek to copy ideas may find difficult to overcome.

South West Tourism (2002) argues that the market for farm attractions is significant and worthy of attention. They cite 13% of the UK population who have visited an open farm within the past year and 26% who had visited a farm shop. Research by the UK Research Liaison Group (2005) showed that in 2002 of 1.1 billion trips taken within the UK 22% (234 million) were to the countryside, with an average spend per trip of $39.30. Examination of the annual survey of UK Visitor Attractions for 2002 (UK Research Liaison Group, 2005) reveals of the 3295 surveyed attractions 3% (99) were farm attractions and attracted 2% (5.68 million) of the 284 million visits to surveyed attractions. The average admission fee charged was $6.77, slightly below the average of $7.17, but with a longer than average time of stay at 182 min (UK Research Liaison Group, 2005). Nationally, estimates suggest there may be 1200 farm attractions attracting 10 million visitors each year (BBC, 2001). Work by the Scottish Agricultural College (2005) explains the farm attractions in Scotland, 41% remained open throughout the year and received an average of 51,300 visits per year, although the smallest attraction received only 500 visits and the largest 350,000. Such figures serve to illustrate the importance of studying each attraction individually to understand the value of diversifying into a business that appears at an aggregated level to either offer little financial assistance to farming, or threaten to swamp traditional farming completely.

Any tourism which is farm-based is inseparable from the farm setting and the context of rurality as a whole. This can be seen as a fundamental difference between small, typically family-run tourism businesses in urban areas where such an explicit dependence upon another industry or employment sector is not evident. There is general consensus in the literature on farm-based tourism that tourists desire the rural setting and its associated imagery which is often related to ideas about idyllic and romantic scenery (see for example, Busby, & Rendle, 2000; Walford, 2001). Nevertheless, there is some debate over whether the farm tourism experience requires as part of this broader rural image an actual working farm with its traditional agricultural activities and farmer and other individuals present as visible, if somewhat stereotypical elements (Morris & Romeril, 1986). Pearce (1990) believes the appeal of rural tourism is derived from the ordinary and everyday happenings of a rural community. While, from their findings on farm-based and other rural accommodation enterprises in Israel, Fleischer and Tchetchik (2005) argue that the working farm is not a necessary attribute for tourists, but leave unasked the question of whether tourists need to know that a related farm does exist somewhere and to some extent. South West Tourism (2002, p. 41) provides an opinion, stating, 'While visitors will want some kind of farm experience with animals, they are looking for a sanitised version, reinforcing the rural idyll imagery'. Busby and Rendle (2000) also question the extent to which a working farm is necessary and consider issues of authenticity (MacCannell, 1976), while Morris and Gladstone (2001, p. 244) write of the invariably 'staged quality' to encounters between farm hosts and guests.

Therefore, it could be argued that the former existence or vastly scaled down activities of a once busy working farm are sufficient, so long as the staged imagery and traditional authenticity of the farm is ensured for the tourist as guest. However, although this might be the case from the standpoint of the tourist as consumer of the farm attraction product, it is the contention of the authors that this may not be appropriate from the perspective of the farming family who must negotiate the delicate balance between the domain of the working farm as an agricultural production unit and the domain of the tourist attraction. Although they may be interdependent, each has differing needs and emphases, which cause the farmer and their family to reflect on their views towards and relationship with both. This research therefore posits arguments according to the standpoint of the enterprise owner *per se* rather than the tourist.

Study Methods

The empirical research adopts a multiple embedded case study design (Yin, 1993). Three key criteria determining the selection of cases were employed. The first is that the farms need to be, or have been at some point in the past, a working farm. The second is that the research is limited to tourism businesses run independently by a 'farming family' or by clearly identifiable individuals, as opposed to a large-scale agribusiness corporation. The third is geographical location as the two regions of Yorkshire and East Anglia were chosen as the areas within which cases would be selected. The empirical data collection was divided into two phases. The first involved a detailed analysis of 10 cases in the Yorkshire region whilst the latter involved 6 cases in East Anglia. The rationale for research locations is based on a number of important characteristics pertaining to each geographical region. Yorkshire was chosen as the research context because it is a highly rural region, dependent on farming where agriculture contributes $1.35 billion to the regional economy (fifth largest industry) through 19,000 holdings and directly supports 40,000 farmers in employment, but it was badly affected by foot and mouth disease (DEFRA, 2005). East Anglia is described as the 'bread basket of the UK' (NFU, 2004) and contributes $2.07 billion to the regional economy (fourth largest industry) and employs 53,000 on 20,000 farms (DEFRA, 2005), but has suffered from the decline in prices for agricultural products, so creating a greater incentive for diversification.

Sample frames were derived from the online database directory hosted by the National Farm Attractions Network (an adjunct to the UK National Farmers Union). Contact was made with the farms identified as meeting the research criteria, and face-to-face in-depth interviews and on-site visits were consequently arranged. The average length of interviews was two hours, and all interviews were recorded and later fully transcribed to facilitate the analysis process. Both researchers also took observational notes whilst in the field which were duly compared and incorporated into the primarily inductive research framework. Raw textual data were analysed by the use of the MaxQDA qualitative analysis software package for the purposes of data management, coding and retrieval. The analysis employed allowed for a grounded understanding of the nature of the individual actors engaged in farm diversified tourism businesses. A vital component of the research involved the use of the actors' own definitions and views as categories by which the data were coded and interpreted, ensuring that the findings are necessarily context-driven and reliable.

Findings

The Farming and Tourism Relationship

From the interviews a clear continuum emerged. At the one end, farmers were keen to embrace diversification from farming towards tourism and saw it as a desirable and creative enterprise, whilst at the other end of the continuum farmers resented the need for change and hence the diversification. These farmers saw themselves primarily as farmers as opposed to managers of tourism enterprises, and this led to comments which appeared both disdainful of the tourism industry and resentful that farming had declined to such a point as to necessitate diversification. There is a feeling of resentment at having to pursue an alternative strategy characterised in some cases as 'alien' in order to increase financial revenue generated by the farm. Therefore, the self-identity of the participants is found not to be dependent upon the level of income generated by a particular activity, be it tourism or farming, or the time devoted to that endeavour, or even recognition of the future direction of the countryside. Instead, it is found to depend upon those highly emotive and intangible elements associated with being a farmer, and a resentment of what are seen to be the lower status, and less inherently altruistic pursuits involved in a tourism enterprise. Tourism as an industry is afforded less legitimacy by the farmers, particularly those who have only recently sought a diversification strategy. It is perceived as having an indirect purpose or value in the countryside when compared to more directly defined agricultural activity. Tourism enterprise is thus regarded as a means to an end and therefore more transient in nature in terms of its inherent value to the countryside. This view is reflected in the following interview excerpts which demonstrate the reluctance by some participants to move into tourism, a strategy that would involve a fundamental and highly personal renegotiation of their sense of self and how they define, characterise and project their role;

> I should maybe have said look, I'm not a farmer anymore, I'm going to be an attraction land. You see … Flamingo Land started as a farm and when they started it was a pig house and a chicken house, and now of course it's come along. We had never any intention of going down that way …
>
> People don't understand this is the part time job, we have got the full time job to do after they leave.

Those more positive about the shift in orientation did acknowledge an increased opportunity to educate others about the countryside and to use tourism as a means to continue their chosen rural lifestyle. Where these sentiments were expressed, participants were very vocal about how they viewed the tourist's experience on a farm and felt a responsibility to present what they regard as an *authentic* farm experience. However, the ability to design a successful business model was often in conflict with the provision of an authentic farm experience that placed tourists in potentially dangerous situations. Some attractions are highly integrated into normal farming activities while others are kept separate from the farm allowing less interaction between the tourist and the farm environment. The following interview excerpts are from those with a desire to integrate everyday farm activities into the experience of the attraction in order to provide an *authentic experience* (Cohen, 1979). Thus, naturally occurring farm scenes are appreciated as real by the tourists.

> ... we are still a working farm, and hopefully that's what keeps attracting them.
> We've tried to keep ours as much a farm. It's not a farm park, it's not a museum ... it's a working farm. But we are now being pushed into the play areas and the pedal trucks.

Others view separating aspects of the farm from those areas where tourists are allowed to venture as more important than the notion of authenticity, as described above, by integrating farm and tourism activities more closely. Reasons for this include legal concerns and health and safety, as well as the view that more rigid separation would be operationally superior in terms of efficiency. There is also a psychological need for physical boundaries to be preserved in order to maintain a distinction between 'front' and 'back' locations (Smith, 1977). This is demonstrated by the following view which shows the boundaries set up between both functions. Whilst this may not always involve a physical separation due to practical restrictions, the coping mechanisms adopted to separate the two domains involve strategies such as creating greater temporal distance in order to restrict overlapping boundaries;

> They fit in fairly well because we're milking at seven in the morning and we go through all the feeding and milking by ... half past nine and then we're ready for opening at half past ten. We don't milk until half past five, and we shut at five, so the two fit together fairly well.

The following excerpts illustrate the perceived clash to be inherent in any attempt to combine both domains, with farming activities being seen as undesirable from a tourism perspective. Similarly, the need to tend to tourists is viewed as impeding 'proper farming' activity;

> Steve built an ice-cream parlour ... he's the best cowman in the county — he's superb. But he built an ice-cream parlour in the middle of the farmyard. The silo smells, there's muck-spreading smells. Who'd want it? I'm sorry but who'd want it?
> You can't farm and have an open farm. No way, not proper farming.
> To be frank with you, tourism and the farming side don't mix. You cannot be working at something on a farm and take a few minutes out to deal with the public. Your focus when you're dealing with the public has got to be public, not farming.

For the owner concerned primarily with running a profitable rural attraction, the need for authenticity can be seen to be of secondary importance, while for the owner concerned with still being seen as a farmer, the desired projection of authenticity can be an impediment to the ability to run a profitable business. There is a general recognition that the ideal business model from the perspective of operational efficiency and profitability would be either to abandon farming production altogether or to ensure a rigid separation of farming and tourism activities. The latter division may result in creating only a pretence or sanitised veneer of farming within the realms of the attraction for the purposes of tourism consumption. As a result, this would constitute *staged authenticity* (Cohen, 1979) whereby scenes and activities are staged for tourists, such as milking cows or feeding livestock, and the experience is viewed as a real reflection of genuine activities taking place on a farm, albeit on a different scale or modified to facilitate their viewing/interaction. At the extreme, particularly in cases where purpose-built attractions are implemented as part of a growth-oriented business diversification strategy where the farm bends to the wishes of the tourists, there is a danger that the farm will disappear completely. This leaner portfolio of activity is unproblematic from an operational perspective but has dramatic implications from an authenticity perspective. It could result in an experience of *contrived authenticity* (Cohen, 1979), which involves the staging of scenes by the owners that are recognised as staged by tourists, thus severing the strength of ties between farming and tourism. An example of this was when the authors visited a farm attraction which had diversified to such an extent that one of the purported highlights of the attraction for the children was a life-sized fibreglass replica cow possessing replica rubber teats. This too was housed in a small all-weather building.

However, for those who resist change, and still cling to an ideal occupation of purely or predominantly farm-related production, decisions to diversify into tourism are difficult to make. As an alternative to a more explicit 'switch', these individuals are more likely to attempt to temporarily 'modify' their farming activities through the diversification route in order to accommodate both farming and tourism activities together. This is exemplified by the following excerpt:

> Our main income now is from the diversification, but the farm side is so important because that's what attracts them here … the farm, the conservation, the tourism, it's a triangle that works quite well together.

Beyond the physical and ideological relationship between the farm and tourism, important issues were voiced about the human qualities needed to run a successful tourist venue. Farmers have been educated to run a business producing a traditional product where there is little new product development, limited control over price and little need for marketing. In addition to this, the required personality for farmers who are required to spend long periods of the day alone or with animals can be seen to be at variance with that desired for a 'tourist attraction' manager. A report by the Scottish Agricultural College (2005) advising farmers of the advantages and disadvantages of diversification into tourism makes no mention of the need to ensure a match of skills. The implication would appear to be that being a farmer is an adequate preparation for being able to run a tourist attraction. By contrast, Acumenia (2002) argue that farmers are less inclined to diversify when the farmer is older, has been on the farm for longer, is from farming stock, does not have off-farm work experience, has higher farm income, has received less external advice, is a NFU member and has a tenured farm. While recognising the importance of personal characteristics, this also produces a danger of a template being developed for a purported ideal candidate for diversification, thereby ignoring more subtle, but no less important individual characteristics. Those interviewed understood the potential source of disharmony between the farming

and tourism. Indeed, there was a clear awareness of these tensions as illustrated in the following excerpts;

> I think we really need to look at managing the business better. He's a farmer,
> and a farmer is not a businessman.
>   Farmers don't really socialise with people do they?
>   I don't think that diversification into tourism and the interface with the
> public is something that just any farmer can do. You have to have certain
> skills and an interest in people, and many, many farmers are not of that ilk.
> They are farmers, first and foremost. I suppose you can't be all things to all
> people anyway.

'Modifiers' and 'Switchers'

Table 1 shows the conceptual map of the findings of the research with four groups of farmers; the first of which have not diversified and have no plans to, the second are currently
considering diversifying and can be at varying stages of planning, the third group have
diversified and the fourth group have diversified but have subsequently reverted back to
pure farming. Acumenia (2002) describes the current diversifiers as potentially being either
'major' or 'minor' diversifiers, but their categorisation is based on the financial extent to
which the farm has diversified. Hence, a farm that derives much of its total income from
non-farming sources is considered to be a major diversifier. However, the interviews
conducted for this chapter show Acumenia's groupings to be limited by ignoring a suite of
factors, but particularly the psychological position of the farmers, the potential importance
of relatively small amounts of additional income, the ability to fit a diversified business
alongside farming and so the ability to be more or less diversified, as well as human resources
and succession planning. Hence, this chapter suggests referring to current diversifiers not

Table 1: Conceptual map of the research results.

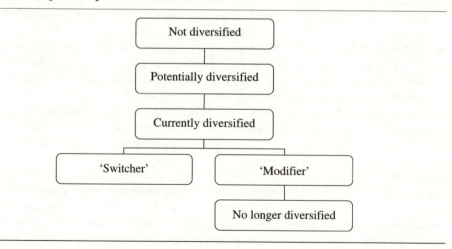

as 'major' or 'minor', but instead as 'modifiers' and 'switchers'. Dewhurst and Horobin (1998, p. 30) sum up the farmers in this research, 'their business success might best be measured in terms of a continuing ability to perpetuate their chosen lifestyle'. As such, the financial extent to which diversification has taken place is somewhat irrelevant. What matters instead is whether the diversification meets the goals for which it was established. Given recognition of these factors internal to the farming household, including the lifestyle approach to diversification, the 'modifier' and 'switcher' labels provide a pronounced representation of those interviewed.

The first type identified by the research is the 'modifier'. These are owners who need to diversify but essentially wish to remain in farming. They recognise the need to temporarily diversify their business model but identify themselves strongly as farmers. They strive to combine both activities, and seek to manage any inherent conflict between farming and tourism. Their long-term aspiration is to have the financial means to return exclusively to farming, ideally through changes that allow farming to become economically viable.

> A lot of them now, it's either a tourism business or it's a farming business, and we don't want to do that if we can.

This group may successfully balance the need to project themselves as farmers and earn enough money in order to subsidise the farming side of the business. However, the corollary of wanting to be seen as a farmer is the burden to the business of maintaining an authentic working farm. The increased cost and exposure to risk from tourists having accidents, plus the reluctance to invest money on necessary product improvements or acquiring the human skills coupled with a generally negative motivation for having tourists on the farm, may ultimately weaken the ability of the farmer to subsidise the farming side of the business. Many examples were found with a mixed tourism/farming identity but who struggled to accommodate farming and tourism together. Getz and Carlsen (2000) found their farm tourism respondents to be low in innovation because of the ease of being copied, but this was not the case in this research of farm attraction managers. Instead those interviewed tended to be very creative, but generally lack focus or the business skills to operate multiple diverse activities without successfully exploiting opportunities to meet their business goals.

> I've got to identify bad spots in my business. We've had our heads down, particularly me, perhaps so much that we haven't seen the whole of the picture.
> … maybe I should cut out a couple of branches, but I don't know which branch to cut out.

The second type identified is the 'switcher', for whom the long-term goal is to separate from farming altogether. Having faced economic pressure to diversify, this group now positively embrace the need to diversify. The physical resources of the farm may mean that it is impossible to colocate tourism and farming effectively and so a decision has been made to move away from farming to the extent that all that remains is what is necessary for the purposes of the attraction. Interestingly, this group has come to see tourism as a means to the end which is continuing life in the countryside, rather than to the end which is the continuance of farming. Lane (1994, p. 105) describes how 'farmers are the guardians of the rural landscape' and yet following the approach of the switchers, farming is the industry through which the countryside has been maintained until this point in time, but the future will require a new industry to achieve the desired outcome of continuing rural life. DEFRA (2005) note that 'it is useful to think of diversification as a transition rather than an end-state', but the question remains as to what the desired end-state is for the individual farmer.

Freed from the constraints of trying to maintain an authentic working farm, there were several examples encountered of switchers who have been extremely economically success-ful and manage purpose-built, growth-oriented, farm-based tourism attractions.

> On any one given day you've got about 35 to 40 people working here in the café and the shops ... We're going to put a two-storey building up for the small animals; we're going to knock down the old small animal building and put a two-storey building there and a single storey. We're going to do more people shelters, school groups having their dinner and things like that.
>
> I mean in three years we had one butcher and now we've got about six. So, that has shot up. The farm is more or less steady at 200,000 and 220,000 visitors, but then there are lots of under threes and we've done a new play-ground, which has been very, very popular. The café gets it's regulars ... The toyshop is fairly new, but again, kids who go round the farm, they always like to buy a little something. There are train sets and lots of cameras, every-thing with our name on.

Although those interviewed were identified as fitting within one of these two categories at the point of data collection, it must be emphasised that owners may transfer from one to another over time. Thus, the categories should be viewed neither as temporally fixed nor as mutually exclusive.

Conclusions

Various situational factors can promote or inhibit the potential success of the farm-based tourism enterprise and the farm. These include motivations for business start-up; longer-term goals; skills of the farming family running the enterprises; extent and value of any advice received; physical resources and on-site aesthetics; range of facilities available to the public (the 'fit' of the farm with tourism); level of perceived and projected authenticity and the location and size of the farm and its accessibility from key urban centres. Other con-cerns that are increasingly important also are planning requirements, insurance liabilities, health and safety concerns and government and animal welfare safeguards. The develop-ment of a list of factors that are important for the consideration of the fit between tourism and farming represents an advance on current knowledge. This would enable farmers and advisors to perform a check on how appropriately configured their farm is to diversifying into tourism and more specifically, farm tourism attractions. Determining commonality amongst the owners may also enable groups of farmers to be identified who possess similar aspirations. This would enable strategies to be developed for particular groups, including training or business advice that enables owners to progress onto a more sustainable position, for themselves and their families, their businesses and the wider image of farm-based tourism. However, discussions held with farmers for this research reveal the complexity of issues involved. It is therefore also imperative that advice be tailored to individual circumstances, recognising the interaction of the issues identified in this chapter.

Further research is necessary in the specific area of farm-based attractions and agricultural diversification more broadly. The implications of the research relate to both the commonality and difference of views among farmers seeking to diversify. In terms of the differences, all participants embrace the label of 'farm attractions' and collectively identify their businesses as such. Yet, it was also found that a number of attractions using the label of 'farm attraction' have very tenuous links with traditional forms of farming. The extreme variability in the quality of the product could lead to a risk to the image of farm tourism that could weaken the future prospects of tourism as a vehicle for diversification. Furthermore, as tourism is certainly advocated as a diversification strategy by farming organisations, more consideration of the cumulative impact of this approach from the perspective of the tourism industry is required. Research also needs to be focused on the attributes of those farmers who are now seeking to diversify, despite the pressure farmers have faced to diversify for more than 20 years. If farmers who are now diversifying into tourism are more open-minded, then the future of the countryside using tourism as a vehicle may hold cause for optimism. By contrast, if current diversifiers are less prescient farmers who have finally conceded to the inevitable fate of 'having to' diversify, then there is cause for concern for both the tourism industry and the countryside.

Acknowledgements

The authors would like to gratefully acknowledge the financial assistance from the School of Management and the University Research and Scholarship Fund at the University of Surrey.

References

Acumenia. (2002). *Farm tourism supply*. Exeter: Acumenia.

Bateman, D., & Ray, C. (1994). Farm pluriactivity and rural policy: Some evidence from Wales. *Journal of Rural Studies*, *10*(1), 1–13.

BBC. (2001). *Double blow for farmers*. www.news.bbc.co.uk/1/hi/business/1194940.htm. Accessed on 5 November 2003.

BBC. (2003). *Health farm for horses*. www.news.bbc.co.uk/1/hi/england/2666663.stm. Accessed on 5 November 2003.

Busby, G., & Rendle, S. (2000). The transition from tourism on farms to farm tourism. *Tourism Management*, *21*, 635–642.

Chaplin, H., Davidova, S., & Gorton, M. (2004). Agricultural adjustment and the diversification of farm households and corporate farms in central Europe. *Journal of Rural Studies*, *20*, 61–77.

Cohen, E. (1979). Rethinking the sociology of tourism. *Annals of Tourism Research*, *6*, 18–35.

Countryside Alliance. (2001). *Planning and agricultural diversification*. http://www.countryside-alliance.org/policy/010214coun.htm. Accessed on 20 April 2005.

DEFRA. (2005). *Economic position of the farming industry.* www.defra.gov.uk. Accessed on 1 March 2005.

Dewhurst, P., & Horobin, H. (1998). Small business owners. In: R. Thomas (Ed.), *The management of small tourism and hospitality firms* (pp. 19–38). London: Cassell.

Fleischer, A., & Tchetchik, A. (2005). Does rural tourism benefit from agriculture? *Tourism Management, 26,* 493–501.

Getz, D., & Carlsen, J. (2000). Characteristics and goals of family and owner-operated businesses in the rural tourism and hospitality sectors. *Tourism Management, 21,* 547–560.

Lane, B. (1994). Sustainable rural tourism strategies: A tool for development and conservation. *Journal of Sustainable Tourism, 2*(1–2), 102–111.

MacCannell, D. (1976). *The tourist: A new theory of the leisure class.* New York: Schocken Books.

McInerney, J., Turner, M., & Hollingham, M. (1989). *Diversification in the use of farm resources.* Agricultural Economics Unit Report no. 332, University of Exeter, Exeter.

Morris, A., & Gladstone, J. (2001). Farm tourism, agricultural heritage and the social and economic regeneration of farm women. In: C. Di Domenico, A. Law, J. Skinner, & M. Smith (Eds), *Boundaries and identities: Nation, politics and culture in Scotland* (pp. 237–253). Dundee: University of Abertay Press.

Morris, H., & Romeril, M. (1986). Farm tourism in England's Peak National Park. *The Environmentalist, 6*(2), 105–110.

National Farmers Union. (1999). *The farming economy.* London: National Farmers Union.

National Farmers Union. (2004). Farming in East Anglia. www.nfu.org.uk. Accessed on 6 December 2005.

Peachey, P. (2003). The common agricultural policy: Rural tourism to benefit from diverted funds. *The Independent,* 27 June, 10.

Pearce, P. (1990). Farm tourism in New Zealand: A social situation analysis. *Annals of Tourism Research, 17,* 332–352.

Scottish Agricultural College. (2005). *Farm attractions.* http://www1.sac.ac.uk/management/external/diversification/DivContents.asp. Accessed on 31 March 2005.

Smith, V. (1977). *Host and Guests: An anthropology of tourism.* Philadelphia: University of Pennsylvania Press.

South West Tourism. (2002). *Farm tourism within the context of rural tourism.* Exeter: South West Tourism.

UK Research Liaison Group. (2005). *UK Statistics on tourism and research.* http://www.staruk.org.uk//default.asp. Accessed on 31 March 2005.

University of Exeter. (2003). *Farm diversification activities.* Exeter: University of Exeter.

Walford, N. (2001) Patterns of development in tourist accommodation enterprises on farms in England and Wales. *Applied Geography, 21,* 331–345.

Whatmore, S., Munton, R., & Marsden, T. (1990). The rural restructuring-process: Emerging divisions of agricultural property rights. *Regional Studies, 24,* 235–245.

Yin, R. (1993). *Applications of case study research.* London: Sage.

Chapter 3

Implementation of Mass Customised Manufacturing in the Flight Catering Industry

Yevvon Yi-Chi Chang and Peter Jones

Introduction

In recent years, the flight catering industry has undergone a revolution in response to the changing nature of the airline business post 9/11 and a significant shift in industry concentration (IATA, 2005). Flight caterers face the pressure of lowering their product prices to meet the demands of airlines without compromising quality of their products. To stay ahead in this competitive environment, many flight caterers not only have to provide bulk volume of meals but also have to constantly develop new menus and dishes to appeal to airline passengers. The flight catering industry is thus, faced with the dilemma of coping with high variety of products while operating at high volume.

Mass customisation (MC) has been identified as the synthesis of two alternative approaches to production, namely job shop and assembly line (Brown, Bessant, Jones, & Lamming, 2000). MC enables the high-volume production of a wide variety of products by adopting a range of policies, procedures and techniques in relation to the supply chain, production design and order fulfilment processes (Gilmore & Pine, 1997). The flight catering industry has been selected for this investigation because there is an *a priori* case that typical flight kitchens engage in MC due to their high daily outputs and great variety between airlines, seat classes and day parts. Apart from exploring the concept of MC, the main purpose of this chapter is to investigate the polices and practice of MC and the extent to which these have been applied in current flight catering operations.

The Flight Catering Industry

A single flight by a long-haul Boeing 747 may require over 40,000 separate items loaded onto it. Flight caterers at major hubs, such as London Heathrow, Frankfurt and Atlanta may be handling twenty or more Boeing 747s, as well as many smaller flights per day. Therefore, it is very clear that flight caterers handle a considerable volume of products on a daily basis (McCool, 1996; Jones, 2004). In essence, airlines require caterers to provide all types of meal, beverages and perhaps other products such as paper goods, blankets, magazines, headsets and amenity kits. Although referred to as 'flight kitchens', the food production part of the operation is relatively small. The focus of attention is on assembly — dish assembly (placing hot entrees and other meal components in service dishes); tray assembly; bar cart assembly and trolley loading.

On most scheduled airlines, there is more than one seat class, and for long-haul flights there is more than one meal for each passenger. In addition, airlines operate menu cycles or 'rotations' to ensure that frequent flyers are not always served the same menu. Moreover, most airlines cater for specific dietary needs of passengers that result from religious persuasion or medical conditions. Typically, a flight caterer may have to offer more than 26 different types of 'special meal', such as kosher, halal, low-fat, low-salt and vegetarian. In addition, crew meals are required for safety reasons to be different from passenger meals, and the crews are engaged in active work and require higher energy intake (McCool, 1995; Jones, 2004). Thus, even within one airline there exists a wide variety of menus, meals and dishes.

Most flight caterers contract to supply more than just one airline, as there are few airports where a single airline has enough flights to justify the exclusive use of a kitchen, except for the 'hub' airports of major carriers. So within the flight catering business, variety derives from:

- Number of airlines.
- Types of airline — scheduled, charter, low-cost, executive.
- Duration of flight — short-haul, long-haul.
- Seat class — first, business, economy and chatter flight.
- "Day-part" — breakfast, mid-morning, lunch, mid-afternoon, dinner.
- Frequency of rotations.

Evidently, flight caterers have to deal with large volume and wide variety.

Mass Customisation

Hayes and Wheelwright (1979) explained the trade-offs between five different manufacturing processes that can produce different levels of variety and volume. Job shops, for example, can produce a wide variety of products but can only produce them in low volume. In contrast, mass production can produce large quantities of products but only offers low variety. Schmenner and Swink (1998) further described that the phenomenon of cross-factory productivity differences can be explained by the Theory of Swift, Even Flow. This theory illustrated that productivity decreases as variety of products/services increases. An extension to Hayes and Wheelwright's (1979) typology has been the inclusion of mass customisation (MC), as shown in Figure 1. MC is a synthesis between job shop and assembly line (Brown et al., 2000). Consequently, MC lies in the position where high volume is achievable while having to cope with variety.

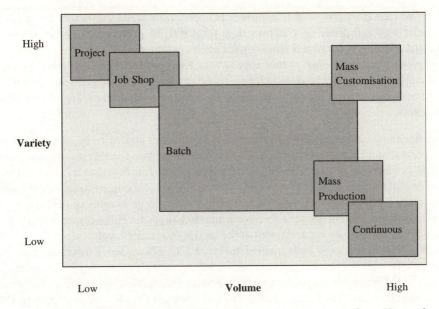

Figure 1: Volume and variety in different operation processes (from Hayes &
Wheelwright, 1979, pp. 135–137).

Types of Mass Customisation

Mass customisation is a relatively straightforward concept, but a review of the literature
reveals a great deal of confusion with regard to how it is put into practice. This is specially
the case when it comes to different types of MC.

Gilmore and Pine (1997) identified four distinct approaches to customisation,
which were *collaborative*, *adaptive*, *cosmetic* and *transparent*. They advocated that when
designing or redesigning a product, process or business unit, managers should choose an
approach or a mix of some or all of the four approaches to serve their own particular set
of customers.

- *Collaborative customisation* — this approach follows three steps: first to conduct a dia-
  logue with individual customers to help them articulate their needs; second, to identify
  the precise offering that fulfils those needs and third, to make customised products for
  them. Collaborative customisation is most appropriate for businesses whose customers
  cannot easily articulate what they want and grow frustrated when forced to select from
  a plethora of options.
- *Adaptive customisation* — adaptive customisers offer one standard, but customisable,
  product that is designed so that users can alter it themselves. This approach is appropriate
  for businesses whose customers want the product to perform in different ways on different
  occasions, and available technology makes it possible for them to customise the product
  easily on their own.

- *Cosmetic customisation* — this approach is appropriate when customers use a product the same way and differ only in how they want it to be presented. In other words, the standard offering is packaged specially for each customer.
- *Transparent customisation* — this approach is appropriate when customers' needs are predictable or can easily be deduced, and especially when customers do not want to state their needs repeatedly. Offerings are customised within a standard package for individual customers.

Alford, Sackett and Nelder (2000) proposed three distinct strategies of customisation — core, optional and form customisation. To illustrate these three strategies, the purchase of a vehicle is taken as an example. In *core* customisation, the customer is involved in the vehicle design process such as low-volume specialised vehicles. In *optional* customisation, the customer is able to choose their vehicles from a very large number of options. In *form* customisation, customers are able to have limited changes or enhancements made to the actual vehicle which may be dealt with at the dealer or retailer level.

In 2001, Zipkin proposed three main elements of MC: *Elicitation* (a mechanism for interacting with the customer and obtaining specific information); *process flexibility* (production technology that fabricates the product according to the information) and *logistics* (subsequent processing stages and distribution that are able to maintain the identity of each item and to deliver the right one to the right customer). Zipkin's (2001) conceptualisation of MC has many similarities with the Lampel and Mintzberg (1996) model.

Anderson (2003) proposed that there are three ways to customise products: adjustable, dimensional and modular customisation.

- *Adjustable customisation* — mechanical or electrical adjustments are a reversible way to customise a product. Adjustments could be infinitely variable. These adjustments and configurations make the product customisable by factory, dealer or customer.
- *Dimensional customisation* — dimensional customisation involves a permanent cutting-to-fit, mixing or tailoring and could be infinite or have a selection of discrete choices.
- *Modular customisation* — modules are literally building blocks that can customise a product by assembling various combinations of modules.

Despite these typologies, the actual implementation of MC is not clearly established. However, it is clear that manufacturers have to adopt policies and procedures that affect one or more of the stages identified in Table 1 — design, fabrication, assembly, packaging and distribution. Moreover, these policies and procedures should facilitate mass production without limiting variety, or customisation without adding cost, or preferably both. Manufacturing practices that achieve these goals include modularity, labour flexibility, JIT, lean production and agile manufacturing.

Modularity

'Modularisation of components to customise end products and services' is one of the five basic approaches to MC proposed by Pine (1993, p. 196). Hudson (1997, p. 82) explained modularisation as a process by which 'a product's components are broken down into modules,

Table 1: Summarises the similarities and differences between these key frameworks in the literature.

MC generic levels	MC approaches		MC strategies	Stages of MC	Types of customisation	
	Gilmore and Pine (1997)	Zipkin (2001)	Lampel and Mintzberg (1996)	Pine (1993)	Spira (1996)	Alford et al. (2000)
8. Design	Collaborative, transparent	Elicitation	Pure customisation			Core customisation
7. Fabrication		Process flexibility	Tailored customisation			
6. Assembly		Process flexibility	Customised standardisation	Modular production	Assembling standard components into unique configuration	Optional customisation
5. Additional custom work				Point of delivery customisation	Perform additional custom work	
4. Additional services				Customised services; providing quick response	Providing additional services	
3. Package and distribution	Cosmetic	Logistics	Segmented standardisation		Customising packaging	Form customisation
2. Usage	Adaptive			Embedded customisation		
1. Standardisation			Pure standardisation			

Adapted from Da Silveria, Borenstein, and Fogliatto (2001, p. 3).

each mass-produced at low cost, which are then assembled efficiently in a variety of configurations to meet individual needs'. In short, modularity is the application of unit standardisation and substitution principle to product and process design to create modular components and processes that can be configured into a wide range of end products to meet specific customer needs.

There are six forms of modularity (Pine, 1993) that are summarised below:

- *Component-sharing modularity* — this refers to same component being used in multiple products. For example, in a fast food restaurant, the burger which is a common component is used in a number of menu items.
- *Component-swapping modularity* — in this case the same product has different components in order to produce a wide variety. This is essentially what the Swatch watch company does.
- *Cut-to-fit modularity* — this idea takes basic components and adopts them to meet the needs of individual customers. For instance, the National Bicycle Industrial Company can manufacture 11 million different bicycles out of 18 basic components of various sizes or styles.
- *Mix modularity* — this approach is based on the idea of a recipe, so that components become something different when mixed together. This has been applied to paints, fertilisers, breakfast cereals and many other processes in which ingredients are mixed.
- *Bus modularity* — this is based on the concept of a standard structure to which different items can be added. The obvious example is the light track where different lights can be fitted.
- *Sectional modularity* — this refers to making components in such a way that they can fit together in all sorts of different procedures. The classic example of this is 'Lego' toys. Aircraft manufacturers, airlines and caterers are increasingly researching for ways in which aircraft galleys and the equipment can be modularised in this way.

Labour Flexibility

Flexibility is the key characteristic of an agile organisation. Indeed, the origin of agility as a business concept lies in flexible manufacturing systems (FMSs). Functional flexibility is the key issue of workforce as the process of increasing the skill repertoire of workers in such a way that the employees acquire the capacity to work across traditionally distinct occupational boundaries (Muller, 1992; Cordery, Sevastos, Mueller, & Parker, 1993).

Just-in-time

Just-in-time (JIT) is the organisational principle on the basis of which every working activity must be supplied with the necessary components in the necessary time and in the necessary quantity (Forza, 1996). JIT delivery and inventories are the heart of lean production systems (Levy, 1997). With JIT the company gives up the expensive security supplied by excess resources and relies on the synchronisation of its various departments (Oliver, Delbridget, Jones, & Lowet, 1994).

Lean Production

Womack, Jones and Roos (1990) defined the term 'lean production' as the lean model that requires less stock, less space, less movement of material, less time to set up the machinery, a smaller workforce, fewer computer systems and more frugal technology. As well as responding to the need to be cost effective, this characteristic also constitutes a general principle that inspires a philosophy of essentiality and which makes every superfluous element seem wasteful. Lean production is the minimum amount of materials, parts, space, workers, time, etc. required for a job, and it improves processes on an operational level as well as contact with suppliers. In addition, lean production is not only about minimal materials, parts, space, movement and time, but also about increasing the efficiency of the workers to be more productive through elimination of waste. Waste in this sense is defined as anything that does not add value to the worker's productivity.

Agile Manufacturing Strategies

Agility is the ability of a company to produce a variety of products with high quality at a low cost. In other ways, agility is a business-wide capability that embraces organisational structures, information systems, logistics processes and, in particular, mindsets (Christopher & Towill, 2000). This demands that the manufacturing system be simple and flexible.

Research Design and Methodology

The purpose of the study reported here is to determine if MC has been adopted in the flight catering industry. However, MC is a general concept which may include a number of dimensions such as modularity, labour flexibility, JIT, lean production and agile manufacturing strategies. These were investigated in order to try to understand their level of adoption. The first stage of this study was exploratory and was conducted through a qualitative research design. Data were collected from three alternative sources in order to provide 'triangulation' of data. Triangulation is regarded as a strategy to overcome problems of validity and bias (Patton, 1990; Mason, 1996; Arksey & Knight, 1999). A triangulated approach facilitates the cross checking of results by using different methods. The first source was secondary data, principally a recently published textbook (Jones, 2004), as well as trade publications. The second source of data derived from observational studies of six flight kitchens in the United Kingdom. The third data set was obtained through structured interviews with flight catering managers who had knowledge of the operational process in the industry. This led to a basic understanding of flight kitchens and how they operated.

The second stage involved an in-depth study of four carefully selected flight kitchens. In order to select these, data from 134 flight kitchens were analysed and ranked using data envelopment analysis. Four kitchens were selected — two in the UK and two in Germany — based on their size and relative ranking from the data envelopment analysis (DEA) analysis. The case method is defined by Yin (2003, p. 13) as an in-depth investigation to gain comprehension of a contemporary phenomenon within its real life context especially when the boundaries between phenomenon and context are not clearly evident. Based on these observational findings, factors that were relevant to the study were identified so that the structured interviews could be conducted in order to confirm or otherwise secondary, observational and fieldwork study findings. The face-to-face interviews were carried out following an interview protocol to guide the discussion towards the determination of the types of MC dimensions in their operational processes. With the aid of a digital recorder, the raw data from the interviews were transcribed into a verbatim transcript; with all references to the catering company's name deleted to ensure confidentiality.

Findings

Stage One — Preliminary Investigation

The preliminary fieldwork began with unstructured observations based on visits to six flight catering companies in the UK. From initial observations, a grasp on the general idea of the operation processes in the flight catering industry was achieved. This enabled questions in relation to the MC processes identified in Table 1. The fieldwork then went on to conduct structured interviews with eleven experienced senior managers from international flight catering companies.

Although all the catering companies surveyed were located in different parts of the world (Asia, Middle East and Italy), there was clearly commonality across the industry. First, all the companies showed that they have to cope with large volume of daily meal production (3000–8000 per day). At the same time, they all had to serve several airline companies per day (20–30 flights daily). Hence, they possessed the characteristics of having to cope with high volume and high variety.

Starting with the menu design process, caterers would present airline companies with a list of different food items for them to pick and/or mix, to form menus they desired. To meet the ever-changing needs of passengers, items in menus had to change constantly to provide passengers with a wide range of choices. All the caterers employed the services of professionals (chefs and nutritionists) or even a dedicated team to handle the design of new menus or products at the request of airline companies. Most caterers suggested that the typical lead time from design to production of a new menu or product, took about 1–2 weeks. Whenever a new menu or product was created, caterers invited airline companies and some invited passengers as well to test the new product. Feedback from airline companies and passengers was noted, and then modifications were made to meet customers' requirements.

At the process engineering stage, a certain set of manufacturing procedures and rules had to be enforced to ensure that the same product could be manufactured again and again. In a typical manufacturing environment, bills of materials were generated along with guidelines on routing and processing instructions. Regarding the generation of bills of materials, the commonly used method to estimate the amount of food/ingredients necessary to provide enough meals for a flight, was calculated by multiplying the weight of ingredients with passenger counts. Some had computer–assisted systems and one relied on the size of aircrafts to estimate the amount. Once the amount of raw materials to provide for a certain flight was known, the next step was to assemble the different food items, for examples, salads, biscuits, butter and so on, onto the tray. This process was facilitated with the use of conveyor belts or workstations. In economy class (E/C), the variety of meals to choose from was very limited; and had to be served in large volumes. Therefore, conveyor belts were used for the production of economy class meals in large volumes.

As for first and business classes, workstations were utilised exclusively to produce tray sets for passengers. All the above–mentioned measures could confirm the manufacturability of product design and establish a set of manufacturing processes and rules. If passengers could pre-order their meals at the same time when they booked their tickets and airline companies inform caterers in advance, many caterers would be able to customise the tray set for each passenger. This would promote flexible services to passengers and reduce any wastage.

Regarding the forecast of the number of tray sets to prepare for each flight, some companies replied that they preloaded the meals 24 hours before departure; and a final load was performed 4–6 hours before flight departure. Some had accounted 10% more on top of their estimated tray sets by their reservation systems informed by airline companies.

Business and first class meals were made in-house with the exception of economy class or some special meals, which were outsourced. To ensure correct dispatch of meals to passengers and to assure food safety procedures and systems such as Hazard Analysis and Critical Control Point (HACCP) system and ISO9001 standard were in place. Besides HACCP, some companies adopted the ISO9001 standard. ISO9001 is a standardisation process that can help both product and service-oriented organisations achieve standards of quality that are recognised and respected throughout the world.

Before meals could be served, there must be enough galley equipment to set up trays for passengers onboard. Methods like push system running (PSR), material handling system (MHS) and warehouse inventory stock check ensured that caterers provide enough galley equipment to set up trays for passengers. PSR is a systematic method of scheduling work based on demand so that the output is controlled without any excess or shortfalls. MHS ensure efficient movement of materials throughout various processes like production, assembly, delivery and so on.

All companies suggested they followed a standard operational management protocol to control their processes, so that meals are delivered on time. HACCP was one of the two operational standards companies employed to control the processes needed to operate or assemble meal sets for delivery to flights on time. Other companies applied JIT in their flight catering operations.

In addition, all the caterers interviewed had strategies to manage flight delays. Sometimes flight delays were due to air traffic congestion and bad judgment from assembly workers which then led to error in predicting the provision of correct amount of food onboard. Some had buffer meals to curb with the shortfall in meal sets. One caterer suggested setting 2 hours of cold holding time before loading meals to keep the food fresh. Investigations of flight delay issues were immediately followed up and rectified. Managing flight delays such as the use of buffer meals to make up the necessary amount, suggested that the companies were flexible in their allocation of resources in the event of flight delays.

These findings led to the development of a systems diagram of a 'typical' flight kitchen, as illustrate in Figure 2.

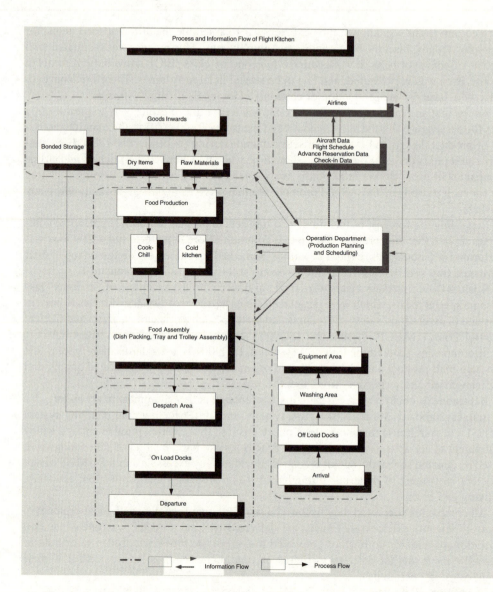

Figure 2: Systems diagram of 'typical' flight production unit (*Source*: Authors).

Stage Two — Case Studies

In order to achieve targeted goals and standards, all the four catering units employed certain key performance indicators (KPIs). The KPIs ensured the elimination of any idle time, which does not contribute to the workers' productivity. Forecasting was a crucial factor in the prevention of overstocking and all four units were found to have MRP implementation via IT systems. The production planning was heavily reliant on the actual flight figures and estimated quantities of ingredients generated by their computer systems, which then allowed them to eliminate waste. In addition, all the four flight catering companies employed the concept of 'first in first out', where food items that arrived in the store first, were utilised since they would expire earlier than other items that arrived later. In this way, any unnecessary waste that arose from expired items was prevented. As such, the implementation of forecasting and MRP had enabled the units to realise both lean production and JIT.

To supplement the shortage in workforce during peak seasons, temporary workers were employed in all four units. Sometimes, workers in different departments were shuffled to work in other departments where more manpower was needed. Generally, the shuffling of workers was within the same process. However, case C further extended the cross functionality of workers in other processes, for instance, drivers taking up the task of washing in the wash up area. During peak seasons where there were a lot of loadings and unloadings, the drivers not only had to perform the primary task of delivery, but also washed up all the unloaded equipment from the aircraft. Instead of allocating more manpower, case C set up a chill area, where all the unloaded equipment were placed; while the drivers continued their delivery work. The chill area not only prevented the unloaded equipment from over-crowding the wash area, but also removed any smell from the remaining food on the equipment by keeping the temperature cool. When the drivers had completed their loadings and unloadings, they then picked up the unloaded equipment from the chill area for washing in the wash area. Similarly, the functionality of drivers in case D extended beyond their main process; where they were required to take up the task as storemen during their off duty hours. Thus, the concepts of functional and temporal flexibilities were clearly exhibited by all the four flight catering companies.

The nature of the flight catering business dictated the need for their operations to be agile, evidenced by last minute meal requests before flight departure, special meal requests and the need to change menus regularly. To cope with the high variety of menus and special meals, common food items were adapted to provide the wide range. The concept of modularity was also observed in the wash up area of the four flight catering companies. Cases A and B installed a machine that could process the different items that included glass, metal and plastic all at the same time. As such, the issue of variety was eliminated. Further, cases C and D grouped together items to be washed by the same airline, albeit different flights. This meant that the belt was not required to re-setup again for each different flight and therefore, would not cause any disruption to the workflow. By grouping together items of the same airline, standardisation across the different flights was achieved, which evidently advocated the concept of modularity.

The analysis of dish packing and food assembling showed that there was not much difference between the performance of economy meal dish packing on table top or conveyor belt, with the conveyor belt slightly faster than the table-top. The efficiency of the conveyor belt was largely dependent on the first person in the line, who was responsible for maintaining the same speed as the belt. Tabletop was still widely adopted not only for assembling dish packing by the small units, but also broadly used for assembling business class or first class meals. The food preparation of long-haul flights was more complex and the labour hours spent were higher than those serving short-haul flights or charter flights only.

Discussion

The key features of MC are modularity, labour flexibility, JIT, lean production and agile man-ufacturing. Since the industry has always had to cope with volume and variety, some elements of these practices have existed in the industry for some time. However, evidence from the research suggests that a number of new practices have been adopted over the last 3–5 years.

Modularity

The flight catering industry had already adopted some key aspects of modularity, as they had modularised service equipment, trays, trolleys and galleys onboard aircraft. Modularity was also evident in the menus across the different classes (economy, first and business classes). In all four cases, common food items — such as pasta and lamb — could not only be used for first and business class meals but also for economy class meals. Similarly, fresh fruits or vegetables could also be used as common ingredients for the different classes. Another indication of modularity was exhibited in the special meals provided by the four flight catering companies that included diabetic, low cholesterol and child meal. All these meals could be made up with existing food items based on modified recipes.

Modularity was also evident in relation to the equipment used for their production and assembly processes. Cases A and B used the same work stations for the assembly of meals in different classes (economy, first and business classes), and in cases C and D, the conveyor belt was used to assemble the trays for different airlines. Likewise in the flight wash up area the machines enabled the processing of glass, plastic or metal.

Labour Flexibility

The findings of this study showed that all the flight catering companies demonstrated flex-ibility in their practices by transferring workers from tray assembly to cold assembly or despatch department in the event of any shortage in workforce. Generally, the shuffling of workers was within the same process. During peak seasons, temporary workers were employed in all four units to supplement the smaller core of workforce. The notion of flex-ibility was thus a very important role for the flight catering company to maintain smooth workflow while coping with high demands. However, the transferring of workers was nor-mally within the same process, for instance, dish-packing worker to work in food assembly. In addition, during seasonal peak periods, temporary workers were hired to supplement the smaller core of workforce in order to produce the increased number of meals for the holiday makers. In the nature of the business, the flight caterers often had to cope with unexpected circumstances that ranged from flight delays to last minute special meal requests.

Just-in-Time

To assure food safety and stock rotation, caterers routinely operate on a 'first in first out' basis. Based on this concept, if there were two items but one arrived in store earlier than the other, the item with the longer storage period would be utilised first. Similarly in the hot food production, items that were produced earlier were utilised first, followed by the same items produced at a later time. In essence, the implementation of this concept allowed food items to be used within their expiration dates and in turn, reduces any waste that arose from expired food items. The items were colour labelled with stickers to distinguish the day they arrived into the store or the day they were produced.

However, a new element of JIT was evidenced in the procurement of raw materials. All the flight catering companies could use their IT systems to monitor and manage the amount of stock they held and ensure JIT purchasing.

Likewise, airline companies were able to estimate the number of trays, trolleys and equipment held in each unit. They would then automatically replenish the stocks for the flight caterer if they saw that the quantity was low. Hence, the airline companies contributed their parts in value creation in the supply chain process by the elimination of unnecessary procedures, where the need to constantly notify the airline companies' designated suppliers of the stock level was necessary.

Lean Production

As mentioned earlier that the notion of lean production is necessary not only in the elimination of unnecessary resources or materials, but also to include any step or process that does not add value. This was exhibited in the external processes of all the four flight catering companies, where they tried to create a global standardisation with airline companies. For example, the elimination of the unnecessary step of transporting meals to airlines' carts before being loaded onto the aircraft saved both time and resources for the flight caterers. Apart from the flight catering company's efforts to eliminate waste in their external process with the co-operation of airline companies, some airline companies such as BA and LTU, went further to help to realise lean production by minimising procedures in the supply chain management through the provision of a webpages for flight caterers and suppliers.

Machinery setup was also one of the ways to achieve lean production. This principle was exhibited in case D, where the production manager would set up the conveyor belt during the break-time of workers. All the items needed to be assembled would be ready for the worker before they started to assemble.

Outsourcing had become a direct solution to achieve lean production in all flight catering companies interviewed. In case B, all economy frozen meals were outsourced and the only meals produced in-house were first class and business class. Fruits for packing as a fruit salad dish were outsourced from other manufacturers which arrived in the store as already washed and pre-peeled. As a result, workers could start to assemble immediately and not waste any time on preparatory work.

Agile Manufacturing

Forecasting is the crucial factor in the prevention of overstocking and all four units were found to have MRP implementations via IT systems. For instance, cases A and B had a flight catering management system and likewise, cases C and D had a X-Net system. The production planning was heavily reliant on the actual flight figures and estimated quantities of ingredients generated by their computer systems, which then allowed them to eliminate any unnecessary waste. Cases A and B indicated they tried to produce meals as fresh as possible that resulted in the company's work schedule of producing meals in the morning for afternoon and night flights. Vice versa, meals produced in the afternoon and night were for the morning flights. In particular for Emirates airline, one chef would come in at 2 am in the morning to prepare and cook all ingredients.

Conclusion

The flight catering industry was found to have many traits of MC, but the industry has not yet fully implemented MC. This is for three main reasons. First, the practices that are associated with MC adoption have not been implemented as part of a MC strategy, but rather as individual cost-cutting measures. In particular, the adoption of JIT has helped to reduce cycle time in processes. Second, caterers operate with uncertainty about the long term, due to the length of contracts they have with airlines. This means that they have made incremental changes to their practices based on relatively low levels of investment. Third, airlines themselves are not driving the adoption of MC, as their focus is on simplifying and reducing onboard provision to cut their costs. Technically, with the adoption of internet-based technologies, it is possible for airline passengers to have a much wider choice of dishes and for them to select what they would like just before they fly, as they would in a restaurant. Some airlines, such as Air India have conducted small trials of this. Were this to be adopted by a major airline, it is highly likely that the full implementation of MC would be necessary in order to cater the aircraft.

References

Alford, D., Sackett, P., & Nelder, G. (2000). Mass customisation: An automotive perspective. *International Journal of Production Economics, 65*, 99–110.

Anderson, D. (2003). *Mass customization, the proactive management of variety, build-to-order-consulting.* Available at www.build-to-order-consulting.com/mc.htm. Accessed on 7 January 2006.

Arksey, H., & Knight, P. (1999). *Interviewing for social scientists.* Thousand Oaks, CA: Sage.

Brown, S., Bessant, J., Jones, P., & Lamming, R. (2000). *Strategic operations management.* Oxford: Buterworth-Heinemann.

Christopher, M., & Towill, D. R. (2000). Don't lean too far-distinguishing between the lean and agile manufacturing paradigms. *Proceedings MIM conference, Aston* (pp. 178–188).

Cordery, J., Sevastos, P., Mueller, W., & Parker, S. (1993). Correlates of employee attitudes toward functional flexibility. *Human Relations, 46*(6), 705–723.

Da Silveira, G., Borenstein, D., & Fogliatto, F. S. (2001). Mass customization: Literature review and research directions. *International Journal of Production Economics, 72*, 1–13.

Forza, C. (1996). Work organization in lean production and traditional plants: What are the differences? *International Journal of Operations and Production Management, 16*(2), 42–62.

Gilmore, H. J., & Pine, II. J. B. (1997). The four faces of mass customization. *Harvard Business Review, 75*(1), 91–112.

Hayes, R. H., & Wheelwright, S. C. (1979). Link manufacturing process and product life cycles. *Harvard Business Review*, January/February, 133–140.

Hudson, B. T. (1997). Industrial cuisine revised. *Cornell Hotel and Restaurant Administration Quarterly, 38*(3), 81–87.

IATA (2005). *International Air Transportation Association: ANSP harmonisation and airline perspective.* Available at http//www.iata.org/pressroom/speeches/2005-01-31-03.htm. Accessed on 29 December 2005.

Jones, P. (Ed.). (2004). *Flight catering* (2nd ed.). Oxford: Elsevier.

Lampel, J., & Mintzberg, H. (1996). Customizing customization. *MIT Sloan Management Review,* *38*(1), 21–31.

Levy, D. L. (1997). Lean production in an international supply chain. *Sloan Management Review,* Winter, 94–102.

Mason, J. (1996). *Qualitative researching.* London: Sage.

McCool, A. C. (1995). *Inflight catering management.* New York: Wiley.

McCool, A. C. (1996). Pricing and cost management for the in-flight catering food service industry. *The Bottomline,* October/November, 14–19.

Muller, W. S. (1992). Flexible working and new technology. In: J. Hartly, & J. N. Stephenson (Eds), *Employment relations: The psychology of influence and control at work.* Oxford: Blackwell.

Oliver, N., Delbridget, R., Jones, D., & Lowet, J. (1994). World class manufacturing: Further evidence in the lean production debate. *British Journal of Management, 5*(Special issue), S53–S63.

Patton, M. Q. (1990). *Qualitative evaluation and research methods.* London: Sage.

Pine, II. B. J. (1993). *Mass customization: The new frontier in business competition.* Boston: Harvard Business School Press.

Schmenner, R. W., & Swink, M. L. (1998) On theory in operations management. *Journal of Operations Management, 17,* 97–113.

Womack, J., Jones, D., & Roos, D. (1990). *The machine that changed the world.* New York: Rawson Associates.

Yin, R. (2003). *Case study research: Design and methods* (3rd ed.). Thousand Oaks, California: Sage.

Zipkin, P. (2001). The limits of mass customization. *MIT Sloan Management Review,* Spring, 81–87.

Chapter 4

Tourism in The Gambia — Ten Years On

Richard Sharpley

Introduction

Tourism has long been regarded as an effective vehicle of development. Over the last half century, not only has it evolved into one of the world's largest economic sectors, now accounting for some 10% of global GDP and approximately 7% of the worldwide export of goods and services but also, for many countries, it has become an 'important and integral element of their development strategies' (Jenkins, 1991, p. 61). The reasons for this are well rehearsed; among other factors, tourism is considered to be an important source of income, foreign exchange earnings and government revenues, as well as providing significant opportunities for employment and backward linkages throughout the local economy (Sharpley, 2002).

At the same time, tourism has also proved to be a consistent growth sector; global international arrivals and receipts continue to increase annually — albeit at a decreasing rate — while, perhaps more importantly, ever more countries play host to tourists. Although approximately half of all international arrivals are still received by just 10 (principally developed) nations, many new destinations have claimed a place on the international tourism map. Indeed, throughout the last decade the East Asia Pacific and Middle East regions have witnessed the highest and most sustained growth in arrivals globally while, in recent years, a number of least developed countries, including Cambodia, Myanmar, Samoa and Tanzania, have experienced higher than world average growth in tourism. Consequently, tourism has assumed an increasingly important developmental role in many less developed countries — although frequently as an option of 'last resort' (Lea, 1988) — not only as a dominant economic sector but also as a potential means of redistributing wealth from the richer nations of the world. As the 2001 UN Conference on Trade and Development noted, 'tourism development appears to be one of the most valuable avenues for reducing the marginalisation of LDCs from the global economy' (UNCTAD, 2001, p. 1).

Importantly, however, the introduction of tourism does not invariably set a nation on the path of development. That is, the unique characteristics of tourism as a social and economic activity, the complex relationships between the various elements of the international

Developments in Tourism Research
Copyright © 2007 by Elsevier Ltd.
All rights of reproduction in any form reserved.
ISBN: 978-0-080-45328-6

tourism system and transformations in the global political economy, of which tourism is a part, all serve to reduce its potential developmental contribution. Not only is it highly susceptible to external forces and events; such as political upheaval, natural disasters or health scares; but also many countries have become increasingly dependent upon tourism as an economic sector, which remains dominated by wealthier, industrialised nations (Reid, 2003). Therefore, a particular economic, political and socio-cultural characteristics of destinations, especially in less developed countries, may themselves limit the extent to which opportunities presented by tourism may be realised. Limited financial and human resources, poor infrastructure and a narrow local economic base are, for example, some of the widely recognised factors that serve to restrict tourism's role in development (Mowforth & Munt, 2003). In short, as a number of countries have discovered that development, however defined, is not an inevitable consequence of tourism.

One such country is The Gambia. Prior to 1965, The Gambia was unknown as a tourist destination. However, following the arrival of just 300 mostly Scandinavian tourists during the 1965–1966 winter season, its potential as a winter-sun destination was increasingly exploited and, over the next 30 years, the country's tourism sector grew steadily, though remaining relatively insignificant in global tourism terms. By the 1993–1994 winter season, almost 90,000 arrivals were recorded and tourism was contributing some 10% of GDP (Dieke, 1993a, 1993b). The introduction of summer-sun package holidays to The Gambia in 1993 further boosted arrivals, and confidence in future development of the tourism sector was manifested in the country's *1995–2000 National Policy for Tourism Development*; this forecast that arrivals figures would reach 150,000 by 1999–2000 (Ministry of Tourism and Culture, 1995, p. 28). It is also interesting to note that, during the 1980s and 1990s, The Gambia also attracted significant academic interest, with a number of commentators exploring the role of tourism in the country's development (for example, Wagner, 1981; Farver, 1984; EIU, 1990; Dieke, 1993a, 1993b, 1994; Thomson, O'Hare, & Evans, 1995; Sharpley & Sharpley, 1996).

However, the last decade has witnessed a reversal in the fortunes of The Gambia's tourism industry, particularly since 2000 (as well as declining academic interest in it). Following the military coup in 1994 and the subsequent collapse of the tourism sector during the 1994–1995 winter season (Sharpley, Sharpley, & Adams, 1996), overall arrivals have remained stagnant. In 2004, for example, 90,098 tourist arrivals were recorded (GTA, 2005), virtually unchanged from 1993–1994 total. This contrasts starkly with the increase in international tourist arrivals in both the African region as a whole and in West Africa in particular (Table 4.1).

Thus, while arrivals regionally have demonstrated significant growth, exceeding the overall growth of 42% in world arrivals during the same period, not only has tourism to

Table 4.1: International tourist arrivals 1995–2004 ('000).

	1995	**2000**	**2004**	**Growth 1995–2004 (%)**
Africa	20,438	28,154	33,222	66
West Africa	1913	2451	2960	55
The Gambia	90[a]	78	90	0

Source: GTA (2005); WTO (2005).
[a]Arrivals based on 1993–1994 season, the nearest comparable figures prior to the 1994 coup *d'état*.

The Gambia remained static but the country has also lost market share. Accurate data with respect to tourist receipts in The Gambia are not available, an issue returned to later, but it is perhaps no coincidence that, since 1995, the country has not developed economically — per capita GDP in 2003 was $280, roughly the same as a decade earlier (www.afdb.org, 2005). Indeed, according to some indicators, poverty in The Gambia increased throughout the 1990s, a trend that has yet to be reversed (Republic of The Gambia, 2003).

It is, of course, overly simplistic and naïve to suggest a positive correlation between the performance of the tourism sector and the lack of economic development in The Gambia. Nevertheless, it can be argued that the problems facing tourism in The Gambia have contributed to the wider continuing socio-economic problems that the country continues to face. The purpose of this chapter, therefore, is to consider tourism in The Gambia over the last 10 years, exploring in particular the reasons for the lack of continued development of the sector, and to suggest ways in which tourism may be planned in the future so as to contribute more sustainability to the country's development. In so doing, it will also contribute to the tourism literature on The Gambia that, since the mid-1990s, has been noticeably lacking.

The Gambia: An Overview

The Republic of The Gambia, situated in West Africa, is the smallest county on the African continent. Following the course of the River Gambia, it is bordered by Senegal to the north and south, and by the North Atlantic Ocean to the west. It has a total land area of 11,300 km^2, and is 350 km long and just 48 km wide at its widest point (see Figure 4.1). Lying equidistant between the Equator and the Tropic of Cancer, some 6 hours flying time from northern Europe, The Gambia experiences a tropical climate of a hot rainy season from June to November and a cooler dry season from November to May.

Established as a British Crown Colony in 1889, The Gambia gained independence in 1965 and became a republic in 1970. Prior to the 1994 coup, The Gambia claimed to have

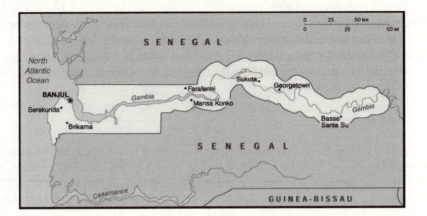

Figure 4.1: The Gambia.

one of the oldest multi-party democracies in Africa, although to what extent a genuine and stable democracy existed is disputed by some (Edie, 2000). After 2 years of post-coup military rule, presidential elections were held in 1996. The new President, Yahya Jammeh, was subsequently re-elected in 2002 and his party, the Alliance for Patriotic Reorientation and Construction (APRC), maintained a strong majority in the 2002 National Assembly elections, which were boycotted by opposition parties. At the time of writing, President Jammeh is expected to be re-elected to a third term in 2006 and, as Saine (2002, p. 171) observes, 'The Gambia remains a long way from being the functioning democracy that it once was'.

The population of The Gambia is approximately 1.6 million and comprises a number of ethnic groups, each maintaining its own language and traditions. Approximately 90% of Gambians are Muslims and some 60% of the population lives in rural villages. The official or natural population growth rate currently stands at 2.7% per annum, although this is boosted to some 4.2% per annum by immigration from less politically stable neighbouring states. With one of the continent's highest population densities (142 per km^2), managing future population growth represents a significant challenge.

The Economy of The Gambia

The Gambia has few natural resources. Consequently, the dominant activity is subsistence agriculture, accounting for approximately 75% of employment but just 35% of GDP that, in 2002, amounted to US$356 million (www.worldbank.org). One of the principal agricultural sectors is groundnuts (peanuts) and groundnut products that, prior to the development of tourism, was the country's main source of foreign exchange earnings. Groundnut production currently represents 7% of GDP, while other agricultural activity is based on crops, fishing, livestock and forestry. A limited industrial sector accounts for 12% of GPD while services, including tourism, account for 53%. Tourism itself is estimated to contribute 12% of GDP although, according to WTTC data, the wider tourism economy in The Gambia accounts for 23% of GDP. Some 10,000 people, or 2.5% of the working population, are employed directly and indirectly in tourism. However, it is suggested that, given the high level of subsistence agriculture and other informal economic activity, tourism accounts for 20% of formal employment (Bah, 2004).

With its limited resources, its small industrial base and principally agrarian economy, not only does the country suffer a significant balance of payments deficit and high levels of external debt, but also it has a narrow tax base that limits revenue generation opportunities. Thus, economic progress remains largely dependent on international aid that, in 2003, amounted to almost US$60 million.

Development Indicators

The Gambia is one of the poorest countries in the world. It is one of the 50 officially recognised Least Developed Countries (LDCs), and is ranked 155th out of 173 nations on the UNDP's Human Development Index (UNDP, 2005). With a per capita GDP in 2003 of US$278, average household income falls below the $1 per day poverty threshold; however, with over half the country's wealth owned by just 20% of the population, between 50% and 70% of the population are estimated to live in extreme poverty. Despite efforts to

Table 4.2: The Gambia: selected development indicators (2003).

Population under 15 years old (% of total)	40.6
Population over 65 years old (% of total)	2.9
Life expectancy at birth	55
Under-five mortality rate (per 1000 births)	123
Adult literacy rate (% of over 15 years old)	30.9 (female)
	45 (male)

Source: UNDP (2005).

address this little progress has been made and, according to the country's first Millennium Development Goals Report (Republic of The Gambia, 2003), there is a high risk that the goal of reducing the incidence of extreme poverty in the country by 50% by 2015 will not be met. Table 4.2 provides other selected indicators of (under-)development in The Gambia.

In most respects, therefore, The Gambia displays the 'typical' characteristics of under-development and undoubtedly falls within the category of so-called 'non-viable national economies' (de Rivero, 2001), or countries that are unlikely to achieve development without substantial and sustained aid. It is against this background that the development of tourism in the country should be considered.

Tourism Development in The Gambia

Tourism was first considered as means of fostering socio-economic development in The Gambia in the mid-1960s, when the global markets for groundnuts/groundnut products were becoming increasingly unstable. Thus, there was a recognised need to diversify into other sources of foreign exchange earnings. With its attractive winter climate and undeveloped coastline, the potential existed to market The Gambia as an exotic winter-sun destination and, as noted above, the first tourists arrived in 1965. However, tourism development was initially driven by overseas (Swedish) tour operators and limited growth was experienced, and it was not until 1972 that a major effort was made by The Gambia to develop tourism (Dieke, 1993b).

Since then, there have been two distinct phases in the development of tourism in The Gambia: a period of relatively stable growth up to 1994 and, following the military coup that year, a decade that has experienced erratic arrivals figures and no overall growth. The focus of this chapter is, as stated earlier, on the latter phase, the development of tourism up to 1994 being well documented in the literature. Nevertheless, it is important to review briefly the first phase as a basis for comparison with more recent developments.

Phase 1: 1972–1994

As noted above, relatively few tourists visited The Gambia in the years immediately following its 'discovery' by the Swedish tour operator Vingressor. However, once proactive steps were taken to develop the sector, the country experienced a rapid increase in the annual number of tourist arrivals, although a number of fluctuations demonstrated the sector's

Table 4.3: Tourist arrivals (air charter) in The Gambia 1972/3–1994/5.

Year	Arrivals	Year	Arrivals
1972–1973	15,584	1984–1985	45,861
1973–1974	20,383	1985–1986	47,926
1974–1975	18,651	1986–1987	45,759
1975–1976	21,116	1987–1988	47,734
1976–1977	19,505	1988–1989	54,149
1977–1978	15,769	1989–1990	47,012
1978–1979	25,907	1990–1991	58,026
1979–1980	23,822	1991–1992	65,771
1980–1981	19,209	1992–1993	63,940
1981–1982	13,331	1993–1994	89,997
1982–1983	26,745	1994–1995	42,919
1983–1984	39,491		

Source: Central Statistics Department (2005) www.gambia.gm/Statistics/Publications.htm.

Table 4.4: Tourist arrivals in The Gambia by country, 1982–1991 (% share).

	1982–1983	1983–1984	1984–1985	1985–1986	1986–1987	1987–1988	1988–1989	1989–1990	1990–1991
UK	37.8	38.1	51.8	59.1	53.6	55.0	56.6	57.2	54.1
Sweden	22.7	14.4	13.1	12.1	14.6	13.9	12.8	13.2	13.5
Denmark	8.8	6.7	5.7	5.3	5.7	5.9	5.4	5.0	3.7
Norway	1.7	2.4	1.5	2.0	4.3	3.2	2.3	1.8	1.4
France	8.9	10.3	9.4	7.8	11.6	12.1	12.8	9.0	5.3
Germany	4.1	6.2	4.6	3.5	3.5	3.5	4.2	9.2	9.6
Others	15.8	22.7	14.0	10.1	6.5	6.5	6.0	4.6	12.3

Source: Adapted from Dieke (1993a).

vulnerability to both internal and external events (see Table 4.3). In a foretaste of 1994, for example, arrivals in 1981–1982 fell dramatically as a result of a failed coup attempt. It should be noted that, for the purpose of comparison, these figures are for air charter arrivals only; figures for non-charter air arrivals are not available from 1996 onwards. However, virtually all leisure tourists travel on package/charter flights from Europe. It should also be noted that, during this first period, arrivals figures relate to a 12-month tourism season (July–June) as opposed a calendar year.

During this period, two principal characteristics of tourism to The Gambia immediately emerged. Firstly, the country became dependent on a small number of key tourist markets, specifically the UK and Scandinavia. As Table 4.4 indicates, during the 1990s, the UK became the dominant market, accounting for well over 50% of annual arrivals throughout the period.

Secondly, tourism became highly seasonal — as a winter-sun destination, the majority of visitors arrived during the peak season of November to April, with over 80% of arrivals occurring during this 6-month period. Although efforts were made to develop a summer market, the country remained uncompetitive compared with Mediterranean summer-sun destinations.

With respect to accommodation supply, the number of bed spaces increased rapidly. By the late 1970s, tourist bed capacity had reached around 3000 and, by the mid-1990s, some 5000-bed spaces were available. The great majority of these were in hotels and guesthouses located in a 15 km strip of land along the coast designated in 1974 as a Tourism Development Area. Most hotels were of tourist, mid-range quality; by 1994, the country boasted only one five-star hotel, the 312-bed Kairaba Hotel. The government of the day provided a variety of incentives for and controls on hotel development, as well as establishing a number of specific bodies responsible for policy development and implementation. However, as Dieke (1993b) notes, the influence of the public sector was limited by inefficient administration and a lack of funding to support tourism development and promotion. In the country's first 5-year development plan, for example, Dalasi 16.8 million, less than 4% of the national budget, was allocated to tourism development; in the second 5-year plan (1980–1985), this sum was halved (Bah, 2004). Consequently, tourism development was largely driven by the overseas-dominated private sector, with grants from international agencies funding some infrastructural developments, while The Gambia's Hotels Association became the country's marketing body.

As tourism to The Gambia grew, particularly during this period, so too did its economic importance. By 1992, it was estimated that tourism was generating approximately US$26 million, or around 10% of GDP (Jeffries Associates, 1992). However, the contribution of tourism to the economy was limited by the fact that most tourists were on pre-paid package tours and, as a result, spent as little as $8 per day within the country (reflecting few spending opportunities outside the hotels). Moreover, as the majority of food and drink consumed by tourists had to be imported, the tourism sector suffered significant leakages, to the extent that only around 20% of the holiday price paid by tourists remained in The Gambia. Nevertheless, the tourism sector accounted for some 7000 direct and indirect jobs.

By 1994, then, tourism had evolved into a major economic sector in The Gambia, although the sector displayed the typical characteristics of dependency — high leakages, significant foreign ownership of tourism assets, dependency on two principal but highly seasonal markets and on international tour operators both for the supply of tourists and for air links with northern Europe. Such dependency was evidenced in the collapse of tourism following the 1994 coup (Sharpley et al., 1996) yet, by the following year, the country was optimistic about the future development of tourism (Ministry of Tourism and Culture, 1995). However, as the next section reveals, such optimism was misplaced.

Phase 2: 1995–2005

In the year following the coup, the tourism sector recovered well and, by 1997, pre-coup figures had been exceeded. In 1999, a record 96,000 tourists visited The Gambia but, since then, annual arrivals figures have fluctuated. As noted in the most recent tourism development plan (DSTC, 2005, p. 26), the tourism industry 'completely lost momentum in the period 2000–2005' (Table 4.5).

Table 4.5: Tourist arrivals in The Gambia 1995–2004.

Year	Arrivals	Year	Arrivals
1995–1996	72,098	2000	78,710
1996	76,814	2001	75,209
1997	84,751	2002	78,893
1998	91,106	2003	73,000
1999	96,122	2004	90,098

Source: GTA (2003, 2005).

Interestingly, most recent figures point to some recovery; for the first 10 months of 2005, arrivals were 27% higher than for the same period in 2004, suggesting that the 100,000 mark would, for the first time, be exceeded (GTA, 2005). However, dependence on the UK market has intensified, rising to 62% of all tourists in 2004, whilst other traditional markets have declined. Conversely, Holland has emerged as an important market, providing14% of air charter arrivals in 2004.

Against this background of variable tourist arrivals, a number of developments during this second phase are of significance:

• There has been an increase in the supply of accommodation. By 2005, 32 recognised hotels and guesthouses offered almost 6400 bed spaces, supplemented by a number of houses/apartments available for private rent. In addition, new developments away from the coastal strip, such as the Mandina eco-lodges at the Makasutu Forest, a small up-market project developed according to eco-tourism principles, have added to the supply of accommodation that is now estimated to total 7000 bed spaces. More accommodation is also planned; an 80-bed three-star hotel was due to open in 2006 while, significantly, a 200-room five-star hotel is currently under construction, allegedly to become part of the Sheraton chain. However, the majority of hotels remain under foreign ownership; despite favourable terms in acquiring land within the Tourism Development Area (see below), a 31% bank-lending rate discourages local investment.

• Infrastructural developments have included a $10 million beach recovery project funded by an African Development Bank loan, a $150,000 street lighting system in the main tourism development area, a new road bypassing Serrekunda, the country's largest urban conurbation, which has dramatically improved access to the tourist area, and upgrading of the coastal road south to the Senegalese border. A large housing development, aimed at the overseas investor, is also being constructed near to the site of the five-star hotel development referred to above, suggesting the potential for an integrated resort area (see www.tafgambia.com). The international airport has also benefited from a new terminal building, although facilities remain basic. However, landing and handling fees at the airport are relatively high (for example, some 50% higher than at London Gatwick), reflecting the low level of traffic yet acting as a major disincentive to airlines and tour operators.

• There has been a reduction in the number of tour operators offering The Gambia as a winter-sun destination. According to one report (Actionaid Gambia, 2005), some 43 European operators brought tourists to The Gambia in 1994 but, by 2002, the number of operators had more than halved. Just eight major UK operators now feature the country in their winter-sun brochures, one of which, the specialist Gambia Experience, offers a year-round programme. This company now accounts for some 60% of all UK arrivals as well as operating a weekly 'scheduled charter' flight from Gatwick throughout the year — the only scheduled air link between The Gambia and Europe is a weekly flight to Brussels. Thus, tour operators remain highly influential in the development of tourism in The Gambia and, through their dominant role, are able to negotiate low contract prices with hotels. According to one commentator, the average per person contract price (bed and breakfast) is between £10 and £12 ($13 and $16) per night and, as a consequence, few hotels are profitable and in a position to reinvest in upgrading facilities (Nyang, 2005).

It is also suggested that the decline in arrivals in 2002 and 2001 (see Table 4.5) resulted from the collapse of a German operator, Frosch Touristik International, which had been running four flights a week into The Gambia (DSTC, 2005, p. 21). The extent to which the decline in arrivals is fully attributable to the loss of this business is uncertain, though it serves to demonstrate the country's continuing and total dependency on overseas tour operators and the consequential fragility of the tourism sector in The Gambia.

- A continuing problem (recognised by the country's tourism authorities) is the lack of data, particularly with respect to the economic value of tourism to the country. Thus, although reliable and contemporary arrivals figures are available, only general statistics, such as tourism's contribution to GDP, are regularly provided. However, specific studies provide additional data that contribute to the overall 'picture'. In 2004, the tourism sector accounted for 13% of The Gambia's GDP, with net foreign exchange earnings estimated to be $40million (DSTC, 2005, p. 22). Leakages are estimated to be 45% of gross expenditure, although this may well be a conservative figure — relatively little progress has been made in developing backward linkages in the local economy and one-third of the country's total imports of food and beverages go to hotels to meet the needs of tourists. Most hotels, for example, import eggs as it is cheaper than using domestic sources as the feed for hens must also be imported at high cost.

Additionally, relatively few opportunities still exist for significant levels of additional expenditure outside the hotels (hence the short-lived policy of banning all-inclusive holidays in 2000). For example, a survey in 2000–2001 found that tourists spent, on average 596 Dalasis per day (£25 at the prevailing exchange rate), though almost two-thirds is spent on food, drinks and excursions in the formal sector (Bah & Goodwin, 2003). A pro-poor tourism project running since 2001 has significantly increased the earnings of specific groups within the informal sector (see Bah & Goodwin, 2003) although this has had little overall impact on spreading the economic benefits of tourism throughout the local economy. Conversely, a significant number of overseas charities have been established, often by people who have visited The Gambia as tourists, usually to assist the development of schools and education (www.friendsofgovi.org.uk/links.html), while some tour operators, such as Gambia Experience, have established charitable funds to support local education projects. However, no comprehensive record of the activities and spending of these organisations exists.

A further source of revenue for the government is the 15% tax imposed on all sales within the formal tourism sector. In 2004, this provided 54 million Dalasis (£1.08 million/ $1.45 million) in revenues, augmented by a £5 arrivals tax that is imposed on all international air arrivals. In 2004, this boosted government revenues by £450,000 ($600,000).

- Over the last decade, there have also been a number of developments with respect to the institutional organisation of tourism in The Gambia. At the governmental level, tourism has, since 1995, been the responsibility of the Department of State for Tourism and Culture (DSTC), the principal tourism policy and planning body. Implementation and operational activities are undertaken by the Gambia Tourism Authority (GTA), which was set up in 2001 by an Act of the National Assembly as a statutory body to develop, regulate and promote the Gambian tourism sector. Although an executive arm of the DSTC, the GTA is funded by annual fees paid by the formal private tourism sector, principally hotels and the four major ground-handlers in the country. Therefore, the relationship between the GTA, the DSTC and the private sector remains unclear.

   In addition to these two bodies, the Responsible Tourism Partnership, members of which include representatives of the public, private and voluntary sectors, and the Association of Small Scale Enterprises in Tourism (ASSET) have been established in recent years. These two organisations work towards developing a more responsible approach to tourism development, particularly with respect to helping small-scale businesses benefit more from their participation in tourism.

Over the last decade then, a number of positive developments have occurred that, in principle, have laid the foundations for the further growth and development of tourism and for increasing its contribution to wider economic development. However, as observed, such growth and development has not materialised. The next section suggests why this has been the case.

The Last Ten Years: A Review

The Gambia's tourism policy for 1995–2000 (Ministry of Tourism and Culture, 1995) set ambitious targets: an increase in arrivals to 150,000, growth in accommodation supply to 10,000 bed spaces and the somewhat contradictory objective of shifting 'from the mass charter tourism to the sale to and attraction of high-spending individual travellers, and special interest groups' (1995, p. 14). Ten years later, little progress has been made other than an increase in accommodation supply, some of which falls within the small-scale, high-quality category. Moreover, a new 'Master Plan' for tourism (DSTC, 2005) has recently been produced, financed by 40 million Dalasi (approximately $1 million grant from the African Development bank), which, recognising the lack of progress, sets out a path for tourism development through to 2020. In short, The Gambia has experienced a 'lost decade' of tourism development.

   This can be explained, in part, by the characteristics of The Gambia both as a country and as a tourist destination:

- As a destination, it has limited appeal to an equally limited (winter-sun) market. The potential to compete in the summer-sun market is restricted by the climate, costs, a lack of facilities and health requirements (a variety of inoculations plus malaria prophylaxis).
- Other than a wide variety of bird species, The Gambia offers little in the way of natural or cultural attractions to tempt the special interest tourist.

- It retains a reputation for 'hassle' — the problems associated with so-called 'bumsters'.
- The dependence on tour operators and lack of alternative air links has severely limited opportunities to expand/transform the tourist market.
- The development of up-country tourism is restricted by poor infrastructure and a lack of resources.
- The Gambia lacks the financial resources to invest in tourism infrastructure and promotion. Moreover, in a developmental context, it has not yet reached the 'take off' stage (Rostow, 1967) where it is able to take advantage of the opportunities offered by tourism.

This is not to say that efforts have not been made to develop tourism and increase its developmental potential. The institutional changes, particularly the establishment of the GTA, have been a positive development, while the recent pro-poor initiative, though of limited benefit in the wider context, has been successful. Through the GTA the government provides incentives to prospective investors in tourism, including tax breaks and 'free' land — investors merely pay application and processing fees amounting to just $500 to secure, subject to planning approval, a 50-year lease on land in the TDA, which now extends along the full length of the Gambian coastline. The imposition of the tourist arrivals tax may also be seen, in principle, as a positive means of revenue generation.

However, in addition to the problems summarised above, it is evident that the greatest barrier to tourism development in The Gambia has been the lack of governmental support in general and, according to some commentators, the exploitation of tourism as a short-term source of revenue in particular. It has long been recognised, for example, that limited funding has been available to support tourism development and promotion yet it is remarkable that, given the potential importance of tourism, the GTA's Marketing plan 2002–2006 (GTA, 2002) is 'the first of its kind in The Gambia'. More specifically, substantial revenues are earned through tourism-related sales taxes (the level of which further reduces the limited profit margins of hotels), which also create the perception that the Gambia is an expensive destination, yet relatively little is re-invested in tourism. Moreover, the tourist arrivals tax, introduced in 2002, was intended to support tourism development and promotion. Initially, proceeds were channelled through the GTA and financed projects such as the street lighting referred to earlier. However, 60% of this tax income now goes towards general government revenue expenditure, with just 40% specifically earmarked for tourism. In short, there appears to be unwillingness on the part of government to invest in the country's future development through tourism.

Tourism in The Gambia: The Way Forward

As a tourist destination, The Gambia is caught in a vicious circle of low and static arrivals, limited income and limited funds for investment. The country's lack of air links and dependence on tour operators restricts further developments while the low number of tourists results in high airport charges to cover fixed running costs and relatively high taxes to optimise government revenues. What, then is the way forward?

Although contemporary wisdom might suggest focusing on the high-spend, specialist market, the conclusion must be that, currently, the tourism industry in The Gambia is unsustainable. What is needed is a substantially higher number of tourists, spread more evenly throughout the year. Such an approach would result in increased foreign exchange earnings, greater overall 'out-of-pocket' expenditure in both the formal and informal sectors, higher levels of employment and, hence, more income circulating in the economy, significantly increased governmental revenues for investment in promotion and infrastructure, greater opportunities for economic support through charities, and a platform for developing more specialist forms of tourism. At the same time, however, both direct government spending and grant aid should focus on establishing and developing backward linkages throughout the local economy in order to reduce leakages and to stimulate wider entrepreneurship and economic growth while, in general, are more proactive commitment to tourism development should be adopted by the government.

Not surprisingly, perhaps, the recent Master Plan proposes a similar, pragmatic policy for tourism development, as well as a number of specific actions necessary (DSTC, 2005). It also recognises that, if nothing is done, The Gambia will continue to lose market share and an opportunity will have been lost forever. What is certain is that tourism still provides the one viable means of achieving development in The Gambia and that, after a problematic decade, the industry should receive the support and investment it deserves.

References

Actionaid Gambia. (2005). *Problems and benefits of tourism in The Gambia*. www.actionaid-gambia.org/pdfs/Tourism%20-%20final20action%20aid%20tourism%20research%20doc.pdf.

Bah, A. (2004). *Integrating tourism into the productive sector: The Gambia*. www.intracen.org/execforum/ef2005/tourism_mega_clusters_papers/4Gambia.pdf.

Bah, A., & Goodwin, H. (2003). *Improving access for the informal sector to tourism in The Gambia*. PPT Working Paper no. 15, London: Pro-poor Tourism Partnership.

Central Statistics Department. (2005). *Arrivals by Mode of Transport*. The Gambia: CSD. www.gambia.gm/Statistics/Publications.htm.

Dieke, P. (1993a). Tourism and development policy in The Gambia. *Annals of Tourism Research*, *20*(3), 423–449.

Dieke, P. (1993b). Cross national comparison of tourism development: Lessons from Kenya and The Gambia. *Journal of Tourism Studies*, *4*(1), 2–18.

Dieke, P. (1994). The political economy of tourism in The Gambia. *Review of African Political Economy*, *62*, 611–627.

DSTC. (2005). *The Gambia tourism development master plan: The challenges for 2005–2010 and the 2020 vision*. Banjul: Department of State for Tourism and Culture.

Edie, C. (2000). Democracy in The Gambia: Past present and prospects for the future. *Africa Development*, *25*(3&4), 161–199.

EIU. (1990). *Senegal and The Gambia*. International Tourism Reports, no. 3, London: Economic Intelligence Unit. (pp. 49–66).

Farver, J. (1984). Tourism and employment in The Gambia. *Annals of Tourism Research*, *11*(2), 249–265.

GTA. (2002). *Marketing plan 2002–2006*. The Gambia: Gambia Tourism Authority.

GTA. (2003). *Peace, stability and growth*. The Gambia: Gambia Tourism Authority.

GTA. (2005). *Monthly provisional arrival of tourists 2004–2005*. The Gambia: Gambia Tourism Authority.

Jeffries Associates. (1992). *Study of tourism in The Gambia*. Final Report. Sanderstead: J.D. Jeffries Associates.

Jenkins, C. (1991). Tourism development strategies. In: L. Lickorish (Ed.), *Developing tourism destinations* (pp. 61–77). Harlow: Longman.

Lea, J. (1988). *Tourism and development in the Third World*. London: Routledge.

Ministry of Tourism and Culture. (1995). *National policy for tourism development 1995–2000*. Banjul: Ministry of Tourism and Culture.

Mowforth, M., & Munt, I. (2003). *Tourism and sustainability: Development and new tourism in the Third World*. London: Routledge.

Nyang, T. (2005). *Tourism Consultant*. Banjul: Personal communication.

Reid, D. (2003). *Tourism, globalization and development: Responsible tourism planning*. London: Pluto Press.

Republic of The Gambia. (2003). *First national millennium development goals report*. www.undp.org/ mdg/gambia_report.pdf.

de Rivero, O. (2001). *The Myth of Development: Non-viable Economies of the 21st Century*. London: Zed Books.

Rostow, W. (1967). *The stages of economic growth: A non-communist manifesto* (2nd Ed.). Cambridge: Cambridge University Press.

Saine, A. (2002). Post-coup politics in The Gambia. *Journal of Democracy, 13*(4), 167–172.

Sharpley, R. (2002). Tourism: A vehicle for development? In: R. Sharpley, & D. Telfer (Eds.), *Tourism and development: concepts and issues* (pp. 11–34). Clevedon: Channel View Publications.

Sharpley, R., & Sharpley, J. (1996). Tourism in West Africa: The Gambian experience. In: A. Badger, P. Barnett, L. Corbyn, & J. Keefe (Eds.), *Trading places: Tourism as trade* (pp. 27–33). London: Tourism Concern.

Sharpley, R., Sharpley, J., & Adams, J. (1996). Travel advice or trade embargo? The impacts and implications of official travel advice. *Tourism Management, 17*(1), 1–7.

Thomson, C., O'Hare, G., & Evans, K. (1995). Tourism in The Gambia: Problems and prospects. *Tourism Management, 16*(8), 571–581.

UNCTAD. (2001). Tourism and development in the Least Developed Countries. Third UN Conference on the Least Developed Countries, Las Palmas, Canary Islands.

UNDP. (2005). *Human development report 2005: Country sheets — The Gambia*. www.undp.org.

Wagner, U. (1981). Tourism in The Gambia: Development or dependency? *Ethnos, 46*, 190–206.

WTO. (2005). *Tourism market trends 2005 edition*. www.world-tourism.org.

Chapter 5

Measuring and Reporting the Impact of Tourism on Poverty

Harold Goodwin

At the 2002 World Summit on Sustainable Tourism in Johannesburg, the World Tourism Organization (UNWTO) launched *Tourism and Poverty Alleviation*. The report argued that tourism is one of the few development opportunities available to the poor and constituted a call for action (WTO, 2002). In 2001 the WTO had, with UNCTAD, published *Tourism in the Least Developed Countries*. The report sought to "support the development of tourism as one of the driving forces in the refocusing of economic development strategies" of Least Developed Countries (LDCs). As Frangialli, Secretary-General of the WTO, argued in his foreword to the report, it is necessary.

> "... to redress the traditional and still prevailing or even deepening inconsistencies of the tourism market ... an exceptional goal because, so far, tourism development has largely emerged as a by-product of economic advancement and well-being of societies ... the tourism market has been organized by adapting to the needs of tourism sending, hence economically advanced countries" (WTO/UNCTAD, 2001, p. 5).

The tourism industry has been and remains market driven; it is a buyers' market. Although as Ghimire (2001) has demonstrated, domestic tourism has been of increasing importance in the developing world, if not in the LDCs, Frangialli's point holds: whether the tourists are international or domestic, tourism adapts to the needs of the economically advanced tourism-originating areas whether they be Delhi, London or Manila.

Akama (1999) argues that tourism development "accentuate[s] the economic structure of dependency on an external market demand" and that this leads to an 'alien' development to which locals cannot relate and respond, both socially and economically. Tourism is often used to demonstrate the contemporary potency of dependency theory (Clancy, 1999; Scheyvens, 2002) and there is considerable scepticism amongst academics and development practitioners who point to the negative socio-cultural and environmental impacts, high

Developments in Tourism Research
Copyright © 2007 by Elsevier Ltd.
All rights of reproduction in any form reserved.
ISBN: 978-0-080-45328-6

leakages and the capture of benefits by metropolitan and local elites (Harrison, 2001; Scheyvens, 2002).

The Millennium Development Goals and Tourism

It was a significant shift of emphasis by the WTO when it sought to address the Millennium Development Goals (MDGs). The WTO's Global Code of Ethics adopted in 1999 had referred to the fight against poverty, and the UN Commission on Sustainable Development in the same year had called on governments to "maximize the potential of tourism for eradicating poverty by developing appropriate strategies in cooperation with all major groups, and indigenous and local communities" (UN, 1999).

As de Villiers, WTO Deputy Secretary General asserted at the UNCTAD Conference in 2001, the WTO is "convinced that tourism can make a meaningful contribution to the reduction of poverty, but not without the intervention of the multilateral and bilateral aid agencies and banks". de Villiers argued that this would be achieved by engaging in "pro-poor and destination based development projects that would demonstrate the benefits of such strategies" (WTO/UNCTAD, 2001, p. 13).

It is a considerable challenge to demonstrate the benefits of tourism in addressing poverty because there is very little data. "The industry has been managed for foreign exchange benefits rather than as a pro-poor development strategy." (WTO, 2001, p. 63) Traditionally, tourism development has been measured and reported in macro economic terms — numbers of international visitor arrivals, contribution to employment and to the balance of payments in foreign exchange earnings. Tourism Satellite Accounts and the multiplier have been used to identify the economic contribution of the industry in world trade and to support assertions about the importance of the tourism industry at the national level (Jamieson, Goodwin, & Edmunds, 2004). It has generally been assumed that, through a 'trickledown' process, local communities gain benefit from employment (direct, indirect and induced) and through the local economic development impact of spending in the destination, but there is little hard evidence to support this view (WTO, 2002).

Tourism and Development

Encontre, an UNCTAD economist, has argued that since the LDCs were identified and labelled in 1971, only one country, Botswana, has graduated out of LDC status — tourism made a significant contribution to that achievement. There have been four potential graduation cases since 1994 — Cape Verde, Maldives, Samoa and Vanuatu — and in all of them tourism has been "the single most important factor explaining the socio-economic progress that would induce graduation." (Encontre, 2001, p. 105)

In the context of the MDGs, the challenge is to demonstrate positive impacts on poverty, to demonstrate that tourism can contribute to the eight MDGs and that the impacts can be scaled up to make a significant contribution to the eradication of poverty. The targets are not defined in terms of growth; they relate specifically to poverty, for example, by 2015 to reduce by half the number of people who live on less than one USD per day (UNGA,

2000). In this context, international visitor arrivals and spend figures, tourism satellite accounts and multipliers have little utility as they cannot be used to measure the impact of tourism on local economic development in general and poverty reduction in particular. In order to increase the poverty reduction impact of tourism development, and to demonstrate it to the satisfaction of the development agencies and banks sought as partners for pro-poor tourism development initiatives, it is necessary to demonstrate that tourism can make a significant contribution.

Yunis (2004) Chief of Sustainable Development at the WTO, argued at a World Bank Conference in Brussels in May 2004 that tourism often plays a major part in the economies of poorer countries. Tourism is growing faster in developing countries than in developed countries and there are many reasons why tourism is particularly well placed to meet the needs of the poor (Ashley, Roe, & Goodwin, 2001; WTO, 2002; Yunis, 2004). Yunis points out that tourism "will not address poverty automatically". The UNWTO announced at the World Summit on Sustainable Development in 2002 that it was going to establish a foundation to use tourism to address poverty, a decision that resulted in the formal launch of ST-EP (Sustainable Tourism — Elimination of Poverty) in 2006. The purpose of the Foundation is to secure funding for tourism and poverty reduction initiatives, and the Foundation will also seek to identify best practise and demonstrate impact, the monitoring and 'validating' of the results of particular initiatives being regarded as central to this process (WTO, 2002).

In the initial articulation of the case for harnessing tourism for poverty elimination (Goodwin, 1998), it was argued that monitoring and evaluation would be a necessary part of the process of encouraging development agencies and banks to support initiatives in this area. Yunis (2004) points to the importance of "developing simple indicators and systems to measure the impact of tourism on poverty". Unfortunately, there are still very few cases where the poverty impacts of particular tourism initiatives have been researched or monitored and reported. The impact of a Dutch Development Agengy (SNV) initiative in West Humla, Nepal, was retrospectively analysed using a livelihoods approach (Saville, 2001) and in The Gambia poor producers involved in a market access initiative participated in research to identify how much their incomes increased between two seasons (Bah & Goodwin, 2003). SNV has engaged in major programmes on three continents. The British development agency DFID has funded some significant initiatives through the Tourism Challenge Fund and latterly the Business Linkages Challenge Fund. South Africa has funded a programme of poverty alleviation projects linked to tourism, and other banks and donors have funded particular initiatives. Data on the impacts of these interventions have not been published.

The MDGs set a number of targets for some of the major dimensions of poverty — hunger, access to drinking water, daily income, maternal mortality, education and a range or other priorities (UNGA, 2000; World Bank, 2005). Given the multi-dimensional character of poverty, the socio-cultural elements of the definition, and the fact that poverty is a relative concept (Boltvinik, nd), the measurement and reporting of tourism impacts on poverty is difficult.

Pro-Poor Tourism

Recognising that poverty is multi-dimensional, the Pro-Poor Tourism Partnership identified a broad range of strategies for using tourism to address the issues of poverty, from the primarily economic (employment and business development) to the mitigation of environmental impacts which adversely affect the poor and addressing social and cultural impacts. The Pro-Poor Tourism Partnership argues that tourism has a broad range of impacts on the poor, amongst which are financial, livelihood (human, physical, social, natural capital, access to information) and that cultural values, optimism, pride and participation, exposure to risk and exploitation are all aspects which need to be considered (Ashley et al., 2001).

Pro-Poor Tourism (Ashley et al., 2001; WTO, 2002) is defined as tourism which generates net benefits for the poor — it is neither a product nor sector. Any form of tourism can be pro-poor. Pro-Poor Tourism seeks to unlock economic and other livelihood opportunities for the poor — what constitutes poverty will vary from destination to destination. The pro-poor approach also recognises that measuring net impacts is necessary because in some circumstances there are negative impacts on the poor through, for example, loss of access to resources or land price inflation. These negative impacts should not be ignored. Expanding the tourism industry may assist with achieving pro-poor impacts through tourism, but it is not in itself sufficient. The focus on poverty reduction as a test of the efficacy of the interventions requires that the impacts of the initiatives on the poor be measured; to rely on general assertions about the impact of the multiplier and trickledown is unlikely to secure support for further initiatives.

The UNWTO (2004) has identified seven different ways in which spending associated with tourism can reach the poor:

1. employment of the poor in tourism enterprises;
2. supply of goods and services to tourism enterprises by the poor or by enterprises employing the poor;
3. direct sales of goods and services to visitors by the poor (informal economy);
4. establishment and running of tourism enterprises by the poor (SMMEs or community based enterprises);
5. taxes or levies on tourism revenues or profits with proceeds benefiting the poor;
6. voluntary giving of resources (money, goods, time) by tourists and enterprises in ways which benefit the poor;
7. investment in infrastructure which provides livelihood benefits to the poor.

It is clear, both from the work of the UNWTO and the Pro-Poor Tourism Partnership, that the impacts of tourism on the poor are diverse, and that both positive and negative impacts need to be considered.

Monitoring Impacts

The challenge is to develop "simple indicators and systems to measure the impact of tourism on poverty", and to develop and use "reasonably robust yet simple indicators of poverty alleviation." The WTO usefully distinguishes between broad indicators that would track such factors as income per head and quality of life, and correlate these with measures of tourism growth and specific indicators relating to particular initiatives. The report goes so far to suggest that "Such reporting may be made a condition of any assistance given" (WTO, 2004). The broad indicators may demonstrate that tourism growth — domestic or international arrivals and spend — correlates with increases in average per capita income. However, such broad indicators are unlikely to convince decision makers in development agencies, government or industry that particular initiatives have had, or will have, any particular impact on poverty, however it is defined.

Specific indicators linked to particular initiatives are more likely to have utility in demonstrating impacts and identifying best practise in particular circumstances. This information is of most use in demonstrating the efficacy of initiatives and in guiding the identification and replication of best practise. The Pro-Poor Tourism Partnership (2005, p. 1) argues that an initiative can only be described as pro-poor where it is possible to demonstrate a net benefit for particular individuals or groups. It follows from this that beneficiaries need to be identified so that the net benefit can be measured and reported, as "only in this way can a pro-poor impact be demonstrated, although there may also be some additional, initially unidentified, livelihood benefits."

Experience suggests that the collection of data is difficult unless this activity is made part of the intervention strategy (Jamieson et al., 2004), in part for resource reasons but most importantly because without baseline data it is difficult, if not impossible, to measure the impact in any reliable way. The desk research undertaken by the Pro-Poor Tourism Partnership and reviews of work in Asia suggest that to "collect reliable and useful data" it is essential "that interventions are focussed on particular poverty impacts and particular individuals and communities." (Jamieson et al., 2004, p. 19)

There is an additional advantage to be gained in identifying beneficiaries and requiring that the intervention logic is made clear in the project's logical framework, or that it is renegotiated as the intervention proceeds — such initial identification means that it will be easier to identify the intended impacts of projects and to measure those impacts. This in turn makes it possible to assess the efficacy of interventions and to identify, in particular circumstances, what interventions result in what impacts — a process essential to identifying best practise.

Jamieson et al. (2004) undertook a literature review and identified a number of methodological issues, which need to be considered in assessing positive and negative impacts. The project proposal should make clear the methodology to be used, and funders will thus be able to see and evaluate impacts.

Assessing Positive Impacts:

- Care needs to be taken to exclude poverty impacts which may be coterminous with the intervention but not a result of it.
- The methodology chosen needs to address seasonality, lead times and sustainability. The latter is the most difficult to fund as it may require follow-up work two or more years after the intervention is complete.
- Baseline data on the incomes and livelihood strategies of the target group of poor beneficiaries need to be collected prior to the intervention in order to enable impact to be measured.

Assessing Negative Impacts:

- Attempt to identify the value of losses in natural capital, for example, by using monetary values or loss of income measures.

- Consider whether any increased conflict resulting from tourism has reduced social capital.
- Consider whether tourism development has increased the vulnerability of the poor in anyway.

This is a preliminary list of considerations; methodology in this field is a work in progress. The scale and significance of the impact of the intervention, positive or negative, on the livelihoods of individuals and households would generally require a livelihoods analysis. This is generally beyond the resources of an intervention project and it is very difficult to secure funding for this kind of research. The views of the poor themselves are of particular importance.

The indicators to be used will be a function of the intended impacts and should be discussed and agreed with the beneficiaries and other stakeholders. There is no single method that can be used to assess impact from a range of very different interventions and approaches in diverse situations. The particular methodology should be designed for the purposes of the specific intervention and the stakeholders in it — including both beneficiaries and funders. The data generated should be shared with the stakeholders and should be in a form, which they can reliably use for evaluation and decision-making.

The kind of "reasonably robust yet simple indicators of poverty alleviation" called for by the WTO in 2004 can be used to make the case for interventions and their up-scaling, to identify best practise (and by implication poor practise), and by funders and managers to hold practitioners to account. There is an understandable tendency to argue that the measurement of impact is expensive and fraught with difficulty and that in the circumstances nothing can be done.

The three examples of "reasonably robust yet simple indicators of poverty alleviation" are reported and discussed here in order to address the question of what can be done. This approach is predicated on the assumption that only by attempting to measure impacts and discussing the results can better methodologies be evolved and best practise identified. Researchers working primarily on poverty and measurement will point to a wide range of serious inadequacies in the way that poverty is not measured and impacts are reported in a limited way. However, the methods reported and discussed here have the considerable benefit that they can realistically be used in the field to assess defined impacts of tourism on poverty.

In the first case, Egypt, primarily secondary data is analysed to estimate the contribution of tourism to household incomes in the Nile Valley. In Tanzania monitoring data is presented from a coffee plantation project. (The location of the project is not revealed because those involved in the project feel that while they are willing to share the methodology, it is early days yet and they do not want publicity.) In the third case, data from an intervention in The Gambia reports on pre- and post-intervention incomes and employment.

Egypt — The Analysis of Secondary Data

The development of tourism in South Sinai from 1980 was part of a national strategy to relieve development pressure in the Nile Valley by creating centres of development and population in desert areas. Tourism was one of the industries that was identified as a potential source of livelihoods for communities in desert areas. There was also a strategic imperative for the development and population of South Sinai. The impacts were not entirely positive, for example, the access of the Bedouin to the sea for fishing declined as the numbers of hotels increased along the South Sinai coast (Ali Dina, 1998).

Staff attracted to work in the tourism sector in Sharm El Sheikh is mainly composed of single or "bachelor" men. Of the population of Sharm El Sheikh, 15.5% are reported as Bedouin and 15.5% as permanent residents with family. 39.4% are reported as permanent residents without family and 29.6% temporary residents without family — two-thirds of the resident population are composed of "single" males. Most of them live in dormitories and remit some or all of their earnings to their home (SEAM, 2004b). The work-shift pattern tends to be 23 days on and 7 days off, with the employer providing transportation home to Cairo or elsewhere in the Nile Valley where the men's families continue to live. Three quarters of those who work in tourism in South Sinai plan to return home permanently at retirement. The cost of living, water and housing and the lack of social and physical infrastructure all discourage resettlement; migration has tended to be temporary (SEAM, 2004a).

Resources were not available for a full labour force survey, so the number of direct employees was estimated using a ration of 1.3 employees per room across all categories of hotels. The average number of staff per room depends to a significant degree upon the number of bars and restaurants maintained within and by the hotel. The ratio was checked with hotel managers and other local experts on tourism. Indirect employment was calculated assuming that indirect employment is an additional 80% of the direct labour, with the same rate of growth as for direct labour (Goodwin & Makary, 2005).

Makary Consulting conducted a survey of all staff in four representative resorts and hotels in Sharm El Sheikh and asked them to estimate the proportion of their earnings being remitted home. Only 23% of employees remitted less than 50% of their earnings to their family elsewhere in Egypt; 53% remitted between 20% and 80% of their earnings; 24% remitted more than 80%. The average was 63% (Goodwin & Makary, 2005).

The same survey recorded an annual average net salary per employee of 7500 LE[1] plus tips of 800 LE per annum producing annual average net earnings per Egyptian employee of 8300 LE (1347 USD). Earnings per employee in indirect tourism employment were estimated at an average net earnings of 12,500 LE (2029 USD) (Tables 5.1 and 5.2).

Calculations based on estimated numbers employed and estimated average earnings of indirect employees and a small sample survey of employees in direct employment were used to determine gross earnings and the average remittance home to the Nile Valley. It was assumed that the average remittance home of 63% of earnings determined for direct employees would also apply to indirect employees. The figures can only be regarded as indicative, but they provide a broad indication of the scale of the contribution of tourism earnings by internal migrant labour in South Sinai to households in the Nile Valley, a significant impact on poverty. There were not sufficient resources to include survey questions about the incomes of the households to which money was remitted. Had this been feasible it would have been possible to draw conclusions about the relative importance of these tourism remittances to households in the Nile Valley and to determine how poor the beneficiary households were.

---

[1] Egyptian Pounds.

Table 5.1: Remittances home by direct and indirect tourism employees in South Sinai, 2003.

	Average earnings		Remitted home	
	LE	**USD**	**LE**	**USD**
Direct employees	8300	1347	5229	849
Indirect employees	12,500	2029	7875	1278

Source: Calculations based on estimates by Makary Consulting (Goodwin & Makary, 2005).

Table 5.2: Total remittances home by direct and indirect tourism employees in South Sinai, 2003.

	Employees	Average earnings		Total remitted home	
		LE	**USD**	**LE**	**USD**
Direct employees	21,600	8300	1347	112,946,400	29,095,200
Indirect employees	17,280	12,500	2029	136,080,000	35,061,120
				249,026,400	64,156,320

Source: Calculations based on estimates by Makary Consulting (Goodwin & Makary, 2005).

Tanzania — *Monitoring and Reporting Impacts at Individual and Household Level*

At the request of a coffee co-operative in Tanzania, a tourism consultant has worked under the auspices of the Dutch Green Development Foundation with the farmers to develop a coffee tour and a campsite. A tour operator has been a partner in the initiative and a relatively small investment has produced significant local incomes. Data from this project are presented here with permission; a condition of the use of the data was that the location of the project should not be revealed. The early results are very good; one-third of the investment has been 'earned back' in revenue. There is a significant risk of over-visiting; additional capacity is in the process of being developed to meet demand. These results relate to work in progress; they are reported here because of the exceptional quality of the impact monitoring and reporting.

Currently the average sized one-hectare farm plot produces two bags of coffee worth 160–200 USD. This produces an annual income of around 180 USD to support a household — an income of 50 c per day for farming coffee. By contrast tour guides gets 5 USD per tour as an additional supplementary income. The tourism income data has been collected from the arrival of the first groups in June, which means that there is a complete record of earnings (Table 5.3).

Records have also been kept of the distribution of these revenues (Table 5.4). The majority of the revenues (35%) are retained for the Community Development Fund controlled by the producers cooperative and 22% is used to fund the tourism office of the co-operative.

Table 5.5 presents estimates of net income (income less direct costs) for each of the individuals involved in the tourism initiative. This is significant additional income and supplements the household incomes of coffee farmers.

Table 5.3: Revenue from coffee tours and campsite, June to December 2005.

Month	No. groups	Campsite pax	Coffee tour pax	Lunch pax	Total sales in USD
June	3	0	47	12	553
July	12	70	183	64	2484
August	10	102	164	46	2264
September	10	81	154	59	2131
October	11	97	154	44	2025
November	2	31	30	0	417
December	4	52	52	8	752
Total	52	433	784	233	10,626

Source: Local project records.

Table 5.4: Distribution of revenues, June to December 2005.

	Total earnings in USD	Percent
Coffee co-operative office	2383	22
Community development fund	3685	35
Tour guides (farmers)	779	7
Food	967	9
Camp. maintenance	794	7
Campsite office	72	1
Camp. security	218	2
Miscellaneous. fund	28	–
Farmers for visits to their land	31	–
Total distributed	8956	84
Retained undistributed	1670	16

This example demonstrates what can be achieved by recording the impacts of a pro-poor tourism intervention and the way in which it can demonstrate to the funder the return on investment — through simple book keeping, and engaging the producers in the process of recording income and its distribution.

The Gambia — Pre- and Post-Intervention Incomes and Employment

The data presented here were collected as part of a Tourism Challenge Fund project in The Gambia which used a multi-stakeholder approach to improve market access and earnings for a range of informal sector producers in 2001–2002 (Bah & Goodwin, 2003). The juice pressers, fruit sellers, guides and craft market vendors were engaged in the project which sought to reduce the barriers to market access which reduced their ability to earn from tourism.

Table 5.5: Estimation of net income accruing to individuals by group.

	Campers	Tour	Group	People	Beneficiaries	Net earnings/ individual in USD	Total individual net earnings
Tour guides	0	5	15	3	6	130	780
Food preparation	0	15	15	4	12	28	336
Cleaning	1	0	5	2	2	60	120
Campsite office	3		3	1	1	72	72
Security	9		9	3	3	73	219
Chairman	3	3	1	3	1	143	143
Farmers for visits to their land		2	2	3	100	3	300
Total					125		1970

Table 5.6: Changes in weekly income of informal sector in The Gambia.

Informal sector group	Weekly net earnings in dalasi		% Change 2001/2002	Net increase in number of jobs
	2001	2002		
Juice pressers	333	736	121	0
Licensed guides (S)	345	408	18.2	0
Licensed guides (K)	285	380	33.3	0
Craft market (K)	41.2	122.8	198	43
Craft market (S)	162.1	316.9	95.5	19

Note: K = Kotu Beach; S = Senegambia.
Source: Bah and Goodwin (2003).

In the peak season of the first quarter of 2001, each of the producers was asked to record daily their purchases of inputs and expenditures on rent, as well as sales of goods and services. The total number of people engaged in each producer group was also recorded. The process was supervised by one of their fellow producers and by the local research manager. The data were collated and analysed so that average daily earnings could be calculated for each producer, and the average net weekly earnings was calculated for the ten-week period. One year later, after the intervention, the process was repeated. This enabled a comparison to be made between average earnings before and after the intervention for each individual and each producer group and to identify any increase in informal sector employment.

One producer group, the female fruit sellers, were unwilling themselves to collect the data and it was decided in consultation with the group to ask the male responsible for collecting together the fruit pressers' data to take responsibility for collecting the fruit sellers' data. When the 2001 and 2002 data were compared, it was apparent that the women had systematically understated their earnings in 2001 and this meant that only estimates were available for the increase in their earnings as a result of the intervention (50–60%).

Had there been any significant change in the number of visitors between the two seasons, the data could have been adjusted to reflect this. In the event, there was no significant change in visitor numbers between the two years in the ten-week period covered by the research (Table 5.6).

There were not sufficient resources to determine how much of household income came from these informal sector tourism sector activities. However, it was clear from the research that tourism was the primary source of income for all of those engaged in the survey. Tourism to The Gambia is highly seasonal and the survey was conducted only in the peak season — the purpose was to determine the scale of the change in earnings from year to year; not to measure total earnings over the year. As with the Tanzania case, the research method was primarily based on book keeping, and engaged all of the producers in reporting their earnings. This has a secondary but important effect in empowering the producers who, by participating in the data collection and engaging with the results, are in a better position to discuss the benefits and to participate in decision-making.

Conclusion

Practitioners engaged in poverty reduction through tourism need to identify intended benefici-aries and impacts in the preliminary stages of their work and to record sufficient baseline data to be able to reliably report impact. It matters less that all the impacts are captured than that impacts are reported in such a way as to permit assessment of the effectiveness and efficiency of the particular approach. In the last ten years, despite the increasing focus on tourism and poverty reduction, there have been very few reported interventions where any attempt has been made to measure beneficiary impact. With major programmes of intervention underway though SNV and ST-EP there is a pressing need for measurement and reporting of impacts.

Given the diversity of approaches and of the target beneficiaries, no single methodology can be used to measure all of them. Agencies, funders and groups of practitioners need to evolve transparent ways of measuring the beneficiary level impacts of initiatives, and of reporting these both to funders and other stakeholders engaged in the particular initiatives — funders and agencies should demand it, practitioners should accept that it is expected of them as good practise, and recognise that only in this way can best practise be identified and the effectiveness of the interventions be maximised. Case studies and progress reports should routinely report data on impacts — it is not sufficient to rely on assumptions about benefits resulting from capacity building, another variant of trickledown. Practitioners owe it to the funders and those they encourage to commit time and resources to their initiatives, including the poor themselves, to demonstrate significant beneficiary impact.

References

Akama, J. (1999). The evolution of tourism in Kenya. *Journal of Sustainable Tourism, 7*(1), 567–574.

Ali Dina, F. (1998). Case Study of Development of the Peripheral Coastal Area of South Sinai in Relation to its Bedouin Community, Masters Virginia State University.

Ashley, C., Roe, D., & Goodwin, H. (2001). Pro-Poor Tourism Strategies: Making Tourism Work for the Poor. London: Pro-Poor Tourism.

Bah, A., & Goodwin, H. (2003). *Improving access for the informal sector to tourism in The Gambia.* PPT Working Paper 15.

Boltvinik, J. (nd). Poverty measurement methods: An overview. UNDP.

Clancy, M. (1999). Tourism and development: Evidence from Mexico. *Annals of Tourism Research, 26*(1), 1–20.

Encontre, P. (2001). Tourism development and the perspective of graduation form the LDC category in World Tourism Organization and United Nations Conference on Trade and Development (2001). Tourism in the Least Developed Countries, World Tourism Organization Madrid.

Ghimire, K. B. (2001). The native tourist. London: Earthscan.

Goodwin, H. (1998). Sustainable tourism and the elimination of poverty. DFID/DETR.

Goodwin, H., & Makary, S. (2005). Poverty impacts of tourism in South Sinai Supporting Environmental Assessment and Management Programme (SEAM), unpublished.

Harrison, D. (2001). Tourism and the less developed world: issues and case studies. CABI.

Jamieson, W., Goodwin, H., & Edmunds, C. (2004). Contribution of tourism to poverty alleviation pro poor tourism and the challenge of measuring impacts. Transport Policy and Tourism Section, Transport Division UN ESCAP.

Pro-Poor Tourism Partnership (PPTP). (2005). Annual Register Pro-Poor Tourism Partnership, London: PPTP.

Saville, N. M. (2001). Practical strategies for pro-poor tourism: Case study of pro-poor tourism and SNV in Humla, District, West Nepal. PPT Working Paper 3.

Scheyvens, R. (2002). *Tourism for development*. Harlow: Prentice Hall.

SEAM. (2004a). Community consultation findings South Sinai Governorate Residents & Workers Final Draft. SEAM Programme, unpublished.

SEAM. (2004b). South Sinai Governorate Development and Environmental Action Plan Consultation Document. SEAM, unpublished.

UN. (1999). United Nations Commission on Sustainable Development. Seventh Session, 19–30 April 1999, Agenda item 5 E/CN.17/1999/L.6.

United Nations General Assembly (UNGA). (2000). United Nations Millennium Declaration 55/2.

World Bank. (2005). World Development Indicators 2005. Washington DC: World Bank.

World Tourism Organization (WTO). (2001). *The Least Developed Countries and Tourism* in World Tourism Organization and United Nations Conference on Trade and Development. Tourism in the Least Developed Countries. Madrid: World Tourism Organization.

World Tourism Organization (WTO). (2002). Tourism and Poverty Alleviation. Madrid: World Tourism Organization.

World Tourism Organization (WTO). (2004). Tourism and Poverty Alleviation Recommendations for Action. Madrid: World Tourism Organization.

World Tourism Organization and United Nations Conference on Trade and Development (WTO/UNCTAD). (2001). Tourism in the Least Developed Countries. Madrid: World Tourism Organization.

Yunis, E. (2004). Sustainable tourism and poverty alleviation. Brussels, Madrid: World Tourism Organization.

Chapter 6

Productivity and Yield Measurement in Australian Inbound Tourism Using Tourism Satellite Accounts and General Equilibrium Modelling

Larry Dwyer, Peter Forsyth and Ray Spurr

Introduction

In recent years two additional concepts have become part of the tourism lexicon. One is the concept of Tourism Satellite Account (TSA); the other is Computable General Equilibrium (CGE) model. Both have relevance for enhancing our understanding of the economic contribution of tourism to a destination, although the different uses of the two are not always made clear by researchers.

This paper illustrates the use of TSAs and CGE models to measure the productivity and economic yield of inbound tourism. We shall use examples of the applications of TSAs and CGE models, in Australia, to illustrate how each can be used. Specifically, we use the Australian TSA to estimate tourism performance in respect of indicators such as productivity, price, profitability and yield. We use a CGE model to show how the economy-wide yield, or impact on the economy as a whole, can be estimated.

Tourism Satellite Accounts

Tourism differs from many economic activities in that it makes use of a diverse range of facilities across a large number of industrial sectors. Since it is not possible to identify tourism as a single *industry* in the national accounts, its value to the economy is not revealed. The development of *satellite* accounts is an attempt to provide a clearer view of the relative importance of tourism as an economic activity and to trace its interrelationship with traditional industry sectors contained within the national accounts (Spurr, 2006).

Developments in Tourism Research
ISBN: 978-0-080-45328-6

A TSA enables tourism activity to be compared with other major industries in terms of size, economic performance, employment and contribution to the national economy. It comprises a set of concepts, definitions, classifications and accounting rules designed to enable a country to properly understand and evaluate tourism within its overall economy. It thus provides a framework of monetary flows, which can be traced from the tourism consumer to the producing unit or supplier within the economy. In doing so it defines and identifies the various tourism 'industries' or groups of suppliers, which produce or import the goods and services purchased by visitors (UN, et al., 2001).

A TSA enables the relationships between tourism and other economic activity to be explored within the national accounts framework. TSAs contain two dimensions. One focuses on consumption and output, providing a view of the basic economic structure of tourism in terms of supply and demand relationships. This enables the size of tourism relative to other types of economic activity to be quantified. The second dimension presents non-monetary data, for example, employment, so that they can be related to data in the first dimension (Australian Bureau of Statistics, 2000).

Increasing numbers of countries worldwide have developed or are developing TSA consistently with UNWTO guidelines (UN, et al., 2001). They represent the 'official methodology' that enables tourism activity to be compared with other major industries in terms of size of value added, output and employment contributed to the national economy (OECD, 2001). TSAs also facilitate international comparisons of destination tourism industry performance.

Computable General Equilibrium Models

In contrast to TSAs, which are sets of accounts, Computable General equilibrium (CGE) models are simulation models of the whole economy, which can be used to analyse the impacts of various changes affecting tourism expenditure. The term *general equilibrium* refers to an analytical approach where the economy is regarded as a complete system of interdependent components (different markets, industries, households, etc.) and all decisions are taken according to the fully optimizing behavior. Economic shocks affecting any one of theses components may produce repercussions throughout the whole system. Assessing the effects of the shocks is done through simulations, i.e., by measuring the repercussions that are triggered by shocking the system in various ways (positively and negatively). The models are called *computable* in the sense that they can produce numerical results that are applicable to particular situations in particular destinations. To do so, the coefficients and parameters (elasticities) of the model are estimated using real-world data (Kehoe & Kehoe, 1995; Harrison, Jensen, Pedersen, & Rutherford, 2000).

CGE models can incorporate explicit assumptions about government policy settings and about economy-wide constraints on the supply side of the economy. They allow for resource constraints, recognising that an increase in one form of economic activity, such as tourism, will, at least to some extent, crowd out other forms of economic activity — something, which input–output models ignore (Dwyer, Forsyth, & Spurr, 2004). Since CGE models are representations of the way the economy works, they can be used to estimate the net economy-wide impacts of such changes on economic variables such as gross domestic product (GDP) or employment (Dwyer, Forsyth, Madden, & Spurr, 2000).

CGE models are being increasingly adopted as the preferred tool for measuring the impact of shocks or changed policy measures on economies. They have been used to model options under the WTO Uruguay Round and the effects of economic development policies by international agencies such as the World Trade Organisation (WTO), the World Bank and the Organisation for Economic Cooperation and Development (OECD). They are also used by government treasuries, economic think tanks and business and economic consultants in a range of developed countries including Australia, USA, UK and Canada (Dixon & Parmenter, 1996). We are beginning to see their application in modelling tourism-related economic shocks and policy options. Recent uses of CGE modelling in tourism has involved assessment of the economic impacts of government policies (Blake & Sinclair, 2003); economic impacts of changes in inbound tourism (Dwyer, Forsyth, Spurr, & Van Ho, 2003; Sugiyarto, Blake, & Sinclair, 2003; Narayan, 2004; Dwyer, Forsyth, & Spurr, 2006; Polo & Valle, 2006); and economic impacts of special events (Blake, 2005; Dwyer, Forsyth, & Spurr, 2005, 2006).

A CGE model can be developed to embody detailed tourism sectors as part of its structure. Such models essentially contain TSAs, though the TSA may not be set out explicitly. A CGE model, which incorporates a tourism sector, contains a virtual TSA embedded within it (Blake, Durbarry, Sinclair, & Sugiyarto, 2001). The existence of a TSA greatly reduces the task of incorporating a defined and detailed tourism sector within a CGE model. The spread of national TSAs internationally has thus made it easier to develop CGE models, which can deal in detail with tourism. In particular, they offer the opportunity for consistent definitions and data use with the TSA, and they do much of the disaggregation of tourism-related sectors, which would otherwise need to be done by the CGE modellers. Conversely, where a TSA does not exist, CGE models can provide some of the information on input and output relationships, which can be used in building a TSA. If the CGE model has already been developed to incorporate a defined tourism industry or industries, then such models contain within them the information required to construct a TSA.

TSAs and CGE models are different techniques and their roles differ correspondingly. TSAs are sets of accounts, and they are measurement tools. Thus they can be used for measurement tasks. CGE models, on the other hand, are representations of the way the economy works. Thus they can be used to determine the net economy-wide impacts of changes, such as a boom in tourism, on economic variables such as GDP or employment. Both can be used for measuring the impacts of changes, such as a boom in inbound tourism expenditure, though on different variables. Thus, for example, a TSA cannot be employed to estimate the additional contribution of tourism to the economy (addition to GDP, employment, etc.) generated by an increase in injected expenditure from inbound tourists. This is because TSAs take no account, for example, of the possible factor constraints that may present barriers to tourism growth or the impacts that changing prices and wages might have on other (non-tourism) industries. They cannot be used to estimate the economy-wide impacts of a boom in inbound tourism since they do not contain any behavioural equations specifying how each sector responds to external shocks including shocks normally affecting the sector directly and shocks transmitted through intersectoral linkages, via change in prices, wages, exchange rates and other variables. In contrast, CGE models track interindustry relationships, which are ideally based on realistic behavioural assumptions, and allow for resource constraints and prices. They can provide fully simulated economic impacts and welfare estimates. CGE models can be used for measuring economy wide, as well as industry level impacts.

Assessing Tourism Productivity, Price and Profitability

Most TSAs do not report all the variables needed for a productivity or profitability study. Typically they provide measures of tourism output, and they may provide some information about key inputs, such as value added and employment. However, with national accounts data, along with information on the parameters used to construct the TSA, it is possible to develop a comprehensive set of data. For example, if according to the TSA, 11% of the total output of an industry can be ascribed to tourism, then, in the absence of more explicit information, it is plausible to assume that 11% of that industry's capital stock can also be ascribed to tourism. On this basis, an estimate of the tourism capital stock can be developed.

Another useful measure, for present purposes, is value added — this is a measure of the value of the production activities in the industry. With information about inputs (labour, capital) on a comparable basis, it is possible to measure the productivity change in the tourism industry as a whole, and in individual sectors of it. With information about the costs of inputs (labour, capital consumption) it is possible to measure profit, and with information about the value of the capital invested, profitability. Trends in profitability can be noted, and the source of these trends can be identified. Tourism output prices and input prices can be determined from TSA and comparable data. This enables a breakdown in the forces on profitability — productivity, input and output prices.

Measures of tourism industry performance have been developed by Forsyth, Dwyer, Fox, and Rao (2004a, 2004b). Six years of Australian TSAs were available at the time of the study. Value added in tourism was used as the output measure. When tourism value added is deflated by the implicit deflators for each of its component sectors, a measure of the real-value added of the industry can be obtained (Table 6.1). This indicates that tourism output and real value added have been growing only slowly since the boom (Sydney

Table 6.1: Tourism value added, employment and productivity, Australia 1997/1998–2002/2003.

Year	Nominal value added (bnA$)	Real value added (bnA$)	Employment '000	Real value added/ Employee A$ '000
1997/1998	21.894	23.042	509	45.3
1998/1999	23.054	24.000	513	46.8
1999/2000	23.994	24.888	525	47.4
2000/2001	25.044	25.830	538	48.0
2001/2002	25.229	25.229	534	47.2
2002/2003	25.875	25.221	541	46.6

Source: Forsyth et al. (2004a, 2004b).

Olympics) year of 2000. It is well known that the industry has been experiencing difficult times, but this result strongly underlines this perception. It is consistent with the declining proportion, which the industry represents of total GDP, a trend that has been documented in the annual TSAs.

Table 6.1 also reports tourism employment data from the TSA over this period. These enable the estimation of a measure of labour productivity (real value added per employee). This measure indicates that over the whole period, productivity has changed little, although it rose during the boom years, and has fallen since.

Trends in prices and productivity can also be estimated. When industries experience lower than average rates of productivity growth, they are often able to make up for this by achieving a higher than average rate of output price growth. This is so for many service industries. The TSA-based data show that this has not been the case for the tourism industry. Table 6.2 indicates that tourism prices have not risen as much as general prices as measured by the GDP deflator.

Falling relative output prices might not be much of a problem for the tourism industry if input prices were also falling. The main input price is that of labour. An indicator of labour prices is obtained from Compensation per Employee as measured by the labour price index (Australian Bureau of Statistics, 2006) has been growing faster than output prices.

There is a defined link between an industry's productivity growth, its output prices, input prices and its profitability. With declining productivity, increasing input prices and more slowly increasing output prices, we would expect a profits squeeze on the industry. This is strongly confirmed in the data (Table 6.2). Profits for the industry are calculated by deducting capital consumption from gross operating surplus. These are then related to the estimate of the value of the fixed assets employed. This gives a rate of return on assets. The rate of return, as estimated, shows a distinct downward trend. It has fallen consistently over the period and by 2002/2003, by only about two-thirds of what it was in 1997/98. All of this indicates a sharp drop over the period in the profitability of the tourism industry as a whole.

Table 6.2: Tourism output prices, input prices and profitability, Australia, 1997/1998–2002/2003.

Year	GDP deflator 2001/2002 = 100	Tourism output prices 2001/2002 = 100	Labour price 2001/2002 = 100	Net rate of return (%)
1997/1998	91.4	95.1	85.8	3.0
1998/1999	91.3	96.1	88.4	2.9
1999/2000	93.2	96.4	89.6	2.7
2000/2001	97.6	97.0	95.2	2.5
2001/2002	100.0	100.0	100.0	2.3
2002/2003	102.0	102.3	106.8	1.9

Source: Forsyth et al. (2004a, 2004b).

This work is preliminary, but it does indicate the usefulness of TSAs in measuring tourism performance. There are several further directions for this work. It is possible to develop measures of total factor productivity, incorporating capital as well as labour inputs — these would give more reliable productivity measures than partial labour productivity measures. Productivity and profitability measures can be developed for individual tourism industries (accommodation, tour operations, etc.). Productivity could be measured using gross output, rather than value added. Using state or provincial level TSAs, which are now being developed in Australia, cross-section comparisons by region can be made. International comparisons of productivity, prices and profitability can be made using TSA data from different countries.

Estimating Tourism Yield

By tourism yield we refer to the impacts that additional expenditure associated with a particular visitor market segment, (e.g., by origin, demographic market or travel motive) has on economic variables of interest, such as value added, profits and employment. Tourism yield is an indicator, which has a particular importance in tourism marketing and promotion. Yield measures, which have been used to date have tended to be simple, such as gross expenditure per tourist (Dwyer & Forsyth, 1997). Expenditure measures have limited usefulness for several reasons — gross expenditure data does not in itself provide information on the types of goods and services that tourists purchase, or the industry sectors that receive the sales revenues, or the import content of the expenditure items. Recently, attempts have been made to measure yield using a wider set of economic variables (Dwyer et al., 2007). Appropriate yield measures can be devised, and measured using TSAs and CGE models.

Two suites of yield measures are discussed below. The first concerns measures of tourism yield at the tourism industry level — these involve how an additional tourist from a particular market contributes to value added, profits and employment in the tourism industry. These yield measures are estimated for selected niche markets using the Australian TSA. The second concerns measures of tourism yield at the economy wide level — these involve how an additional tourist from a market impacts on national value added, employment, and profits of all industries in the Australian economy. These are estimated using a CGE model.

Estimating Industry Level Tourism Yield Using the TSA

Tourism Research Australia (TRA), the national government's official tourism research agency, has recently estimated tourism yield in Australia (Salma & Heaney, 2004). The purpose of the study was to illustrate how the concept of 'tourism yield' can be measured from the perspective of both tourism operators and destination managers. The measures of yield developed by TRA are essentially *industry-yield* measures, which show how the tourism industry is impacted on by additional tourism from different source markets. Salma and Heaney (2004) estimated yield for eight important Australian inbound niche markets. Three measures are used. The first is tourism gross operating surplus (GOS) per visitor; the second is rate of profit on tourism sales; and the third is employment generated per thousand visitors

Table 6.3: GOS per visitor, yield rates and employment generated in selected inbound markets, Australia, 2001/2002.

Niche market	Tourism consumption per visitor (A$)	Tourism GOS per visitor (A$)	Yield rate (%)	Employment generated per thousand visitors (number)
Japanese honeymooners	3491	483	13.8	25
German holiday makers	5401	693	12.8	29
Backpackers	6158	773	12.6	54
NZ mature	1374	173	12.6	11
Malaysia first timers	1902	237	12.5	17
UK repeat	3662	432	11.8	29
Business	3020	353	11.7	23
Students	11,872	1181	9.9	123
All inbound visitors	3484	427	12.2	29

Source: Salma and Heaney, 2004, Table 6.1. Australian Bureau of Statistics (2004) and Tourism Research Australia (2002).
Note: Yield rate per visitor market = GOS for that market divided by the associated tourist consumption.

from each niche market. The yield measures are estimated from tourist expenditure data and the TSA. The expenditure data comes from Australia's International Visitor Survey (IVS), which reports expenditures and expenditure patterns of tourists from source countries annually (Tourism Research Australia, 2002). The results are shown in Table 6.3.

The steps involved in measuring yield can be set out explicitly (Salma & Heaney, 2004). These are:

- Extract data on itemized tourism expenditure of the visitors included in the selected tourist market from the IVS, and calculate their proportion of total tourism expenditure for each industry;
- Apply the proportions to the TSA estimates of aggregate tourism consumption and GOS in each industry to derive consumption and GOS generated by the tourist market;
- Sum these to estimate total tourism consumption and total GOS due to the tourist market;
- Divide the tourist market GOS by tourism consumption of the market, and the ratio will give the average yield for that market segment;
- The yield measures can be estimated from tourist expenditure data and the TSA. The expenditure data for inbound markets comes from IVS which reports expenditures and expenditure patterns of tourists from source countries annually (Tourism Research Australia, 2002);
- The employment effects produced by a tourist market are estimated by applying the tourism consumption proportion derived from the tourism expenditure data to national industry employment data published in the TSA, and summing these across industries to estimate total direct employment generated by that market.

The highest GOS per visitor for the selected markets is associated with students followed by backpackers and German holidayers. The smallest GOS per visit are associated with New Zealand mature travellers and Malaysian first timers. GOS per visit depends importantly on the expenditure of each market. Average yield rate (GOS per A$ of tourism consumption) for the total inbound visitor market is 12.2%. Five of the selected niche market groups had a rate of yield higher than the average, while three (Students, Business and UK repeats) produced a below-average yield rate. Students were the lowest yielding visitors. In terms of overall contribution to employment per thousand visitors, students generated the highest contribution (12.3%) followed by backpackers and German holidayers. These were the only visitor markets to generate employment at or above the average for all inbound tourism to Australia.

This type of analysis gives partial-equilibrium measures or the direct impacts on the tourism industry alone. Salma and Heaney do not consider the economy-wide effects of the tourist expenditure after allowance is made for interindustry effects of the injected expenditure resulting from changes in prices, exchange rates in the presence of factor constraints. However, the GOS per visitor and the employment generated per visitor are likely to be substantially lower once interindustry effects are recognised. Proper acknowledgement of these effects requires going beyond TSA-based measures to undertake CGE modelling of the tourism expenditure associated with each market segment. In the following section, we discuss some yield estimates, which have been made by the authors using a CGE model.

Estimating Economy-Wide Tourism Yield Using CGE Models

The STCRC for Tourism Economics and Policy Research has developed a CGE model of the Australian and New South Wales economies for analysing tourism impacts and related policy measures (Dwyer, Forsyth, Spurr, & Ho, 2003, 2005). This model, called M2RNSW, is an adaptation of the standard Monash Multi-Regional Forecasting (MMRF) model (Dixon & Parmenter, 1996).

Table 6.4 presents the results of the CGE model simulations using IVS data (with no adjustment for the international airfare component of visitor expenditure overseas but injected into Australia). The annual inbound visitor expenditure data fed into the model was the average for each niche market over the three-year period. The tables contain several yield measures, estimated as outcomes of applying the CGE model to the expenditure data.

Expenditure

Of the identified markets, the highest greatest expenditure injected in Australia is associated with backpackers, followed by business travellers and UK repeaters. The smallest expenditure is associated with Malaysian and Canadian matures. The total expenditure associated with each market depends on total visitor numbers, expenditure per day and length of stay. The economic impact of each market depends both on the volume of expenditure and purchasing patterns.

Table 6.4: Economic impacts of selected inbound market expenditure (annual average period 2001/2002–2003/2004).

Niche market	Total injected spend ($m)	Real GVA per visitor ($)	Real GVA per visitor night ($)	Real GOS per visitor ($)	Real GOS per visitor night ($)	Real GOS per spend (%)	Number of jobs per $m spend
Backpackers	2382.2	671.04	10.09	389.8	5.86	7.67	6.08
Business	1118.1	258.92	22.17	261.2	14.56	8.45	7.32
Canadian mature (+55)	60.83	294.91	11.13	292.2	7.48	8.75	6.35
Convention	169.93	191.96	24.18	108.7	13.47	6.79	6.99
Hong Kong first timers	82.941	296.18	14.33	127.5	6.13	5.36	5.71
Japanese honeymooners	105.40	167.09	27.76	97.4	17.46	8.13	4.56
Malaysia first timers	74.53	229.00	13.50	93.8	5.52	5.20	6.12
Malaysian mature (+55)	27.46	186.41	9.56	109.0	5.69	7.64	5.65
Malaysian repeaters	348.39	458.17	14.81	172.0	5.63	4.81	6.00
NZ mature (+55)	243.79	158.69	10.19	105.4	6.83	8.74	6.45
UK repeaters	903.53	343.50	10.16	229.7	6.79	8.74	6.19

Source: Economic impacts based on author's simulations. Expenditure data from IVS (Salma & Heaney, 2004).

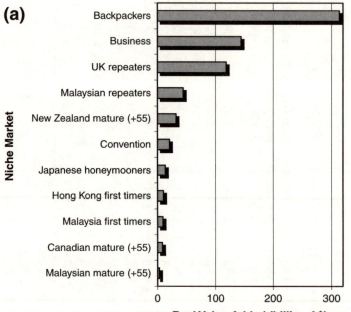

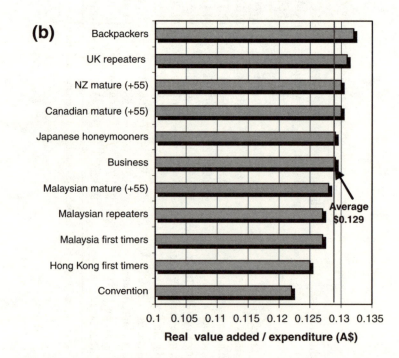

Figure 6.1: (a) Real value added annually, by niche market; (b) Real value added per
expenditure dollar by niche market.

Real Value Added

Table 6.4 indicates that the greatest contribution to real gross value added (GVA) came from backpackers, business and UK repeat visitors, with the lowest contributions from Malaysian and Canadian mature travellers. This information is displayed in Figure 6.1a.

Real value added as a proportion of tourism expenditure for each niche market is displayed in Figure 6.1b. The backpacker market has the highest proportion of value added per dollar of expenditure followed by UK repeaters, New Zealand mature, Canadian mature, Japanese honeymooners and business travellers. The lowest proportion of value added per dollar of expenditure is associated with convention visitors and Hong Kong and Malaysian first timers.

Table 6.4 shows real GVA per visitor night. This is displayed in Figure 6.2. Origins above the average ($12.13) were: Japanese honeymooners, convention attendees, business travellers, Malaysian repeaters, Hong Kong first timers and Malaysian first timers.

The results can be displayed in matrix form as Figure 6.3. The axes cross at the average value added per day for all markets ($12.13) and average real value added per visitor for all visitors to Australia ($332.65). The north-east quadrant, indicating above-average value added per visitor (over total trip) and above average value added per visitor day has only one niche market — Malaysian repeaters. Canadian matures, Malaysian matures, New Zealand matures and business travellers are located in the south-west quadrant, indicating below-average value added per visit and below average value added per day.

Gross Operating Surplus

Table 6.4 indicates that the greatest contributions to GOS came from backpackers, business and UK repeat visitors, while the smallest contributions were from Malaysian matures, Malaysian first timers and Hong Kong first timers.

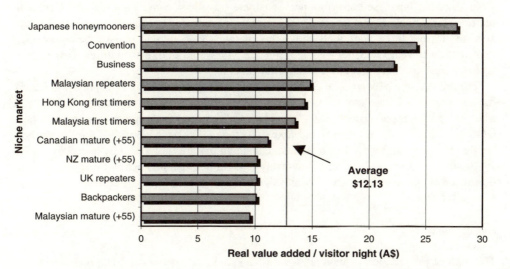

Figure 6.2: Real value added per expenditure dollar by inbound market.

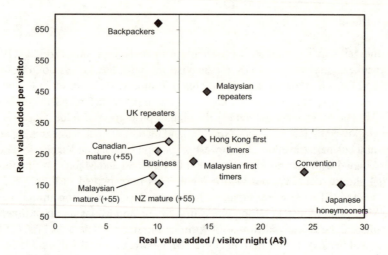

Figure 6.3: Real value added per visitor trip and per visitor night by niche market.

Table 6.4 also provides information on GOS as a percentage of the amount of expenditure injected from the selected niche markets. Those markets above the average (7.16%) are: Canadian matures, UK repeaters, New Zealand matures, business travellers, Japanese honeymooners, backpackers, and Malaysian matures. Below average contributions to GOS as a percentage of injected expenditure are associated with Malaysian repeaters, Malaysian first timers, Hong Kong first timers and convention visitors. This information is displayed in Figure 6.4a.

Niche markets above average in contribution to real GOS per visitor night (average $6.71) were, in order, Japanese honeymooners, business travellers, convention visitors, Canadian matures, New Zealand matures and UK repeaters, as depicted in Figure 6.4b. Of these markets, the former three were well above the average. Markets that make a below-average contribution to real GOS per visitor night are Malaysian markets (matures, first timers, repeater), backpackers and Hong Kong first timers.

The relationship between real GOS per visitor and per visitor night is displayed in matrix form in Figure 6.5. The axes cross at the average GOS per day for all markets ($6.71) and average real GOS per visitor ($184.03). The north-east quadrant indicates above-average GOS per visitor (over total trip) and above-average GOS per visitor day. Origin markets located in this quadrant are UK repeaters, Canadian matures and business travellers. In the south-west quadrant, indicating below-average GOS per visit and below-average contribution to GOS per day, are located Malaysians (repeaters, matures, first timers) and Hong Kong first timers.

Employment

The highest job creation is associated with backpackers, business and UK repeat visitors, while the smallest job creation is associated with visitation from Malaysian and Canadian

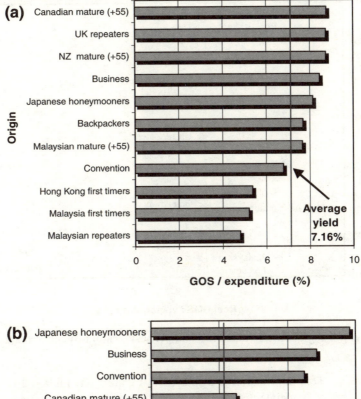

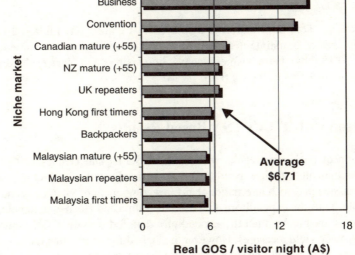

Figure 6.4: (a) GOS as proportion of expenditure by Niche market; (b) real GOS per visitor night by niche market.

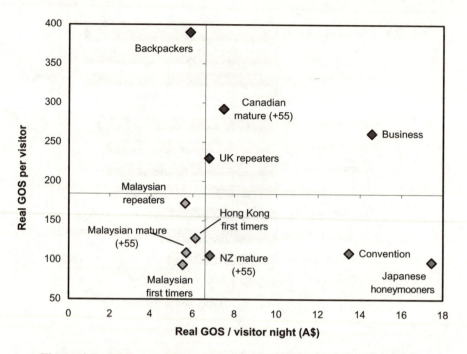

Figure 6.5: GOS per visitor trip and per visitor night by niche market.

mature travellers. This information is displayed in Figure 6.6a. Table 6.2 shows that, in terms of jobs created or maintained per million dollar expenditure, the niche markets above the average (6.13 jobs) were: business, convention visitors and New Zealand matures. This information is displayed in Figure 6.6b.

Comparison with TRA's TSA Based Results

A comparison of the above results with those of Salma and Heaney (2004) needs to be qualified. As indicated, their expenditure data were adjusted to reflect an estimate of the expenditure associated with international airfares component of visitor expenditure injected into Australia. Thus the expenditure data used by Salma and Heaney to develop TSA-based yield measures are greater than the expenditure data fed into the CGE model to estimate the economy-wide yield measures. However the main difference is that the two sets of results report impacts on different variables. The TSA-based results measure impacts on tourism industry level variables, whereas the authors' results measure the impacts on economy wide variables. The authors' simulations include the indirect effects throughout the economy as well as direct effects on the tourism industry. It is noteworthy that all of the authors yield measures — for employment, real GVA, and GOS per visitor day are uniformly smaller than the TSA-based estimates. The reasons for this lie in the interactive, feedback effects reflecting those economic realities that are allowed for in the CGE model. The latter

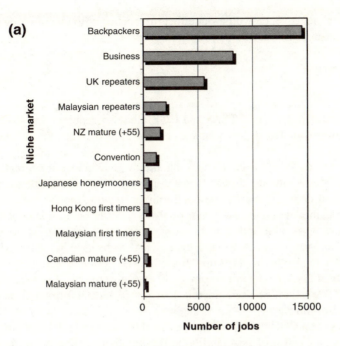

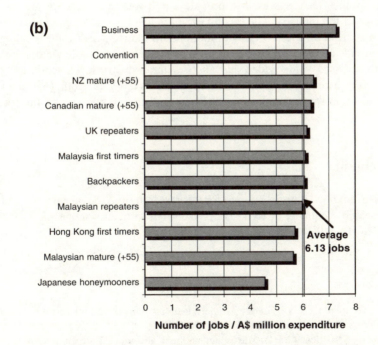

Figure 6.6: (a) Total jobs created/maintained annually, by niche market; (b) jobs created/
maintained per million dollar expenditure by niche market.

allows for substantial negative, crowding-out effects associated with tourism growth, which the TSA-based measures ignore.

Conclusions

This paper has illustrated the use of TSAs and CGE models to measure productivity and economic yield of tourism. The differences and relationships between the two techniques were described.

A key theme of this paper has been to stress that the two techniques are complementary, and can be used for related, though distinctly different purposes. Both can be used for estimating the impacts of changes, such as inbound tourism booms, though not on the same variables. Clearly the model of choice depends on the task. If the interest is in how tourism industry variables, such as value added in the tourism industry or tourism-related employment, are impacted on by a change in demand, then a TSA can be used. A CGE model, which incorporates a TSA can also be used for this. If the interest is in how economy-wide variables, such as national GVA, or overall employment are impacted on, it is necessary to use a CGE model. A TSA cannot be used since it does not include information on anything other than the tourism industry.

The uses of TSAs and CGE models were illustrated in two examples. The first of these involved developing measures of profitability and productivity of the Australian tourism industry. The Australian TSA was used to provide a rich source of data for the analysis of the performance of the industry. The second example involved developing measures of the yield of tourists from different origins to the tourism industry and to the economy as a whole. TSAs provide an appropriate technique to estimate the economic yield, for example, in terms of increased value added and GOS at the industry level, while the CGE approach was used to estimate the yield to the economy as a whole. Both TSA and CGE models are useful tools for economic measurement and policy analysis of the tourism industry.

Acknowledgement

The authors wish to acknowledge the support for this research from the Sustainable Tourism Cooperative Research Centre (STCRC). They also wish to acknowledge the modelling work of Thiep Van Ho, which underpins the yield estimates.

References

Australian Bureau of Statistics. (2000). Feature Article: Australian tourism satellite account. *Australian Economic Indicators*, September, (ABS Cat. no. 1350.0).

Australian Bureau of Statistics. (2004). Australian national accounts; Tourism satellite account 2003–2004, Canberra, April, (ABS Cat. no. 5249.0), http://www.abs.gov.au/Ausstats/

Australian Bureau of Statistics. (2006). Labour price index: Concepts, sources and methods, Australia (ABS Cat. no. 6351.0.55.001).

Blake, A. (2005). *The economic impact of the London Olympics*, Discussion Paper 2005/5, Christel DeHaan Tourism & Travel Research Institute, University of Nottingham, http://www.nottingham.ac.uk/ttri/

Blake, A., Durbarry, R., Sinclair, T., & Sugiyarto, G. (2001). *Modelling tourism and travel using tourism satellite accounts and tourism policy and forecasting models*, Discussion Paper 2001/4, Christel DeHaan Tourism & Travel Research Institute, University of Nottingham, http://www.nottingham.ac.uk/ttri/

Blake, A., & Sinclair, M. T. (2003). Tourism crisis management: US response to September 11. *Annals of Tourism Research, 30*(4), 813–832.

Dixon, P., & Parmenter, B. (1996). Computable general equilibrium analysis for policy analysis and forecasting. In: H. Aman, D. Kendrick & J. Rust (Eds.), *Handbook of computational economics* (Vol. 1, pp. 4–85). Oxford: Elsevier Science BV.

Dwyer, L., & Forsyth, P. (1997). Measuring the benefits and yield from foreign tourism. *International Journal of Social Economics, 24*(1/2/3), 223–236.

Dwyer, L., Forsyth, P., Fredline, L., Jago, L., Deery, M., & Lundie, S. (2007). Yield measures for Australia's special interest inbound tourism markets. *Tourism Economics*, forthcoming.

Dwyer, L., Forsyth, P., Madden, J., & Spurr, R. (2000). Economic impact of inbound tourism under different assumptions about the macroeconomy. *Current Issues in Tourism, 3*(4), 325–363.

Dwyer, L., Forsyth, P., & Spurr, R. (2004). Evaluating tourism's economic effects: New and old approaches. *Tourism Management, 25*, 307–317.

Dwyer, L., Forsyth, P., & Spurr, R. (2005). Estimating the impacts of special events on the economy. *Journal of Travel Research, 43*, 351–359.

Dwyer, L., Forsyth, P., Spurr, R., & Van Ho, T. (2003). Contribution of tourism by origin market to a state economy: A multi-regional general equilibrium analysis. *Tourism Economics, 9*(4), 431–448.

Dwyer, L., Forsyth, P., Spurr, R., & Van Ho, T (2005). *Economic impacts and benefits of tourism in Australia: A general equilibrium approach* (STCRC Sustainable Tourism Monograph Series, Sustainable Tourism Cooperative Research Centre, February. ISBN 1920704108).

Dwyer, L., Forsyth, P., & Spurr, R. (2006). Assessing the economic impacts of events: A computable general equilibrium approach. *Journal of Travel Research, 45*, 59–66.

Forsyth, P., Dwyer, L, Fox, K., & Rao, D. S. P. (2004a). Tourism productivity and performance: New results using the TSA. Paper presented at Sustainable tourism CRC workshop on industry performance, Tourism New South Wales, Sydney, December.

Forsyth, P., Dwyer, L, Fox, K., & Rao, D. S. P. (2004b). Efficiency and productivity measurement methods for the tourism sector. Paper presented at Sustainable tourism CRC workshop on industry performance, Tourism New South Wales, Sydney, December.

Harrison, G., Jensen, S., Pedersen, L., & Rutherford, T. (2000). Using dynamic general equilibrium analysis for policy analysis. In: G. Harrison, S. Jensen, L. Pedersen, & T. Rutherford (Eds.), *Contributions to Economic Analysis* (Vol. 248). Oxford and New York: Elsevier North Holland.

Kehoe, P. J., & Kehoe, T. J. (1995). A primer on static applied general equilibrium models. In: P. J. Kehoe, & T. J. Kehoe (Eds.), *Modeling North American Economic Integration* (pp. 1–31). Boston: Kluwer Academic Publishers.

Narayan, P. (2004). Economic impact of tourism on Fiji's economy: Empirical evidence from the computable general equilibrium model. *Tourism Economics, 10*(4), 419–433.

OECD. (2001). *Tourism satellite account recommended methodological framework*. Co-edition with: UNSD, Eurostat-Tourism Unit, Paris: World Tourism Organization.

Polo, C., & Valle, E. (2006). A general equilibrium assessment of the impact of a fall in tourism under alternative closure rules: The case of the Balearic Islands. *Proceedings second international conference on tourism economics*, University of Balearic Islands, May, 2006.

Salma, U., & Heaney, L. (2004). Proposed methodology for measuring yield. *Tourism Research Report, 6*(1) 73–81. Canberra: Tourism Research Australia.

Spurr, R. (2006). Tourism satellite accounts. In: L. Dwyer, & P. Forsyth (Eds.), *International hand-book on the economics of tourism*. Cheltenham, UK and Northampton, MA: Edward Elgar.

Sugiyarto, G., Blake, A., & Sinclair, M. T. (2003). Tourism and Globalization: Economic Impact in Indonesia. *Annals of Tourism Research, 30*(3), 683–701.

Tourism Research Australia. (2002). International Visitor Surveys 2000, 2001, (IVS), BTR, Canberra.

United Nations, World Tourism Organization, Eurostat, Organization for Economic Co-operation and Development. (2001). Tourism satellite account: Recommended methodological framework (RMF), United Nations Statistics Division, World Tourism Organization, Eurostat, Organization for Economic Co-operation and Development, New York, Madrid, Luxembourg and Paris.

Chapter 7

Assessing Tourism Yield: An Analysis of Public Sector Costs and Benefits

David G. Simmons, Susanne Becken and Ross Cullen

Introduction

This chapter reports on an analysis of the public sector's contributions to tourism provision in New Zealand. It reviews definitional and methodological challenges before reporting on a national level and four local authority case studies. Government agencies' involvement in tourism is both broad (virtually all government departments have some involvement with tourism) and varies at different geographical scales. Tourism also attracts a spectrum of economic and social/developmental perspectives which lead to differing policy perspectives.

Yield has become a central issue in tourism development with many tourism managers seeking "high yield" tourism (Dwyer & Forsythe, 1997). Sustainable development is at the core of the New Zealand Tourism Strategy 2010 (Tourism Strategy Group (TSG), 2001), which seeks to: "Grow tourism demand and financial returns while enhancing the quality of the visitor experience and New Zealander's quality of life" (p. ii). Among its 43 recommendations are a search for "… initiatives to research, develop and promote the use of pricing and yield management strategies to improve financial and economic viability" (no. 29); and the need to "(D)evelop and promote resource use efficiency initiatives and environmental systems" (no. 8). In response to these goals Lincoln University in partnership with the Tourism Industry Association of New Zealand, have recently been funded by New Zealand's Ministry of Tourism, to undertake an extensive programme of research to investigate the nature of tourism yield.

In seeking a robust consideration of tourism yield we have seen the need to reach out from 'profit and loss' and 'residual income' metrics at the firm level (financial yield, FY), to examine the costs and benefits (revenues) of public sector entities (economic yield), and when sustainability is added as a goal, to a consideration of measurements of 'ecological and social services' (sustainable yield) engendered by tourism production and consumption. Our operational definitions have been discussed below.

Developments in Tourism Research
Copyright © 2007 by Elsevier Ltd.
All rights of reproduction in any form reserved.
ISBN: 978-0-080-45328-6

Financial Yield

FY is a measure of a firm's performance by using readily accessible accounting information, making appropriate adjustments to derive 'free cash flow', and computing its 'residual income' (similar to Economic Value Added or EVA® (Stewart, 1991)). Using residual income will afford us a consistent approach to analyse a firm's financial performance, based on its capital cost (debt and equity components) and revenue streams.

Economic Yield

Tourism firms do not exist in isolation; they are part and parcel of the wider economy. As such, tourism firms are dependent on, and contribute to, the economic performance of local communities, regions and the nation. The public sector receives benefits from tourism operators by way of rates,[1] taxes, GST (goods and service tax),[2] and direct levies. In turn, government (national and local) supplies infrastructure, bio-security, customs and immigration services, and promotion of tourism by various bodies (e.g. Tourism New Zealand (TNZ), Regional and District Tourism Organisations (RTOs, DTOs)). Economic yield encompasses all monetary costs/benefits attributable to the public sector (local, regional, and national) relating to tourism production and consumption.

Sustainable Yield

For the tourism sector to be truly sustainable over time, it must be able to provide viable financial and economic returns in the prevailing social and environmental context (Northcote & MacBeth, 2006). Some of the social and environment dimensions to be examined are non-market services provided 'free of charge' (i.e. not transactionally evident). Examples include ecosystem services, culture, and 'life style' advantages. Tourism also brings crowding, congestion, pollution, and biodiversity loss. Some of these costs can be monetised (e.g. CO_2, roading), while others will simply be described.

It should be noted that when a price is paid for a social or environmental benefit (when it is no longer a free good), a transaction results, bringing that benefit within the economic yield definition, as used in the research programme. Thus, the boundary between economic and sustainable yields is not fixed, but shifts over time, depending on whether money has changed hands (Figure 7.1).

Methodology

The full research programme is based upon an eight-step methodology, grouped into three themes, to be developed and implemented over a 3-year timeframe.[3]

---

[1] Local property taxes.
[2] GST — goods and services tax is New Zealand's equivalent of VAT and is charged at 12.5% on all purchases.
[3] A framework for the research programme and ongoing reporting can be found via the programme's web portal at: www.lincoln.ac.nz/trrec/tsmyield.htm

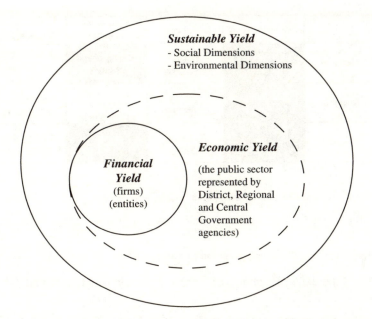

Figure 7.1: Conceptual view of types of tourism yields: Firms exist in, and interact with, the wider economy at the district, regional, and national levels, and society and the environment.

The first theme 'private sector analysis' involves a search for 'financial' yield across the various industries that make up tourism's private sector. In the second theme 'public sector analysis' economic yield is to be assessed by examining three contributing factors — public sector, business, and the visitor. The third integrative theme examines tourists' activities and expenditure to explore the question of who or what constitutes high-yield tourism — taking into account financial, economic, and sustainable yield dimensions.

The public sector examination reported here involves the analysis of national-level costs and benefits, as well as those incurred in four case studies in New Zealand districts, to examine public sector costs and benefits and resource asset cost. The research has studied the public sector's impacts of tourism at two levels: national and local. Figure 7.2 illustrates the types of costs and benefits that have been investigated and the three levels studied.

At a national level, the analysis applied a specific question to identify the costs and benefits of tourism at the national level. *What level of cost or benefit to the national public sector, or to New Zealand, would occur in the absence of tourism?* At a national level it can be argued that resources might be allocated to other sectors following price changes or other events, and that the national economy would, after a lag, return to near full employment. In cases where it is judged that the level of service provided by the public sector is not influenced by the presence of tourism, no cost or benefit is attributed to tourism. If a public sector activity is clearly linked to tourism an attempt is made to estimate the size of public sector costs and benefits associated with tourism. In many cases services and facilities are provided for both general economic or social benefit and for visitors whether domestic or international. In those instances costs and benefits are attributed to tourism based upon their share of total usage. Total cost

	Economic costs	Social costs	Economic benefits	Social benefits
National	International marketing	CO_2 emissions	GST from international tourists	More services in National Parks
Regional	Public transport for visitors	More road congestion	Stimulus to regional development	Seasonal employment
Local	Art gallery operational costs	Increased crime	Rates from tourism firms	More services in small towns

Key:

Black – costs and benefits estimated from existing data sources

Grey – quantified using prices from existing non market valuation studies, or shadow prices

Underline – quantification possible, but not monetized in this report

Figure 7.2: Examples of tourism costs and benefits studied.

data are used to calculate shares of costs in many cases. Occasionally, where marginal cost data are available such as road congestion costs, marginal cost is used to attribute costs to tourism.

In regions and districts,[4] where tourism plays a major role in their economies, it is less plausible that resources could be re-allocated to another activity in the absence of tourism and that the region or district could return to near full employment. The approach taken at region and district level differs from that at the national level and asks, "*What share of costs and revenues might reasonably be attributed to tourism*". At this level it is therefore explicitly recognised that many facilities and services are provided primarily for locals. Decisions have here been based upon tourism's share of usage where the data are available, or proxies of that ratio based on visitor densities in other cases. The choice of average or marginal costs is also considered on a case-by-case basis. The approaches used at regional and district levels are partial equilibrium analyses. No attempt is made to study the effects of tourism upon price levels, labour markets, or employment in the rest of the economy.

Choice of Case-Study Regions

The research plan allowed for the collection of information in four districts, to allow complete calculations of regional yield. However, the choice of case studies was complicated by several competing factors:

- *Capital intensity:* Understanding capital investment structures is a key to understanding business and sector financial and economic yield. Thus, a chosen regional case study should have a broad mix of capital-intensive tourism entities.

---

[4]In New Zealand local governance and resource management is given effect by 'Territorial Local Authorities' (TLAs). Local authorities comprise 74 territorial authorities and 12 regional councils. The 74 territorial authorities comprise 16 city councils and 58 district councils. All are under a single national parliament.

- *Nature of tourist behaviour and visitation patterns:* Tourism hubs depend, to some considerable extent, on the range of tourist activities and attractions in their surrounding regions. Case study regions therefore need to draw on a broad range of 'things to do and see', which are crucial elements in the evolution and health of destination regions.
- *Data availability:* At a more pragmatic level, the choice of regions was also influenced by ease of data collection, including congruence between local, regional, RTO, and Department of Conservancy management jurisdictions. Background data on the size of tourism activity and economies would also assist in contextualising the regions chosen for further analysis.
- *Nature of regions/destinations within a national system:* Tourism in New Zealand, as elsewhere, is manifested in a system of tourist flows, that in turn are supported by a hierarchy of tourist places: gateways, primary destinations, tertiary destinations, and travelling routes (Forer, 2005). Case-study regions that can lead to an elaboration of regional tourism yield should reach across these categories in a way that would enhance generalisation of results to the whole tourism sector and the national economy.

Based on the above criteria four districts stood out as most suitable for this study, namely Christchurch (the South Island's major city and tourist gateway), Rotorua[5] (a significant cultural (Maori and geothermal) tourist destination in the Central North Island), and Hurunui and McKenzie Districts, smaller local authority areas in the South Island.

Approach Taken to Assessing Public Sector Costs and Benefits

There is no clear guidance in economic theory on the correct method to allocate shared costs of a service to users. Any allocation of costs and attribution of benefits to tourism require analysts' judgment about what is appropriate. In many instances there are shared costs of providing a service to both local residents and to visitors whether domestic or international. It is particularly difficult to allocate costs of public sector services to tourism when there have been significant changes in policy and in the role of government in past years or decades.

There are at least two ways that costs could be attributed to tourism: average total costs per visit will attribute costs equally over all users. In contrast, marginal costs per visitor will attribute only change in variable costs to tourism. As an example of average cost allocations, a nation or a region decides to construct a new museum, to achieve three objectives: preservation of culture, display of culture, and provision of a tourist attraction. In this case there is a strong argument for basing cost attribution to tourism on their share of average total costs as the museum was provided in part for tourists to visit, and fixed costs as well as variable costs have been incurred to meet tourism's needs. An example for allocating average costs to tourism is the Christchurch Art Gallery, whose costs are funded from local property taxes. This organisation had an annual total cost of operation in 2004 of $7.419 million and total revenue of $1.279 million (Christchurch City Council, 2004a). Surveys of attendees and other information sources indicate that 57 percent of attendees are visitors to the region

---

[5]Christchurch and Rotorua had recently been the subject of extensive tourism research and planning activity (see Simmons & Fairweather, 2005).

(Christchurch City Council, 2004b). We can calculate tourism share of net cost of operating the Christchurch Art Gallery at (7.419–1.279) × 0.57 = $3.5 million per annum.

Alternatively, a region may for many years have provided a museum to preserve and display its cultural heritage. There are no charges for entry and the costs of the museum are funded by local property taxes collected from local residents (e.g. Canterbury Museum Trust Board, 2004). If the museum becomes a tourist attraction but does not require expansion of capacity to meet a tourism-led increased demand for visits, then a case can be made for using marginal costs (e.g. electricity consumption) to allocate costs to tourism. The case of traffic congestion is an example where marginal costs have been applied. Tourists may have greater discretion over their time of use of roads than locals and therefore attempt to avoid peak use periods. This time of use factor has been recognised when calculating congestion costs associated with tourism using off peak marginal costs provided in a recent Ministry of Transport (2005) study.

In cases where the data did not provide identification of the most appropriate approach (i.e. average versus marginal costs) and the specific revenue or expenses of a service solely attributable to tourism, expenses and revenue were apportioned according to estimated levels of per day visitor density, which were easily derived from national visitor monitors.[6] Tourism's share of local amenity (e.g. parks, botanic gardens) use is an example of this approach. This could be refined in some instances, for example in the case of road usage where roading costs were allocated according to vehicle type. Cars impose much lower roading costs than do heavy trucks and allocation of such costs to tourism cannot be based solely upon their share of total kilometre of driving on the roads. Their share of costs could be adjusted to recognise the low impact that a kilometre of car travel has compared with a kilometre by heavier vehicle.

A number of costs and benefits of tourism are not traded in markets and no prices exist for them. Examples of non-market costs that might be included in estimates of sustainable yield include increased pollution and crime associated with tourism. An example of a non-market benefit is improved access to services for residents of a region as a consequence of regional tourism. Where there are avoided costs of travel, for example to a school, because tourism helps sustain a school in a region, these avoided costs might be estimated as an indicator of the benefits to local residents occurring because of the presence of tourism. Tourism also provides a significant proportion of employment in some regional economies and rural communities, which brings both economic and social benefits, but these have not been quantified. We have searched databases of non-market valuation studies to identify any that may be used to provide estimates of currently non-monetised costs or benefits of tourism in New Zealand, but such studies are rare for tourism.

Results

National Level

Nationally, there are two major net revenue streams from tourism: GST from international tourists of $481 million per annum and excise taxes from international tourists of $35 million

---

[6]The New Zealand Tourism Research Council (hosted by the Ministry of Tourism) collects omnibus International Visitor and Domestic Travel Studies; see www.trcnz.govt.nz

per annum. A surplus of $97.3 million is also reported from roading and fuel levies and taxes (Statistics New Zealand, 2005).

For the economy as a whole, tourism also generates direct taxes of $1430 million per annum, and $730 million of GST on domestic tourism. However, it is argued that a similar amount of direct taxes might be paid by another sector that used the same volume of resources as are used by tourism. While it would be possible to view all taxes ($2.7 billion per annum) generated by tourism as a benefit of tourism and place these alongside tourism's share of all government expenditure, we have focused on only net costs and benefits that are achieved by using resources in tourism rather than in some other sector.

Government expenditure at the national level was grouped into two areas:

- 'Core' public sector tourism activities (e.g. Tourism New Zealand, Ministry of Tourism) ($102 million)

International marketing by Tourism New Zealand costs $64.3 million per annum. The payoff from this state-funded activity is a continuing flow of international tourists to New Zealand and their economic, fiscal, and social impacts. At ports of entry, passenger clearance costs are partly met by the Crown and partly by users (New Zealand Treasury, 2005). We have allocated 59 percent of the Crown contribution to tourism, a total of $21.4 million per annum. Central government also purchases $5.3 million policy advice $5 million for regional development initiatives, and $4.1 million of research through their Ministry of Tourism, which in the 2004 year also had a special allocation of $2.3 million for implementation of the national tourism strategy.

- 'Related' public sector infrastructure tourism activities (predominantly for access to environment, culture and heritage, conservation, border control ($109 million).

While many agencies of the New Zealand public sector provide services that benefit tourism, the largest costs accrue through the provision of site access and activities by the Department of Conservation (DOC). While DOC receives revenues from tourists, it provides services to tourism that we estimate have a net cost of $79 million per annum (Department of Conservation, 2004). This may understate the true tourism-related net cost of conservation activities by $25–50 million per annum, if we were to add in some proportion of the costs of managing natural and heritage values, and potential imbalances in annual capital expenditures. At the national level we similarly judge that Te Papa (the National Museum), the Ministry of Culture, Search and Rescue and Nature Heritage each incur significant net costs because of tourism in the range $5 million–$10 million per annum.

Tourism in New Zealand typically involves significant amounts of travel and we estimate that it contributes 15.5 percent of national road vehicle kilometre. New Zealand captures significant amounts of revenue from road users and we estimate that domestic tourists' travel generates a financial surplus of $109.2 million, and international tourists' travel a revenue outflow of $11.9 million for a combined surplus of $97.3 million. It is similarly estimated that domestic and international tourists also contribute a net $18 million and $1 million per year, respectively, towards Accident Compensation Commission funds but these are held against future claims.

In summary, central government collects tax and excise revenue of over $500 million per annum from international tourists. Beyond this revenue, roading generates an additional net surplus of \$97.3 million per annum. Direct costs for government services to tourists arise largely from offshore marketing, research and policy advice to total \$102 million. Resource conservation (particularly providing access to and services within national parks, culture and heritage) costs incur an additional \$109 million of government expenditure. On this basis it is estimated that tourism's net central government revenues exceed costs at the national level for a net gain just in excess of \$400 million per annum.

Monetised *external* costs for road transport are well documented by the Ministry of Transport (2005). Travel by visitors imposes environmental and social costs as well as financial costs. International visitor's share of accidents is reported as double the percentage share of vehicle per kilometre. The Ministry of Transport (2005) has also identified air and water pollution, noise pollution, CO_2 emissions, congestion, and external costs of transport accidents as significant items whose shadow price can be estimated. Based on information from that study, the annual costs associated with tourists' road travel are estimated to be: road accident externalities \$57 million; congestion costs \$78.6 million; and noise from transport \$3.9 million. Transport uses large volumes of fossil fuel and contributes to climate change and to air and water pollution. It is calculated that tourism's share of these costs is \$80 million per annum, of which carbon costs are \$62 million per annum. These figures are examples of shadow costs and are key indicators of the sustainability costs associated with tourism. Under present resource management and pricing regimes similar cost estimates would be anticipated for other productive sectors (e.g. agriculture, forestry) of the New Zealand economy (Patterson & McDonald, 2004).

For other dimensions of sustainable yield we note that tourism impacts on the environment at a limited number of fragile sites, and imposes noise costs on recreationists in some national parks. Conversely, tourism brings substantial external benefits to many New Zealand residents via improvements in the range and quality of services available in cities, towns, and national parks. Tourism contributes to more diverse cosmopolitan communities that are attractive to many people. The dollar magnitudes of these external benefits have not been estimated in New Zealand; hence, it is difficult to assess their importance and to compare them with the fiscal costs that have been quantified. Notwithstanding this, current assessments of the social impacts of tourism indicate that New Zealand residents consistently list greater benefits from tourism than social and community costs (Shone, Horn, Moran, & Simmons, 2005).

A number of external costs and benefits can be described. Among these, transport externalities have received the maximum attention and have been estimated as \$223 million per annum. Even if they were included in the above comparison, central government funds would still be seen as a net surplus on activities and services to the tourism sector. While not included in our assessment of net revenues we note that tourism also generates direct taxes of \$1430 million plus GST on domestic tourism of \$788 million per annum. As noted above, these have not been included in our assessment on the assumption that deployment of these resources in other sectors would generate similar costs and revenue.

Local Level

Results of the four cases — Christchurch, Rotorua, and Hurunui and Mackenzie districts — show that local public sector costs and revenues are generally of a similar magnitude.

As a percentage of estimated tourism costs, tourism revenues were 15 percent less than costs for Mackenzie District (Mackenzie District Council, 2004), 5 percent less than costs for Christchurch City (Christchurch City Council, 2004a), 13 percent greater for Hurunui District (Hurunui District Council, 2004), and 28 percent greater for Rotorua Region (Rotorua District Council, 2004, 2005). However, the totals (and the derived percentages) cannot be considered robust overtime. They are subject to many assumptions and data limitations and at this stage present a single year snapshot, which does not readily account for significant non-recurrent capital expenditures.

The two small districts studied in Canterbury are very strongly dependent on and impacted by tourism, with visitor/resident densities of 22 percent for Hurunui and 48 percent for Mackenzie. The structure of local public sector activities in rural districts is also quite different from that of districts containing large towns and cities. Local provision of general infrastructure and services may be more limited, but to the extent that it is provided, *per capita* costs are often higher. Tourism impacts on roading costs are, however, mitigated by the fact that most visitor travel is on State Highways with associated costs allocated at the national level. Impacts on other infrastructure are clearly significant, although the use of average rather than marginal costs may have overstated this to some extent. Revenues from specific visitor activities vary greatly within and between regions, but only the Hurunui District-owned Hanmer Springs Thermal Resort stood out as a dominant source of local public revenue (approximately 70 percent of total for this district). In each of the other three cases, local property taxes (general and targeted) attributed to tourism accounted for the majority of tourism revenue.

Tourist densities have increased steadily in New Zealand during the past two decades. The flows of both domestic and international visitors can be a mixed blessing to communities. Quantifying these costs and benefits can be completed in some cases by using existing social statistics or other indicators such as trends in availability of medical services or restaurants in small communities. Wherever possible we have provided examples from existing studies of the ways that tourism has benefited (seasonal employment, better facilities in National Parks, greater frequency of public transport) or imposed stresses or social costs (crowded local parking, increased demands on volunteers, loss of cultural integrity) at national, regional, or local level. Non-market valuation studies have been completed in the USA, Australia (Bennett, van Bueren, & Whitten, 2004), and other countries to estimate dollar values of some of these tourism-related items but few such studies have been completed in New Zealand.

In Rotorua, non-financial impacts of tourism appear to be of more concern than in the other three cases. These impacts included dealing with tensions around inner-city parking arrangements and concerns about tourist involvement in road-traffic accidents. Crime, or at least tourist perceptions of crime, was also of concern (Horn, Simmons, & Fairweather, 2000).

Discussion

Our findings indicate that central government derives a cash surplus from its tourism sector-based activities. Taking 'net' revenues into account we estimate a net annual cash flow to central government of just over $400 million. Notwithstanding this assessment there are a number of caveats that need to be borne in mind. Most of these focus on the core approach — the determination of 'marginal' costs and the relationship between static and equilibrium based conceptualisations of the national economy, and the role that tourism might play within it. There also exist significant temporal elements to government investment and how past costs might be considered in the present (political) economy.

Results at the regional and local level indicate that costs and benefits are broadly balanced especially when the context of the different case study areas are brought into consideration. While not all dimensions of tourism impact have been quantified it appears that in aggregate tourism benefits exceed costs that may disguise some local cases where acute tourism pressures mean costs could exceed benefits.

For the local case studies our method of allocating rates of revenue to tourism reflects economic principles of a demand-driven economy. However, this perspective does not appear to match those of Councils. Local authority rates, whether general or targeted, are based mainly on the capital value of properties. Often the same rates apply to residential properties and businesses. Implementation of user-pays principles is generally limited. We suggest that there are two ways for Councils to ensure that tourism does not impose net financial costs on them. One way is to use targeted tourism rates to cover a wider range of costs. Another is to extend user-pays principles so that rates paid by all rate payers better reflect their individual impacts; tourism-related or otherwise.

Attempts to report on sustainable yield draw attention to the fact that while many of the economic costs and benefits of tourism are measured and recorded in existing financial transactions, revealing the magnitude of some social costs and benefit remains problematic (Northcote & MacBeth, 2006). Some can be quantified by way of non-market valuation techniques or mitigation cost measures, while others can be described but are not easily quantified or measured in dollars. We have used existing financial data where they are available, shadow prices where they are available, and qualitative assessments in cases where there are no financial or economic data available.

Throughout our analysis attempting to unravel why a service or facility is provided or funded by government has emerged as an extremely difficult task and this part of the research programme did not attempt to do that. The objective of this research project has been to evaluate the impacts of tourism upon the New Zealand public sector. This strand of the research project has collected data that will be used elsewhere in the research programme to determine if tourism is generating both economic and sustainable yield.

Notwithstanding these broad statements, the research frames a number of broader policy issues including whether, given tour and travel patterns in New Zealand, central government offers adequate support to peripheral economies where tourists can overwhelm the funding capability of the local resident population. To answer such policy questions adequately it becomes important to separate initial capital costs from those arising during ongoing operations and maintenance (Market Economics, 2003; Cullen, Dakers, & Meyer-Hubbert, 2004). If tourism in New Zealand continues to grow in volume, increasing revenue seems likely to arise from local authorities for infrastructure support, especially. Subsequent analysis would also need to question whether Councils effectively deploy the full suite of cost recovery mechanisms available within existing legislation.

As a second set of questions raised by the research focus on the pricing of traditionally free services, for example national park facilities, and urban facilities such as museums and art galleries. Analysis of such a question would need to take into account that the national (brand image) and local (collection efficiency, substitutes, and complements) issues are being resolved adequately. This question remains particularly salient given the significance in terms of both visitation to (Tourism New Zealand, 2005) and satisfaction from (Tourism New Zealand, 2006) New Zealand's natural environments.

As noted in the introduction, this project comprises one of several themes and approaches in our assessment of financial, economic, and sustainable yield for tourism,[7] which has the twin goals of determining 'high-yield visitor (types)' and developing tools for both the public and private sectors to enhance tourism's performance in the national economy.

References

Bennett, J., van Bueren, M., & Whitten, S. (2004). Estimating society's willingness to pay to maintain rural communities. *Australian Journal of Agricultural & Resource Economics, 48*(3), 487–512.

Canterbury Museum Trust Board. (2004). *Canterbury Museum 2003/2004 annual report.* Christchurch, New Zealand.

Christchurch City Council. (2004a). *Christchurch city council annual report 2004.* Christchurch, New Zealand.

Christchurch City Council. (2004b). *Our community plan 2004.* Christchurch, New Zealand: Office of the Chief Executive, Christchurch City Council.

Cullen, R., Dakers, A., & Meyer-Hubbert, G. (2004). *Tourism, water, wastewater and waste service in small towns.* Tourism Recreation Research and Education Centre, Report no. 57. Canterbury: Lincoln University.

Department of Conservation. (2004). *Annual report of the department of conservation for the year ended 30 June 2004.* Wellington: Department of Conservation.

Dwyer, L., & Forsythe, P. (1997). Measuring the benefits and yield from foreign tourism. *International Journal of Economics, 24,* 223–236.

Forer, P. (2005). Tourist flows and dynamic geographies: Applying GI science to understanding tourism processes. In: D. G. Simmons & J. R. Fairweather (Eds.), *Understanding the tourist-host encounter in New Zealand: Foundations for adaptive planning and management* (pp. 21–52). Christchurch, New Zealand: EOS Ecology.

Horn, C. M., Simmons, D. G., & Fairweather, J. R. (2000). *Evolving community response to tourism and change in Rotorua.* Tourism Research and Education Centre (TREC), Report no. 14. Canterbury: Lincoln University.

Hurunui District Council. (2004). *Annual report: 2003/2004. Hurunui District Council.* Canterbury, New Zealand: Hurunui District Council.

Mackenzie District Council. (2004). *Mackenzie district community plan: 2004–2014 long term council community plan.* Canterbury, New Zealand: Mackenzie District Council.

Market Economics [for NZ Ministry of Economic Development & Ministry of Tourism]. (2003). Effects of tourism demand on water and sewerage infrastructure in four local authorities. Wellington: Ministry of Tourism.

Ministry of Transport. (2005). *Surface transport costs and charges: Main report.* Wellington: Ministry of Transport.

---

[7]Ongoing analyses and reports can be viewed at www.lincoln.ac.nz/trrec/tsmyield

New Zealand Treasury (2005). *Funding of passenger clearance services consultation*. Retrieved 20th April 2005 from the World Wide Web: http://www.treasury.govt.nz/fundingpcs/

Northcote, J., & Macbeth, J. (2006). Conceptualising yield in sustainable tourism development. *Annals of Tourism Research, 35*(1), 199–220.

Patterson, M., & McDonald, G. (2004). How clean and green is New Zealand tourism. Landcare Research Science Series, no. 24. Canterbury: Lincoln University.

Rotorua District Council. (2004). *The ten year plan. Long term council community plan 2004–2014*. Rotorua: Destination Rotorua.

Rotorua District Council. (2005). *Statements of proposal: The annual plan 2005/2006*. Rotorua: Destination Rotorua.

Shone, M. C., Horn, C. M., Moran, D., & Simmons, D. G. (2005). Adapting to tourism: Community responses to tourists in five New Zealand tourism destinations. In: D. G. Simmons & J. Fairweather (Eds.), *Understanding the tourist-host encounter in New Zealand: Foundations for adaptive planning and management* (pp. 83–105). Christchurch, New Zealand: EOS Ecology.

Simmons D. G., & Fairweather, J. (Eds.) (2005). *Understanding the tourist-host encounter in New Zealand: Foundations for adaptive planning and management*. Christchurch, New Zealand: EOS Ecology.

Statistics New Zealand. (2005). *Tourism satellite account 2004*. Wellington, NZ: Statistics New Zealand.

Stewart, G. (1991). *The quest for value — The EVA management guide*. New York: Harper Collins (see also: www.sternstewart.com).

Tourism New Zealand. (2005). *International visitor satisfaction index 2004/05*. Accessed at http://www.tourismnewzealand.com/tourism_info/market-research/visitor-satisfaction/visitor-satisfaction_home.cfm; 15th January 2006.

Tourism New Zealand. (2006). *Consumer needs and motivations*. Accessed at: http://www.tourism-newzealand.com/tourism_info/index.cfm?912DFD3E-BCD8-304B-0EC0-C3CA1BBACE2E; 15th January 2006.

TSG (Tourism Strategy Group). (2001). *New Zealand tourism strategy 2010*. Wellington, New Zealand: Ministry of Tourism.

Chapter 8

Developing a GIS-supported Tourist Flow Model for New Zealand

Susanne Becken, Shane Vuletich and Scott Campbell

Introduction

International visitor arrivals to New Zealand have grown strongly over the past decade, reaching an all-time high of 2.37 million in 2005. The strong growth is expected to persist in the future, with the Ministry of Tourism forecasting 3.21 million international visitor arrivals by 2011 (Ministry of Tourism, 2005). In addition to the rapid growth rate, travel behaviour as manifested in transport choices has changed markedly over time. For example, in 1998 about 27% of tourists reported travelling within New Zealand by coach compared with only 11% in 2005 (year ended March, Ministry of Tourism, 2005). The combination of growth and changing travel patterns requires careful management to avoid adverse tourism impacts and maximize the opportunities created by tourism. A major component in assessing those risks and opportunities of tourism is understanding the spatial distribution of tourism and changes over time.

This paper describes a project run by the New Zealand Ministry of Tourism to provide public agencies with information on past, present and future tourism demand at a sufficiently refined geographic level to make infrastructure-related decisions. The assumption is that a better understanding of the spatial distribution of tourism growth and impacts on publicly provided infrastructure will facilitate informed decision making on where to invest and where to adopt proactive policy, planning and resource allocation practices. The Tourist Flow Model (TFM) consists of an underlying statistical model of tourist movements and a geographic information systems (GIS) front end that allows the user to view the data spatially.

Spatial Analysis of Tourist Behaviour

At its very core tourism is a spatial activity: it involves travel from the tourist's place of origin to the destination and back (Leiper, 1995). Spatial behaviour by tourists is diverse, as, for

Developments in Tourism Research
Copyright © 2007 by Elsevier Ltd.
ISBN: 978-0-080-45328-6

example, different routes might be taken for the journey *to* and *from* the main destination, and many factors influence which route the tourist might consider. In addition to travel between destinations (i.e., overnight stops), there may also be substantial mobility once at the destination. Primary factors that were found to affect route choice include the directness of a journey, safety, amount of congestion and actual distance. Secondary factors are the entertainment value and scenic attributes of a route and how pleasant the traveller perceives the drive to be (Eby & Molnar, 2002).

Oppermann (1995) builds on earlier research (e.g., Lue, Crompton, & Fesenmaier, 1993) to present a categorisation of tourist trips into single and multiple destination patterns. New Zealand is a good example of a destination that induces multidestination travel, with the different attractions having an agglomerative rather than a competitive effect for visitors who come from faraway countries (Kim & Fesenmaier, 1990). The New Zealand 'sightseeing circuit' from Auckland to Christchurch via Rotorua and Queenstown (Forer & Pearce, 1984) matches Oppermann's category of an 'open jaw' multiple destination loop.

Tourist movements, itineraries and tourist flows (i.e., aggregated numbers of tourists on specific routes) have been studied at various levels. At a macro scale, Prideaux (2004) analysed the factors that influence bilateral tourist flows between Australia and other countries. Tourist flows have also been analysed in Europe for both domestic and international travel (Jansen-Verbeke, 1995). Other research has focused on destination-based travel patterns (e.g., Flognfeldt, 1999). Tideswell and Faulkner (1999) found that long-haul visitors to Queensland, Australia, travel more regionally than short-haul visitors; however, this study did not examine in detail where those tourists travelled.

The importance of distance — measured as route distance, time and travel cost — as one determinant of tourist flows to a specific attraction has been analysed in relation to travel patterns to National Parks in China (Zhang, Wall, Du, Gan, & Nie, 1999). The authors found that distance is related to demographic variables (e.g., age) and psychological traits, but not to travel motivations. Tourist profiles (e.g., nationality and age) were also used to predict the movements of international tourists in the South Island of New Zealand (Holt et al., 1998). This model achieved a successful prediction rate of 65%. A similar approach (agent-based modelling) has been taken to predict route choice based on tourists' personal attributes and tourism resources, i.e., the attractiveness of certain places (Sun & Lee, 2004). To better understand complex travel behaviour, Dahl (2000) piloted the use of "space-time budgets" (see also Fennell, 1996) for tourists on coach tours in Scandinavia, suggesting that while there are still challenges relating to data collection, the combination of travel and time is a promising avenue for tourism research.

GIS has been used in tourism research (e.g., see Forer, 2006; Barringer, Walcroft, Forer, & Hughey, 2002), but not extensively. Generally speaking, GIS is used as a tool for managing, analysing and displaying large volumes of spatial data. Tourism planning can be enhanced by GIS applications (Bahaire & Elliot-White, 1999). To date GIS applications in tourism have focused mainly on smaller scales, for example in relation to producing a recreational facility inventory, tourism-based land management and visitor-impact assessment. Boyd and Butler (1996) demonstrated the application of GIS in the identification of areas suitable for eco-tourism in Northern Ontario. A general lack of tourism databases and/or data inconsistencies have limited the application of GIS to tourism analysis and planning, particularly at a national level.

Development of the Tourist Flow Model

The TFM uses national tourist data to estimate the volumes of tourists travelling down the main transport corridors in New Zealand. The model estimates seasonal passenger volumes and is capable of generating forecasts that extend 7 years into the future. The model is visualised and can be accessed through a GIS interface. The data sources, modelling process and GIS interface development are described in more detail below.

Data Sources

The TFM is based mainly on data collected through the International Visitor Survey (IVS) and the Domestic Travel Study (DTS). Both databases contain key information required for transport modelling as argued by Lew and McKercher (2006): trip origin, trip destination and transportation mode.

The IVS time series began in 1997 and is used to produce national and regional reports on visitor behaviour, expenditure, preferences and attitudes. Among other things the IVS collects information on transport modes, accommodation used and attractions/activities visited by tourists, the definitions of which have changed marginally over time. It is also possible to create sequenced travel itineraries from the survey responses (Forer & Simmons, 2002). The IVS is undertaken in the form of an exit survey at New Zealand's main international airports in Auckland, Christchurch and Wellington. Collectively these airports are the exit point for 98% of all international visitors. The sample comprises visitors over 15 years of age who are surveyed face to face by multilingual interviewers. Approximately 5500 visitors are now interviewed each year. The IVS has some limitations based on sample size when it is oversegmented or analysed at spatial levels with low rates of visitation.

The DTS has been administered continuously since 1999 and is populated by around 15,000 telephone interviews per annum. The survey collects data relating to both overnight tourists and day visitors. In addition to general information on their trip and demographics, domestic tourists report their travel itinerary, transport modes and accommodation types. Based on this information 'travel sectors' can be introduced — travel between two overnight stops — where tourists' residential home is the origin of the first travel sector, and the destination of the last sector.

A substantial amount of work was required to develop generic spatial units that allowed the IVS and DTS data to be validly combined in a common framework. The DTS code frame has over 9800 possible locations (although data is only recorded against around 1500 locations) while the IVS captures data for around 185 locations. The TFM collapses the DTS and IVS data into 128 consistent and mutually exclusive catchments. Each catchment is represented by a single 'node', which connects the catchment to the main road, air and 'other' transport networks. The transport linkages between nodes are referred to as transport sectors.

Modelling

Data was sourced from the IVS and DTS to describe the number of passenger movements between each node pair. The passenger movement data was segmented by origin of visitor, type of visitor, transport mode, quarter and year. The sample sizes were generally too small to provide robust estimates of tourist flows when fully segmented, so some augmentation of the data was required to enhance its reliability. The quarterly data was aggregated into summer (December and March quarters) and winter (June and September quarters) seasons. The seasons were designed to pick up the differences in travel patterns between warm (beach) and cool (mountain) periods.

In most cases the sample sizes were still too small to be reliable at the seasonal level, so the majority of data points needed an additional level of temporal and/or spatial aggregation. The need to aggregate data was balanced against the objective to uncover genuine temporal and spatial variations in travel behaviour. To this end, a *minimum acceptable sample size* (MASS) was determined for each market segment, the derivation of which is beyond the scope of this paper (for more detail refer to Vuletich, 2006). Any market segment with sample less than MASS was aggregated further until its sample size equalled or exceeded MASS. The MASS for both the IVS and DTS was 600 sampled trips out of each origin market.

The model uses *conversion rates* to translate trip numbers to estimates of passenger movements along trip segments. A trip segment is a direct movement between two distinct nodes with no stops of one hour or more. The conversion rate is influenced by the attributes of the trip such as what type of trip it is, who is taking it, what season is it being taken in and in which year. Historical conversion rates are derived by dividing the number of passenger flows on each trip segment by the number of trips initiated (total arrivals retrieved from the arrival statistics). This calculation is done for every origin market $\times$ trip segment $\times$ time period $\times$ season $\times$ travel mode $\times$ travel-type combination. The conversion rates derived from temporally and/or spatially aggregated data are assumed to apply to each year and geographic region within the aggregation.

The historical flows are estimated by multiplying the conversion rates by the trips initiated in the selected time period. For example, if the user wants to observe tourism flows by Australians for the month of June 2003, the model calls the Australian conversion rates for June 2003 and multiplies them by the trips initiated by Australians in 2003. If the user wants to observe all international tourist flows for the year of 2003, the model (1) calls the conversion rates for each international market in 2003; (2) multiplies these by the appropriate trip figures (segmented by international market); and (3) sums the results for each market and each month to get an annual total for all international visitors.

The process used to *forecast* tourist flows is the same as that used to estimate historical flows — seasonal conversion rates are multiplied by seasonal trip numbers and aggregated to fit the selected time period. The forecasts of trip numbers are an extension of the Ministry of Tourism forecasting programme and are readily available. Given that there have been provider changes and methodology changes in both the IVS and DTS it is assumed that the conversion rates remain constant over the forecast period. This implicitly assumes that the travel patterns of each *market segment* remain unchanged over time, but it does not mean that aggregate travel patterns will remain unchanged over time because market segments are expected to grow at different rates. Changes in travel patterns are therefore driven by changes in *market composition* over time and not by changes in travel patterns *within* market segments. Identifying trends in travel behaviour would be a major improvement to the current version of the TFM.

Building the GIS Interface

Data Preparation Processes and Methodology   One of the first steps in generating the geographic output of the tourist flows required the creation of travel networks for the whole country and the assignment of tourist flows between each origin–destination pair to specific transport routes.[1] To cover all the possible movements by tourists within New Zealand, three generalised transport networks were created (road, air and other). The first of these, the road network, was the most complex in both creation and content. It was created using standard GIS tools from the following components:

- All state highways
- Selected non-state highway roads (e.g., established tourist routes).
- Link roads (used to connect the nodes)
- Ferry routes (passenger and vehicle)
- Walking tracks (used to show flows into non-road accessed areas, for example, Milford Sound)

Once the network was created, a number of additional operations were carried out including a cleaning process to ensure connectivity and a merging process to combine sections of road into one (where there are no junctions or nodes in between). Finally the roads were each given a drive time/speed attribute based on various factors such as road type and sinuosity. These steps then allowed the building of an ESRI Network dataset, which is a logical representation of the network itself and allows queries to be made such as what is the shortest path from A to B. A custom ESRI ArcEngine application was then written using VB.NET to run these queries for every possible combination of origin and destination. The results were then stored in a table in a form giving the Ids of all the roads traversed for a given origin to destination route. This table could then be used in conjunction with the traveller information to attribute flow numbers to each road segment as described below.

The air network is simpler than the road equivalent and was automatically generated to include all sectors served by Air New Zealand and Qantas as well as tourist sectors served by other airlines. Like the road network, this air network also had the origin to destination calculations done and a table was created to hold these results for querying within the application.

An 'other' transport network is used to present the non-road/air modes of transport as well as the 'all transport modes' option. This network is again generalised and was automatically created. Unlike the other two networks this one did not have any origin–destination precalculations done on it as no routing takes place since every origin–destination combination have one and only link connecting them (a straight line).

---

[1]The following technologies/products were used for the data creation and manipulation process, and the development of the end-user flows GIS application:

- ESRI ArcView 9.1 (+ Network Analyst Extension)
- ESRI ArcObjects
- ESRI ArcInfo
- ESRI ArcSDE
- Microsoft SQLServer
- Microsoft Access (Personal Geodatabase)
- Microsoft Visual Basic.NET

All of the above work took place during the development process in order to produce the prerequisites for the run-time analysis within the GIS application itself. This analysis took place within the ESRI ArcView GIS product with the addition of custom extension, which contained the above and other data tables along with a suitable user interface for creating the queries and interrogating the results.

Assumptions   A number of assumptions are made in the routing of travellers via the three networks. The basic input of analysis is the estimated number of passenger flows between each location pair. In theory there are over 16,000 possible location pairs in the flows model (128×128), although in practice most of these location pairs have no direct flows recorded between them. In some cases there is only one possible route between two locations, and in other cases there are multiple (possible) routes. New Zealand's topography (e.g., corridors in mountainous areas) and the dispersion of attractions means that the transport network is comparatively simple, at least for international tourists who follow the main routes. In general the number of possible routes will increase with the length of the trip segment (all other things being equal). The choice of route will ultimately depend on the preferences and time budget of the traveller — some will opt for the fastest route while others will opt for longer scenic routes (see also Lew & McKercher, 2006).

Unfortunately little is known about the road route decision making of tourists in New Zealand. In the absence of better information an algorithm has been developed that assigns road passenger flows to specific routes based initially on travel time (as calculated based on various estimated factors such as distance and straightness of road) and 'tourist value' (represented by the attractiveness of popular tourist routes). It is acknowledged that this process is reasonably "blunt" when compared with the rest of the model. It should be noted that, due to its simpler nature, routing through the air network is much more accurate and has also been based on detailed route information provided by Air New Zealand.

A couple of other key assumptions were made within the model. Firstly that in routing by air from/to an origin/destination that does not have an airport, the assumption is made that the flow is from/to the nearest airport, which offers that service. However, in many cases the reality may be that a traveller chooses to drive further to another airport, for example for a more convenient service.

Secondly, as a result of collapsing reported tourist destinations into the 128 tourism flows areas (see above), flows may be slightly misrepresented within the catchments. The flow in and out of all locations within a catchment is then attributed to a single chosen key location (normally a significant town or tourist destination) and any intra-region flow is discounted. This can be shown in Figure 8.1 where the flows between A and a, and B and b are not shown. Furthermore, it is assumed that flows from a to b are via A and B whereas another route may be shorter (Figure 8.2).

Results

When aggregating all forms of tourism — international and domestic overnight tourism and domestic day visits — the number of trips made is substantial. The total number of travel segments (i.e., travel between overnight stops) in 2004 amounted to almost 130 million.

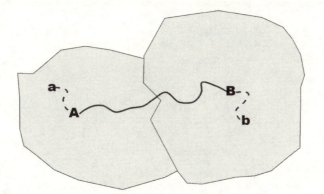

Figure 8.1: Intra-region flows (possibility 1).

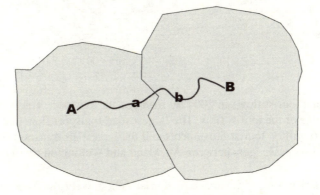

Figure 8.2: Intra-region flows (possibility 2).

The majority of travel segments are generated by domestic day visitors, whereas international visitors generate fewer but longer travel segments. In the following, major tourist flows in New Zealand will be described and compared. An example of using the TFM for the purpose of a regional analysis will also be provided.

Major Tourist Flows

The aggregated tourist flows (i.e., international and domestic) are most pronounced around the main centres of Auckland, Wellington and Christchurch (Figure 8.3). This is because a large percentage of New Zealand's population resides in these areas, making them major source markets as well as destinations for domestic tourism. Furthermore, Auckland and Christchurch are the main entry and exit points for international tourists. The sector between Auckland and Rotorua is the dominant tourist route for both domestic and international visitors. Not surprisingly, the largest air flows are between Auckland, Wellington and Christchurch, respectively. Also of importance are air links into Queenstown and Dunedin in the South Island.

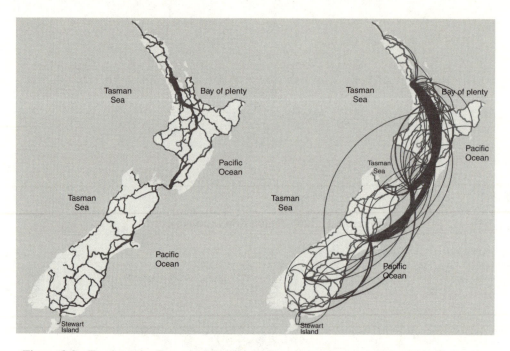

Figure 8.3: Total tourist flows in 2004 by road and air transport. The width of the line represents the size of the tourist flow. The largest road transport flow (Auckland) represents about 30 million tourist movements and the largest air transport flow involves about 2 million passengers between Auckland and Wellington (both directions).

The largest tourism flow is generated by tourists who travel from Auckland to Hamilton (or vice versa) with about 4.7 million international and domestic tourists travelling this route (Table 8.1). While the top three flows are determined by road flows, the Auckland to Wellington sector is largely travelled by air, generating around 2.2 million passenger flows in 2004.

While the TFM displays tourist flows as the total volume of tourists on a given sector, i.e., forward and reverse combined, it is also possible to distinguish the directions of travel. The ability to observe directionality reveals some quite substantial asymmetries in travel patterns in areas where tourists travel predominantly in one direction. The asymmetry is more marked for international travellers because domestic travellers tend to take the same route to their destination and back home. A good example of directionality can be seen on the West Coast of the South Island where international tourists travel predominantly in one direction, namely from north to south (40% more than those travelling south to north). As Figure 8.4 shows, the southbound West Coast flow forms part of the tourist circuit that starts in Auckland and leads toward the south and around the South Island anticlockwise.

Travel Pattern by Market

Different markets show different travel patterns across both space and time. The most marked differences in terms of destinations visited and routes travelled can be found between

Table 8.1: Top 10 tourist flows between stops in New Zealand in 2004 (combined international and domestic).

Travel segment	Air volumes	Road volumes	Total volumes[a]
Auckland-Hamilton	2,897	4,706,325	4,713,741
Auckland-Warkworth	1,252	2,932,197	2,970,852
Auckland-Whangarei	91,904	2,139,866	2,236,294
Auckland-Wellington	1,759,542	357,521	2,188,559
Auckland-Pukekohe	0	2,186,901	2,187,648
Auckland-Rotorua	39,199	2,058,485	2,111,482
Wellington-Palmerston North	534	1,905,581	1,937,516
Christchurch-Ashburton	20,084	1,741,978	1,762,061
Auckland-Tauranga	28,994	1,670,914	1,703,155
Wellington-Waikanae	0	1,474,788	1,574,485

[a]Includes flows conducted using 'other' modes of transport.

"other Europe" (all Europeans except those from the UK, Scandinavia and Ireland) and "Northeast Asia" (mainly China and South Korea). Figure 8.5 shows that the summer tourist flows for "other Europeans" are very dispersed and reach into remote areas such as Northland and around the south of the South Island.

In contrast, the Northeast Asian tourist flows are highly concentrated on the Auckland to Rotorua sector in the North Island and the Christchurch to Milford Sound route in the South Island (Figure 8.6). The majority of tourists travel by air between Auckland and Christchurch (not shown in Figure 8.6), although there is a secondary road tourist flow from north to south crossing the Cook Strait between the two islands. Destinations such as the West Coast or Northland are hardly visited by this market.

Regional Analysis — Case Example of Northland

It is possible to zoom into the map produced for a given query and analyse the generated flows at a more regional level. Figure 8.7 displays the tourist flows of all tourists in Northland in 2004; tourist volumes decrease as the distance from Auckland increases. The map also gives additional information such as place names, airports, conservation areas (green shaded) and Transit New Zealand telemetry road count points (grey circles with a black dot).

Information on a specific travel sectors can be retrieved from the TFM. For example, the sector between Whangarei and Kaikohe (near the Bay of Islands) shows 4,472,800 tourists in 2004 (and 5,077,500 in 2011), of which 2,253,200 travelled south and 2,219,600 travelled north. There is no asymmetry in direction travelled on this road sector. Tourist traffic represents about 45% of all traffic. This proportion is obtained by comparing tourist volumes with road counts provided by Transit New Zealand. The main markets when measured over the whole year are domestic day visitors from Northland and overnight visitors from Auckland. The most important international market on that sector is Australia. In summer, however, UK/Nordic/Ireland becomes the most prominent international market. Also, tourist

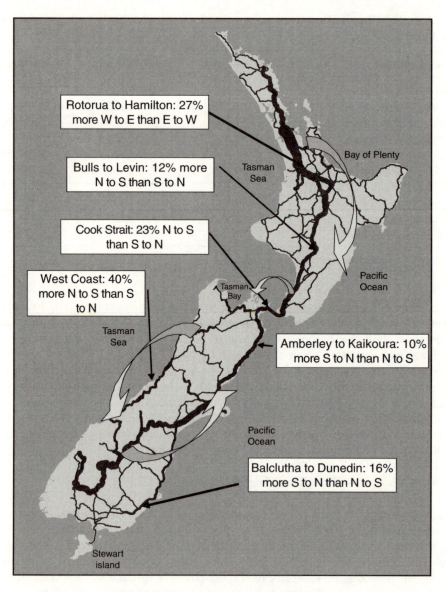

Figure 8.4: Directionality for selected international tourist flows.

traffic compared with all traffic increases to 49% (compared with 40% in winter). It can be seen in Table 8.2 that the international markets grow more than the domestic markets, increasing their market share on that particular sector.

As can also be seen in Figure 8.7, the tourist flow to the far North is much smaller than the flow to the Bay of Islands. In 2004, only 195,200 tourists travelled the sector to Cape Reinga either direction. The main markets on this sector are still day visitors from

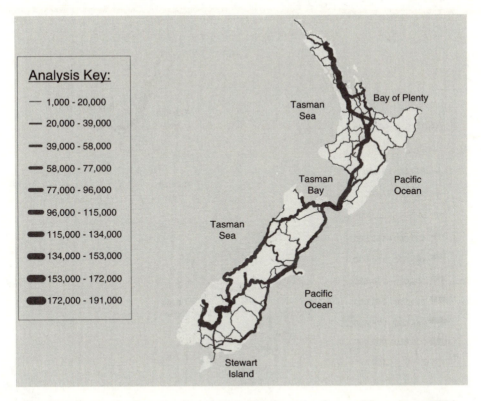

Figure 8.5: Tourist flows by "other European" tourists by road in summer 2004.

Northland and overnight tourists from Auckland; however, the second and third strongest markets are from UK/Nordic/Ireland and Australia, which indicates the relative popularity of the sector with international tourists.

Discussion

As Forer (2006) pointed out: "Flows are not just reflections of tourist geographies; they are prime agents of their creation". Tourist flows are a visualization of where tourists go and what kinds of needs they might have. Flows also allow for inferences on environmental impacts (e.g., air pollution resulting from transport) and economic potential, for example in relation to the development of more remote regions. Those positive and negative impacts as well as infrastructure needs depend not only on total tourist flows but also on flow composition. This paper indicates the usefulness of the TFM to analyse flows generated by different markets as well as market composition for a given flow.

The TFM allows for a wide range of applications with different potential users (Table 8.3). For the Ministry of Tourism, the TFM provides an advanced way to store their core data sets, to verify the data (e.g., by visually detecting outliers and anomalies) and to perform

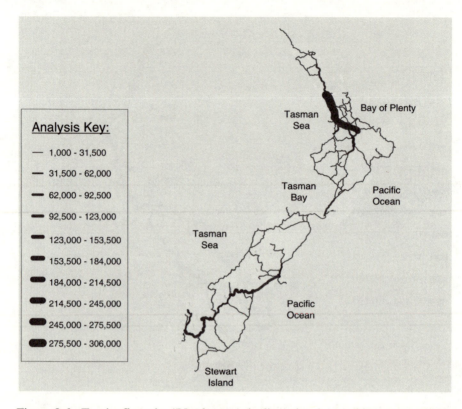

Figure 8.6: Tourist flows by "Northeast Asian" tourists by road in summer 2004.

various kinds of analysis, such as the preferred direction of travel on certain routes. Other users include local and regional planners, marketing agencies and national agencies that are involved in various aspects of tourism, for example, National Park Management or road infrastructure provision. For those users, the TFM can be used as a toolbox (e.g., how many visitors travel on a particular sector in a specified year or season), a decision-making support system (e.g., the development of a new regional airport) or a general application, for example for marketing purposes. The TFM can also be used for research purposes, for example in relation to the oil requirements of different markets and travel patterns in New Zealand.

The private sector may also find the information displayed through the TFM useful. For example, airlines can assess the viability of certain air routes compared with road transport. Similarly, tour operators can identify existing and future volumes on certain sectors and therefore avoid congestion at tourist hot spots. Finally, it is useful to know for an individual operator where tourists come from and what markets dominate on a particular route; this information assists business planning and marketing.

The configuration of the GIS interface allows users to add new layers of data. For example, the New Zealand Department of Conservation maintains a detailed database of their conservation areas and assets. This database can be linked to the TFM, which will allow recreation planners to use information of nearby tourist flows for planning and management

Figure 8.7: Total tourist flows (international and domestic) in 2004 in Northland.

Table 8.2: Tourist volumes by market on the Whangarei — Kaikohe sector in 2004 and 2011.

Market	Volume (both directions) 2004	Market share 2004 (%)	Volume (both directions) 2011	Market share 2011 (%)	Growth
Northland day visitor	1,899,800	42.5	2,056,200	40.5	108
Auckland overnight tourist	639,700	14.3	721,900	14.2	113
Northland overnight tourist	552,100	12.3	584,700	11.5	106
Auckland day visitor	331,400	7.4	383,400	7.6	116
Australian tourist	208,700	4.7	276,300	5.4	132
UK/Nordic/Ireland	179,500	4.0	266,000	5.2	148

purposes. The TFM may also provide information on visitor numbers in the context of carrying capacity assessments.

Several refinements are desirable for the TFM. First of all, the model would be enhanced by more detailed information on actual route choice. Currently, most likely routes between

Table 8.3: Properties of the TFM and potential users.

Property	Potential user
A process: A system for capturing, storing, checking, manipulating, analysing and displaying data which are spatially referenced to the earth	Ministry of Tourism to manage and improve their core tourism data sets
A toolbox: Containing tools for collecting, storing, retrieving, transforming and displaying spatial data, for example route choices	National and local planning agencies, for example, relating to infrastructure management, National Park Management, emergency planning, etc.
A decision support system: Integrating spatial data within a problem-solving environment	
An application: As part of marketing or planning information systems; development of tourism-resource inventories; visitor management, etc.	

Source: Bahaire and Elliott-White, 1999.

two nodes are assumed. In many cases, however, several routes are conceivable and the most 'logical' route (e.g., in terms of travel time) may not necessarily be the preferred one. More research on tourists' actual travel paths between stops would be beneficial to reduce uncertainty around some of the road tourist flows.

Over time, it is also desirable to collect more data on travel behaviour at a local level. The current core data sets (i.e., the IVS and the DTS) have been designed as national surveys and, as a result, some of the tourist flows rely on very small sample sizes. With the help of Regional Tourism Organisations and other providers of local tourism statistics, the validity of the TFM could be increased for smaller tourist flows. Feedback on the release of the TFM in late 2006 will be collected for that purpose and to aid future developments.

Acknowledgements

We wish to acknowledge the input of Tara Druce and Pip Forer and funding from the Cross-Departmental Research Fund.

References

Bahaire, T., & Elliott-White, M. (1999). The application of geographical information systems (GIS) in sustainable tourism planning: A review. *Journal of Sustainable Tourism, 7*(2), 159–174.

Barringer, J., Walcroft, A., Forer, P., & Hughey, K. (2002). Development of an environmental effects and tourist flow data management system. *Proceedings of the 5th New Zealand tourism and hospitality research conference* School of Tourism and Hospitality, Waiariki Institute of Technology, Rotorua (pp. 307–314).

Boyd, S. W., & Butler, R. W. (1996). Seeing the forest through the trees: Using GIS to identify potential ecotourism sites in Northern Ontario. In: L. C. Harrison & W. Husbands (Eds.), *Practising responsible tourism: International case studies in tourism planning, policy & development* (pp. 380–403). New York: Wiley.

Dahl, R. (2000). Tracing complex travel behaviour. In: J. Ruddy & S. Flanagan (Eds.), *Tourism destination marketing*. Dublin: Dublin Institute of Technology.

Eby, D.W., & Molnar, L.J. (2002). Importance of scenic byways in route choice: A survey of driving tourists in the United States. *Transportation Research Part A: Policy and Practice, 36*(2), 95–106.

Fennell, D. A. (1996). A tourist space-time budget in the Shetland Islands. *Annals of Tourism Research, 23*(4), 811–829.

Flognfeldt, T. (1999). Traveler geographic origin and market degmentation: The multi trips destination case. *Journal of Travel & Marketing, 8*(1), 111–124.

Forer, P. (2006). Tourist flows and dynamic geographies: Applying GI science to understanding tourism processes. In: D. Simmons & J. Fairweather (Eds.), *Pathways to sustainable tourism*. Christchurch (NZ): EOS Ecology.

Forer, P., & Pearce, D. (1984). Spatial patterns of package tourism in New Zealand. *New Zealand Geographer, 40*(1), 34–42.

Forer, P., & Simmons, D. (2002). Serial experiences: Monitoring, modelling and visualising the free independent traveller in New Zealand at multiple scales with GIS. In: A. Arnberger, C. Brandenberg, & A. Muhar (Eds.), *Monitoring and management of visitor flows in recreational and protected areas* (pp. 173–180). Vienna: Institute of Landscape Architecture and Landscape Management, Bodenkultur University.

Holt, A., Higham, E., & Kearsley, G. (1998). Predicting international tourist flows using a spatial reasoning system. *Pacific Tourism Review, 1*(4), 299–312.

Jansen-Verbeke, M. (1995). A regional analysis of tourist flows within Europe. *Tourism Management, 16*(1), 73–80.

Kim, S., & Fesenmaier, D. (1990). Evaluating spatial structure effects in recreation travel. *Leisure Sciences, 12*, 367–381.

Leiper, N. (1995). *Tourism management*. Melbourne: RMIT Press.

Lew, A., & McKercher, B. (2006). Modeling tourist movements. A local destination analysis. *Annals of Tourism Research, 33*(2), 403–423.

Lue, C. C., Crompton, J. L., & Fesenmaier, D. R. (1993). Conceptualisation of multi-destination pleasure trips. *Annals of Tourism Research, 20*, 289–301.

Ministry of Tourism (2005). Tourism Forecast 2005–2011. Summary Document. Wellington.

Oppermann, M. (1995). A model of travel itineraries. *Journal of Travel Research, 33*(4), 57–61.

Prideaux, B. (2004). Factors affecting bilateral tourism flows. *Annals of Tourism Research, 32*(3), 780–801.

Suna, Y., & Lyndon, L. (2004). Agent-based personalized tourist route advice system. XXth ISPRS Congress. Geo-Imagery Bridging Continents, 12–23 July 2004, Istanbul, Turkey. Available at (25/01/06) www.isprs.org/istanbul2004/comm2/papers/147.pdf

Tideswell, C., & Faulkner, B. (1999). Multidestination travel patterns of international visitors to Queensland. *Journal of Travel Research, 37*, 364–374.

Vuletich, S. (2006). Tourism flows model — Methodology. Covec Ltd. Available at (10/10/06 www.tourism.govt.nz).

Zhang, J., Wall, G., Du, J. K., Gan, M. Y., & Nie, X. (1999). The travel patterns and travel distance of tourists to National Parks in China. *Asia Pacific Journal of Tourism Research, 4*(2), 27–34.

Chapter 9

Duelling Definitions: Challenges and Implications of Conflicting International Concepts of Tourism

Stephen L. J. Smith

Introduction

Most tourism researchers arguably look at tourism as a demand-side phenomenon — a form of individual or social behaviour. The World Tourism Organization (UNWTO, 2001a) also defines tourism as something people do. However, tourism also represents an internationally traded service. Examining tourism as a tradable service is not only an unconventional perspective for many tourism researchers, it can also be a challenge for trade analysts because they tend to have little or no understanding of the nature of tourism. This paper examines some of the challenges in measuring tourism as a tradable service. It begins with a review of the nature of tourism and its significance as an area of economic activity. This is followed by a review of the World Trade Organization's (WTO's) conception of tourism in the context of the General Agreement on Trade in Services (GATS) and then that of the International Monetary Fund (IMF) in the Balance of Payments Manual (BPM5) methodology. The paper concludes with a discussion of some of the implications of these observations and offers several recommendations.

Being able to measure the magnitude of trade in tourism is important because it allows an assessment of the benefits and costs of tourism development. While tourism researchers usually are familiar with its economic benefits achievable with manageable environmental and social impacts, and relatively modest capital investments, it is often overlooked by policy analysts and economic planners who fail to integrate tourism with the nation and their development policies and strategies. Moreover, tourism development typically is affected by policies and priorities from government ministries such as foreign affairs, trade, immigration, labour, safety/security, environment, transportation, forestry, agriculture, and fisheries that are implemented without considering their impact on tourism. A pre-requisite for ensuring more recognition of tourism in national-policy formation is the development of credible statistics on

Developments in Tourism Research
Copyright © 2007 by Elsevier Ltd.
All rights of reproduction in any form reserved.
ISBN: 978-0-080-45328-6

tourism. These statistics need to be based on coherent concepts of tourism as a form of economic activity and be consistent with national and international economic statistical systems.

The Nature of Tourism as a Tradable Service

It is useful to begin with the UNWTO's definition of tourism. "Tourism comprises the activities of persons travelling to and staying in places outside their usual environment for not more than one consecutive year for leisure, business, and other purposes not related to the exercise of an activity remunerated from within the place visited" (UNWTO, 2001a, Section 2.1). As noted previously, this is a demand-side perspective. There are several important implications of this definitional approach.

First, tourism is not an industry in the conventional sense of the term. An industry is a group of businesses that produce essentially the same commodity using similar technologies. Tourism businesses in the aggregate cannot be an industry because they produce fundamentally different services using very different technologies. For example, the accommodation industry provides temporary accommodation services — a service that keeps people temporarily in one place. The passenger transportation industry provides services that move people around.

Next, tourism is not just pleasure travel. It encompasses travel for education, religion, meetings, conventions, conferences, trade shows, and general business travel. Travel for almost any purpose, other than migration or commuting to work is a form of tourism. The scope of tourism is thus wide and significant in most national economies. In fact, to the degree that international trade generally depends on personal meetings among individuals from different nations, international trade depends on international tourism.

International tourism is characterized by substantial cross-border movements. However, the movement is of consumers coming to suppliers, rather than commodities being shipped to consumer. Trade in tourism services can still be conceptualized as a flow of imports and exports, but the focus has to be on the flow of money, not on the service itself. The delivery of the service occurs in the country being visited. In other words, a tourism export occurs when a visitor comes to a destination country and buys services directly in the country being visited. A tourism import occurs when a person leaves the country of his residence and buys services directly in the country being visited.

The term "activities of persons" is also a distinctive aspect of the UNWTO definition. Most other international classification systems addressing forms of economic activity refer to "productive economic activity" by producers (United Nations, 1993), not to the activity of consumers. The phrase "usual environment" is also distinctive to tourism. Systems such as Systems of National Accounts (SNA93) and BPM5 (see below) refer to households and places of residence. "Usual environment" is a broader term than "place of residence". One's work place is normally part of one's usual environment, although the work place is normally not the same as one's residence. A household refers to a group of individuals sharing a residence and usually have a degree of economic interdependence. Tourism is done by individuals who may or may not belong to the same household. The focus is on the activities on individuals travelling, not on the activities done jointly by people with whom they share a residence.

While tourism is not an industry, *per se*, one can still speak of tourism industries. Tourism industries are those industries that produce services for which a substantial portion of demand comes from persons involved in tourism as visitors. In other words, these are industries that would either be significantly reduced in the absence of tourism or would virtually cease to exist. The services are sometimes called "tourism commodities" or "tourism characteristic products". While industries are labelled according to the core commodity they produce, it is important to note that tourism products may be produced by two or more different industries. For example, food and beverage services are provided not only by restaurants, but also by hotels, airlines, rail lines, and major attractions.

Tourism industries generally consist of enterprises in the following sectors:

- Transportation.
- Food services.
- Accommodation.
- Cultural services.
- Recreation and entertainment.
- Tour operators and travel agents.
- Convention services.
- Miscellaneous tourism services (e.g., tourism equipment rentals, visa issuing services).

The UNWTO (2001a) has published guidelines for the identification of tourism industries and commodities that have been endorsed by the UN Statistics Division. Unfortunately, this conceptualization of tourism industries is not always recognized by other key international bodies. It is to some of these divergences that we now turn our attention.

The World Trade Organization

The WTO is the global organization that deals with the rules of trade among nations. At its heart are agreements negotiated by the majority of the world's trading nations and ratified in their national governing assemblies. WTO's goal is to help producers, exporters, and importers conduct international trade. The original focus was only on the trade of goods, through the General Agreement on Tariffs and Trade. However, in 1995 the WTO launched a new platform to extend the multilateral trading system to services — the General Agreement on Trade in Services (GATS). A key component of GATS is the Services Sectoral Classification List (WTO, 1991), a list of services for which member nations have made commitments about the degree to which they will open up to international trade. Commitments are made with respect to four modes of trade:

Mode 1. *Cross-border supply*: services supplied from one country to another, such as the ability to make a hotel reservation using a computer reservation service in another country.

Mode 2. *Consumption abroad*: the ability of consumers, businesses, and governments to make use of a service while in another country, such as an international visitor staying at a hotel.

Mode 3. *Commercial presence*: a foreign company setting up a subsidiary or branch, such as a multinational hotel chain investing in a hotel in another country.

Mode 4. *Presence of natural persons*: individuals travelling from one country to another to temporarily supply services, such as a hotel chain transferring a general manager to a hotel in another country for a limited period.

Tourism is most closely associated with Mode 2, consumption abroad. However, there is some overlap with Mode 1, cross-border supply, as well. Modes 3 and 4 represent forms of service delivery that are not directly relevant to tourism as defined by the UNWTO. These represent aspects of the operation of tourism businesses but not the consumption of tourism commodities themselves.

One of the service sectors in the GATS schedule is "tourism services". These comprise four sub-sectors:

1. Hotels and restaurants (including catering).
2. Travel agency and tour operator services.
3. Tourist guide services.
4. "Other".

The first observation that can be made is that WTO's definition of "tourism services" does not reflect the array of services consumed by visitors. In particular, air transport services are excluded from GATS. GATS signatories generally prefer to limit negotiations on international air transportation to bilateral agreements outside of GATS. Other tourism activities such as convention services, travel distribution services, recreation and entertainment, cultural services, and sports are categorized in other sectors but are not recognized as tourism.

The UNWTO has expressed dissatisfaction with the WTO's characterization of tourism. A communication recommending the expansion of the WTO's definition of tourism to reflect the full array of tourism services has been proposed by a number of Latin American countries to the WTO's Council for Trade in Services (WTO, 2001). These comments notwithstanding, GATS considers tourism to be the three sectors identified above, and this shapes the extent and form of how the WTO reports and tracks trade in tourism.

Comments on the Tourism Sub-Sectors of the World Trade Organization

Hotels and Restaurants   The WTO's label for this sub-sector is misleading. The sub-sector is intended to encompass all accommodation and food services, not just hotels and restaurants. These include caterers, campgrounds, motels, and resorts. Moreover, the operational and structural distinctions between the accommodation and food services sub-sectors are substantial and conflating them is misleading.

Food service is ubiquitous in virtually every society and is an essential tourism service. Although dining out rarely is a primary motive of travel, tourism would not be possible without food services. However, many, often the majority, of food service establishments serve local customers, not visitors.

Hotels and similar establishments may be the type of business that many people think of when they think about "tourism businesses". They are, as food services, an essential tourism service although not usually a motive of travel. The bulk of accommodation revenues come from visitors. The geographic distribution of accommodation services is more uneven than that of food services. The UNWTO (2001b) estimates that Europe accounts for nearly 40% of total hotel rooms with the Americas supplying nearly 35%. East Asia-Pacific offers nearly 25% of the supply. Ownership of the accommodation sub-sector is more concentrated than the food-services sector, although the degree of concentration varies greatly by nation.

Travel Agency and Tour Operator Services   This sub-sector, though relatively small in terms of the numbers of firms, is vital for international tourism. The sub-sector, often referred to as "the travel trade", consists of tour operators, travel agencies, and tour wholesalers. The boundaries among these can be fuzzy. Tour wholesalers assemble packages of services, typically transportation to the destination, transportation at the destination, accommodation, and attractions/admissions. Food services may also be part of the package. The packages are sold to consumers indirectly, through travel agencies. Tour operators may act as tour wholesalers or they may sell directly to consumers, thus becoming retailers rather than wholesalers. Tour operators include outbound operators who sell tours to foreign destinations, and receptive operators who, as partners with outbound operators, receive visitors in the destination and provide services during the group is in the destination.

Travel agents are retailers of travel services. They are a common source of airline, hotel, cruise, and other reservations services for travellers as well as the retailer for tours developed by wholesalers. Unlike tour operators and wholesalers, they usually do not create tour packages or operate tours. However, some firms in some countries offer both tour operator and travel agency services.

Tours are often classified into three types: (1) escorted, (2) hosted, and (3) fully independent travel (FIT). An escorted tour is a group led by one or more guides who stay with the group from start to finish. Hosted tours refer to a package in which a guide meets an individual or group at one or more specified times during their trip to accompany them on a segment of the trip. For example, a hosted tour might involve having a representative from a tour company meet a person at an airport and accompany her or him to her or his hotel. A hosted tour could also involve the guide taking the person/group on a tour of the city they were visiting. An FIT tour is a package sold to an individual or travel party that includes transportation, accommodation, and some activities that travellers enjoy without a guide.

Tour guide services, whether escorted or hosted, are offered by tour operators and some travel agencies. These may be either tour directors who accompany a tour from start to finish as it travels through one or more foreign destinations, or they may be step-on guides who provide guide services to a group while it is visiting a specific locality. Other guide specializations included hunting, fishing, skiing, rafting, and backcountry services. However, these services are classified as a separate sub-sector by the WTO under GATS.

Tour Guide Services   Tour guides are a fundamental part of tour operations. They may be employees of tour operators or independents. Independent tour guides are an important sub-sector in some nations but insignificant in others, in terms of total employment. Tour guide services can be a critical element in overall visitor satisfaction, especially in the context of international tourism. They require a combination of human relations skills; organizational abilities; language skills; knowledge of local culture, ecology, heritage, or history; and the ability to communicate. The tour guide sub-sector, though, is best seen as a component of travel trade than a sub-sector in its own right, in contrast to the WTO classification.

Tourism is the sector in which the most commitments have been made by GATS members — 125 members to date — making it the most liberalized sector. A study by the Centre for Trade Policy and Law (2003) concluded that GATS is an important long-term force for continuing growth of international tourism. However, the Centre also concluded that the full impacts of GATS on tourism are impossible to model empirically with current data. There are so many forces affecting international tourism that it is not possible to determine quantitatively the impact of trade liberalization in isolation from other forces. Statistics on international tourism arrivals and receipts are generally adequate for time-series and international comparisons. However, data related to tourism employment, tourism's contributions to GDP, and other macro-economic indicators are much more difficult to obtain on a consistent and comparable basis.

A particular data need is information on international investment flows in tourism. There are three types of investment flows: loans, portfolio investments (in which an investor acquires a degree of equity in a business but only at a small level with no control over the enterprise being invested in), and foreign direct investment (FDI), in which the investor acquires a significant stake (nominally, at least 10%) and exercises some degree of control. FDI is of particular interest to most countries, both as a source of capital and, sometimes, as a cause for concern over foreign control of national assets.

Service sector FDI has grown rapidly in recent decades, becoming the dominant sector for foreign investment, even larger than manufacturing. The stock of FDI in services was estimated at 20% in the 1950s, rising to 30–40% in developed countries by the mid-1970s, to 60% or more in most developed countries by the end of the decade (World Bank, 2003). Total value grew from $802 billion in 1982 to $7.12 trillion in 2002 — a 900% increase. By way of contrast, fixed capital formation (the sum of investments in all countries) grew from $2.3 to 6.4 trillion over the same period, less than a 300% increase. Despite dramatic growth, the ratio of FDI to value-added in services is less than half the ratio of FDI to value-added in manufacturing. In other words, there is potential for substantial growth in a wide range of services, particularly financial, insurance, health, and legal services. Tourism, too, represents a significant service sector and one that has historically demonstrated significant growth in most nations. However, because of the fragmented nature of tourism, tracking foreign investment in tourism industries continues to be an area in need of attention by statisticians.

The International Monetary Fund

The IMF promotes international monetary co-operation, exchange stability, and orderly exchange arrangements; fosters economic growth and high levels of employment; and provides temporary financial assistance to countries. The IMF is responsible for developing and disseminating the methodology for calculating Balance of Payments (BOP) in national economies. Its Department of Statistics is in the process of updating the fifth edition of the BPM5.

As a result of IMF's key role in formulating guidelines for BOP calculations, their work on BPM5 has inspired Organisation of Economic Co-Operation and Development's (OECD's) and Eurostat's creation of an Extended Balance of Payments Services (EBOPS) accounting system for trade between residents and non-residents of an economy. The BPM5 methodology has also been consulted by the UN Statistical Division in the creation of its *Manual on Statistics of International Trade in Services* (MSITS). The treatment of tourism is not identical among these various systems, nor are these treatments always consistent with the UNWTO's conceptualization of tourism. The following paragraphs describe some of the key differences.

First, BOP does not include "tourism" within its concepts. Instead, it has a "travel item" covering expenditures for many tourism commodities recognized by the UNWTO. However, the travel item has a notable exception — passenger transportation. The omission of passenger transportation from the travel item substantially under-estimates the magnitude of tourism in an economy and as an internationally traded service. On the other hand, the travel item includes expenses for medical treatment in other countries and expenditures by long-term students, which inflate estimates of the economic importance of tourism.

Whereas the UNWTO's definition of tourism focuses on individuals, BPM5 focuses on households as a basic economic unit. This distinction represents a limitation on the ability of BPM5 to adequately track tourism activity because not all members of a household may participate in any given tourism trip. The sources of data available to BOP compilers normally provide data only for households, not individuals.

A principle within BPM5 is that all members of a given household have the same "economy of residence" (a concept different than "usual environment"). In BPM5, residence is not based on legal criteria but on the household's centre of economic interest — generally the economic territory of a nation. However, this also includes special enclaves such as embassies, military bases, scientific stations, and aid offices physically located in other economies with the formal permission of the host government.

The UNWTO's concept of "usual environment" is based on the assumption that it is always possible to unambiguously determine a person's usual environment. However, BPM5 recognizes that there can be some ambiguity in that some residents of households may have close ties with two or more economies of residence. BPM5 labels such individuals as "non-permanent residents". These are individuals temporarily away from their usual environment but who are in a grey area in terms of where their residence should be deemed to be. They are to be assigned to a single household but, in fact, are associated with two or more households in different economies. These include long-term students, medical patients receiving treatment in a foreign country, and live-in domestic workers who are temporarily residing in a foreign country for a period of over 1 year, or who routinely reside in two or more economies for less than a year in each.

"Household", as used by BPM5 refers to the composition of persons sharing a common dwelling. "Usual environment" normally includes the location of one's household, but may also include the place of employment. Thus, two persons in the same household may share the same dwelling but have different usual environments. As a result, a trip taken by one of these individuals might be considered to be tourism because it is outside his usual environment but would not be for the other individual, if the trip were not outside her usual environment.

Students temporarily living in a foreign country but who are still financially supported by their families share their household but will have usual environments that are very different than that of their stay-at-home household members. The same is true for persons in long-term health care facilities or correctional institutions. They can still be part of a household, yet be temporarily away from their family's residence.

There continues to be different thresholds for the time required to determine residence; BPM5 editors and other interested parties are exploring options. For example, the

International Labour Organization (2003) suggests a minimum of 6 months, as does the *Eurostat Manual on Income Measurement*. In contrast, as noted above, the UNWTO suggests 12 months.

BPM5, MSITS, and EBOPS classify travellers under two broad categories: business and personal. "Personal" is further divided into health-related, education-related, and "other". The UNWTO divides travellers into visitors (i.e., those individuals deemed to be engaged in tourism) and all others. The distinction between business and personal travel is seen as purpose of travel rather than as categories of travellers. Table 9.1 summarizes the similarities and differences of the various classifications of travellers under these systems.

As explained in the notes to Table 9.1, one of the problems associated with these different approaches is that the categories used by the different frameworks are not consistent. BPM5 uses some categories from the UN's Central Product Classification system (CPC) — a standardized list of products used for statistical classification purposes — whereas MSITS uses a classification system associated with EBOPS. UNWTO's categories are fully consistent with CPC.

Some other problems include the following. MSITS includes "other" (1.1.2) as a subcategory of "business" (1.1). However, this captures both business travellers who are visiting to earn money from within the place visited (thus who are *not* visitors) and those who are not earning money from the place visited (who *are* visitors). Visitors are generally the largest source of revenues from international travel and thus combining a set of visitors with non-visitors in the MSITS framework produces misleading results.

There also is a problem with the BPM5 classification of travellers into personal and business from a practical perspective. BOP compilers typically work with border-crossing counts of inbound non-resident travellers and outbound resident travellers as well as measures of currency flows captured through central bank records. These sources, typically, do not provide any information about whether the person is travelling for business or pleasure.

BPM5 (International Monetary Fund, 1993, Section 250) states, "all goods and services acquired by travellers from the economies in which they are travelling and for their own use are recorded under 'travel'". The UNWTO's list of tourism characteristic products is based on the CPC; this list is more inclusive and representative of tourism activities than the breakdown currently used by MSITS. It is significant to note that this characterization of travel expenditures is not based on the distinction between business and personal travel specified by BPM5 or MSTIS.

BPM5 includes total expenditures for the services of travel agents and tour operators under travel expenditures. The UNWTO Tourism Satellite Account (TSA) specifies that the value of travel agency and tour operators' services, including the value of passenger transport services sold by the travel trade should be reported as a margin, not a gross amount (UNWTO, 2001, Sections 4.13–4.19).

Other Issues

One empirical issue not yet adequately handled in either the BPM5 or by UNWTO concerns the treatment of personal expenditures by diplomats and the military while stationed in foreign countries. BPM5 (International Monetary Fund, 2004) notes that such expenditures

Table 9.1: Classifications of travellers in four statistical frameworks.

BPM5	MSITS	Proposed modifications to BPM5	UNWTO (TSA)

1. Travel[a]
1.1 Business
1.2 Personal[b]
1.2.1 Health
1.2.2 Education
1.2.3 Other
	1. Travel[c]
	1.1 Business
	  1.1.1 Seasonal and border workers
	  1.1.2 Other workers
	1.2 Personal
	  1.2.1 Health
	  1.2.2 Education
	  1.2.3 Other
		1. Travel
		1.1 Business
		  1.1.1 Seasonal and border workers
		  1.1.2 Other workers
		1.2 Personal
		  1.2.1 Health
		  1.2.2 Education
		  1.2.3 Other
		
		2. Transport
		2.1 Passenger
		2.2 Freight
		2.3 Other
			1. Visitors[d]
			1.1 Transportation
			1.2 Accommodation
			1.3 Food services
			1.4 Transportation
			  1.4.1 International transportation
			  1.4.2 In-country transportation
			1.5 Other services
			1.6 Goods
			2. Other travellers
			2.1 Seasonal and border workers
			2.2 Other

	Expenditure data by business and personal travellers is collected on: 1. Goods 2. Accommodation and food services (combined total) 3. All other travel expenditures	Expenditure data by business and personal travellers is collected on: 1. Goods 2. Transportation 3. Accommodation 4. Food services 5. All other travel expenditures	Expenditure data by business versus personal travellers could be reported if border surveys are designed to capture purpose of trip. However, purpose of travel is not reflected in CPC codes and is irrelevant to TSA framework.

Modified from WTO's comments on IMF's draft annotated outline of the BPM5 revision, 2003.

[a] Includes CPC classes 7471 (travel agencies and tour operators) and 7472 (tourist guide services).

[b] Includes CPC divisions 92 (education services) and 93 (health and social services).

[c] Travel expenditures are classified as EBOPS component 236; this classification does not have a direct correspondence with the CPC, unlike BPM5, with the exception of expenditures on accommodation and food that correspond to CPC division 63.

[d] Categories of commodities for which tourism expenditure data are collected match CPC codes.

are to be categorized within "government services, not included elsewhere". From the perspective of UNWTO, such people are not within the scope of "international visitors". Military are excluded, by definition, from the concept of visitors. Diplomatic staffs, at an embassy or consulate, are deemed to have travelled between two discontinuous parts of their economy of residence. They enter the host country through special formalities and are not captured within normal visitor statistics. However, when they travel within their host country on personal matters, their consumption could be considered to be a form of internal travel, even if they are not considered to be international visitors. Further discussion both within the context of TSAs and BPM5 is needed.

BPM5 (International Monetary Fund, 1993, Section 250) suggests that "[a]ll goods and services acquired by travellers ... from the economies in which they are travelling and for their own use are recorded under travel. These goods and services may be paid for by the traveller, paid for on his or her behalf, or provided free to him or her without a *quid pro quo*" — for example, accommodation provided free by friends. It is normally impossible to estimate the value of such services. However, BPM5 encourages BOP compilers to estimate the value of such goods and services and to include this within the "travel item". The UNWTO suggests, in its recommended methodological framework for TSAs, ignoring services provided on a non-*quid pro quo* basis because they do not involve any cash flows. However, the guidelines suggest that additional spending by households to host visitors, such as additional groceries or additional automobile expenses, should be recorded as a transfer and thus as visitor consumption (UNWTO, 2004, Section 270).

BPM5 treats business travel expenditures as an intermediate input for the production of a product, whereas personal travel expenditures are considered to be final demand. TSA treats business travel and personal travel the same.

Finally, BPM and MSITS are silent on the treatment of social transfers in-kind such as a social security system that covers medical expenses for a traveller abroad, or subsidized (or free) education for short-term foreign students. These transfers, from the perspective of a TSA, represent expenses made on behalf of a visitor and thus represent a form of tourism consumption and should be captured in demand data.

Conclusion

The key implication of differing tourism definitions is that estimates of the value of international trade in tourism services made by the UNWTO, the WTO, or the BPM5 cannot be legitimately compared. The magnitude of international tourism tends to be either underestimated or seen as not credible by analysts not familiar with the issues described above because of conflicting definitions.

Fortunately, significant progress has been made in international tourism statistics by the UNWTO since the early 1990s. International consensus has been achieved among tourism statisticians on the definition of tourism and related concepts. TSAs are moving from concept to reality in a growing number of nations, and work continues, in many countries, on improving their tourism statistical infrastructure. TSAs offer not only a mechanism for building and reporting data on tourism that is comparable among nations, they provide an internally coherent view of tourism that is consistent with the principles of SNA93 (with the exception of the treatment of business travel). And through their significant data requirements, TSAs can stimulate improvements in a nation's tourism statistical infrastructure. The importance of TSAs as a new methodology for understanding tourism as an economic activity leads to two suggestions.

Recommendation 1

While TSAs have become recognized as the international standard by many national statistical offices and tourism organizations, the level of familiarity with even the basic conceptual foundation of TSAs among academic tourism researchers is inadequate. Tourism researchers, especially those working on aspects of international tourism, need to educate themselves about the core concepts and perspectives of the TSA.

While not every researcher is interested in measuring the magnitude of tourism as an economic activity, the definition of tourism on which the TSA is based as well as associated concepts should be familiar to all international tourism researchers. This definition provides a coherent approach to the conceptualization of tourism that can support objective research on tourism independent of political or personal value-laden definitions, and that has relevant to research perspectives other than the purely economic. Personal definitions may have some utility in certain forms of scholarship, but any tourism researcher should be familiar with the UNWTO's definition and — should he or she chose to use an idiosyncratic definition — be able to explain the need for such definitional divergence.

Recommendation 2

Material on the UNWTO's definition of tourism and TSA concepts (tourism commodities, tourism industries, forms of tourism, etc) should be incorporated into undergraduate and graduate tourism curricula. The level of detail and treatment of these concepts will need to be adapted to the level of student, of course. Introductory students should be exposed to the concept of tourism as a demand-side phenomenon as well as to the importance of understanding tourism as an economic activity. The key features of the UNWTO definition as well as alternative definitions proposed by various tourism educators should be presented and the nature of the divergences discussed. Intermediate-level students can be introduced to more details of tourism commodities and industries, and the structure of the CPC and SNA93 as classification systems that shape how statisticians define and measure economic activity. Fuller examination of TSA methods and some of the issues discussed in this paper should be presented to advanced students wishing to explore such topics in detail.

As the earlier portion of this paper has documented, the definition of tourism and some associated measurement concepts used by certain international organizations, particularly the WTO (GATS) and the IMF (BPM5) diverge from those of the UNWTO. In general, the divergences concern what items are to be considered to be tourism and thus included in an assessment of the economic magnitude of tourism as an area of economic activity. GATS and BPM5 have conceptualizations of tourism that, on the whole, tend to diminish the magnitude of tourism. More fundamentally, the discrepant views of tourism lead to both an under-appreciation of the importance of tourism as well as a misunderstanding of the very nature of tourism as an internationally traded service. This leads to the third recommendation.

Recommendation 3

The Statistics and Economic Measures Division of the UNWTO should continue their current discussions on resolving, to the degree possible, differences in the definitions and concepts related to tourism in the context of BPM, EBOPS, and MSITS. Wider consultations should also be held on examining potential areas for refinement of the TSA methodology and, where appropriate, reaffirming its conceptual foundations. Some of these issues are the stuff of technical detail and consequently not immediately relevant to researchers not working in the worlds of TSA and/or BOP. However, the conclusions that emerge from these possibly arcane differences can significantly distort conclusions about the magnitude of tourism activity. More generally, the UNWTO should more actively assert the essential elements of the recommended methodological framework in terms of making clear, especially to national tourism offices and elected officials, what constitutes a true TSA and what does not (see Smith and Wilton (1997) for an example of this issue).

Differences between the conceptualizations of tourism by the UNWTO and the WTO are readily grasped even by non-experts. The WTO's definition of tourism is much narrower than that of the UNWTO and the exclusion of international air passenger transportation is, in particular, a significant difference. Unfortunately, there is little political will among international trade experts to broaden the WTO's concept of tourism. Political forces keeping passenger air transport out of WTO's definition of tourism are too strong for tourism leaders to overcome. Instead, a strategy other than futilely lobbying for changes in WTO's definition is needed. This observation is the basis for the fourth recommendation.

Recommendation 4

Tourism leaders, policy-makers, and researchers need to learn the language of international trade. The situation is roughly analogous to the development of TSAs in which tourism statisticians and economists had to learn the language of the SNA93. By learning that language, it has been possible to construct a tool — TSAs — that SNA analysts and policy-makers who use SNA data find credible. Without adapting to the conventions and assumptions of SNA93, tourism statistics would still be dismissed by analysts in other industries, policy leaders, and elected officials. Instead, TSAs have given the sector credibility sought for decades. Such credibility is only one leg of a ladder of progress in advancing understanding tourism as a form of international trade. Tourism analysts must accept, at least for the foreseeable future, the definitions, conventions, and assumptions of GATS and learn to work with it from the inside, rather than simply and ineffectively criticizing this large and very complex policy edifice that shapes international trade in services. Only by doing so will tourism be given a seat at trade-negotiation tables where it can represent its legitimate interests and be accorded the respect that conventional industries, long ago learned how to work with GATS, enjoy.

Figure 9.1 describes a highly simplified ladder of progress for tourism as an international service. One foot of the ladder is based on the development of credible tourism statistics by tourism statisticians learning the language and conventions of SNA93. This has been accomplished in principle through TSAs. The next task is to learn the languages and conventions of trade negotiations, particularly through GATS. The task should not be a major one. GATS already recognizes tourism as a sector, albeit in a way in which it currently fails to capture the

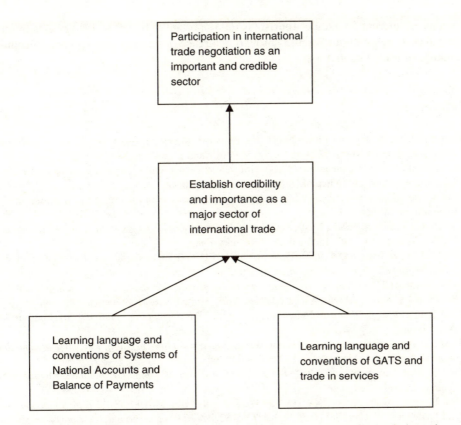

Figure 9.1: The ladder of progress for tourism as an internationally traded service.

richness and size of tourism as an area of economic activity. Moreover, as noted above, tourism has the reputation for already being the most liberalized service sector within GATS.

The challenge for tourism analysts and policy-makers is to resist the temptation to continually criticize GATS and, instead, to learn how to work within it. Once these two foundations are in place, tourism leaders will be in a position to earn recognition as a major player in international trade. Many nations already have the statistical infrastructure or are developing the infrastructure to provide essential tourism statistics. Credible statistics can provide tourism policy leaders and trade negotiators with the leverage needed to earn greater attention and respect from other negotiators once tourism negotiators understand how to work within the realm of international trade policy. This, then, will open the door to having tourism represented more effectively in trade negotiations.

Tourism researchers have a significant role to play in helping to refine and apply methods and concepts associated with measuring tourism as an internationally traded commodity. Their contributions will help to deepen our understanding of tourism as a major component of international trade as well as of the complexities of measuring such a complex and multi-faceted phenomenon. In addition to contributing to the advancement of tourism research, there is also the need for tourism researchers to better learn the conventions, assumptions, and language of international trade. Tourism is too important to be left on the margins of international trade negotiations whether through ignorance of tourism researchers or misunderstandings of trade negotiators.

References

Centre for Trade Policy and Law. (2003). *The costs and benefits of tourism services liberalization.* Ottawa: Carlton University, Centre for Trade Policy and Law.

International Labour Organization. (2003). Household income and expenditure statistics. Report II. 17th international conference of labour statisticians, Geneva.

International Monetary Fund. (1993). *Balance of payments manual* (5th ed.). Washington, DC: International Monetary Fund

International Monetary Fund. (2004). *Revision of the balance of payments manual* (5th ed.). Annotated Outline. Washington, DC: International Monetary Fund.

Smith, S. L. J., & Wilton, D. (1997). TSAs and the WTTC/WEFA methodology: Different satellites or different planets? *Tourism Economics, 3*, 249–263.

United Nations (UN). (1993). *International standard industrial classification of all economic activities,* Revision 1.1, Series: M, No. 4/Rev 1.1. New York: United Nations Statistical Division.

World Bank. (2003). *Global economic prospects and the developing countries.* Washington, DC: World Bank.

World Tourism Organization (UNWTO). (2001a). *Tourism satellite account: Recommended methodological framework.* Madrid: World Tourism Organization.

World Tourism Organization (UNWTO). (2001b). *World overview and tourism topics.* Madrid: World Tourism Organization.

World Tourism Organization (UNWTO). (2004). *Tourism trends.* Madrid: World Tourism Organization.

World Trade Organization (WTO). (1991). *MTN.GNS/W/120 Uruguay round — Group of negotiations on services — Services sectoral classification list — Note by the Secretariat.* Geneva: World Trade Organization.

World Trade Organization (WTO). (2001). Council for Trade in Services: *Communication by Bolivia, Dominican Republic, Ecuador, El Salvador, Honduras, Nicaragua, Panama, Peru, and Venezuela: Draft annex on tourism S/CSS/W/107.* Geneva: World Trade Organization.

SECTION 3:

RESEARCHING TOURISM EXPERIENCES AND CHALLENGES

Introduction

Reference has already been made to the difficulties of identifying a unifying theme for Tribe's *non-business* field of tourism. This is certainly true of the papers that were presented at the conference from which this collection is drawn. The tracks of the conference which included, for example, *ethics and tourism; heritage and cultural tourism; media, popular culture and tourism; nature-based tourism; safety security and new world order; sustainable tourism* give some flavour of the range of research areas that are being pursued. Two broad themes have been used to present the chapters in this section. The first is research that seeks, better to understand the experience of being a tourist. By shifting the focus from the destination and the industry where much of the earlier work was concentrated, to the people who are engaged as tourists, this represents the shift in research from production to consumption. Three of the chapters provide examples of this work. The second broad theme has as its starting point the attempts to understand the responses to the challenges raised by tourism. The three chapters provide just a small sample of the wide range of work in this area, providing examples of the attempts to understand the work of tourism policy makers, the interactions within tourism destinations and the position of tourism in an ideological setting. But perhaps what is more unifying for this collection of work is less the subject matters than the methodological challenges that their exploration raises. Here some of real changes in tourism research, noted in the introduction to this collection, come to the fore. Positivism is joined by a range of new research approaches to solve tourism puzzles. Examples of these are demonstrated in these chapters.

In the first chapter in this section, Cathy Guthrie and Alistair Anderson (*Tourists on Tourists: The Impact of Other People on Destination Experience*) comment on an important gap in the knowledge about the experience of the tourists. As they point out, there have been plenty of studies of tourist–host interactions but virtually none on the relations between tourists, themselves whether within their own group or between groups. In many ways this is very surprising since, as they say, "these interactions form a part of the overall destination experience, and are likely to influence both the tourist's perceptions of the destination and the destination image transmitted to others". Their study, carried out in Edinburgh and Greenwich, begins to uncover some of the dimensions of this relationship but clearly this is a strand of work that is very much at its beginning.

The tourist is also at the centre of the contribution by Bruce Hayllar and Tony Griffin (*A Tale of Two Precincts*), who move away from predominantly descriptive accounts of the tourist destination to arrive at new insights by using a phenomenological approach to reach the perspective of the tourists themselves. In other words they provide an understanding of the destination experience from the perspective of the tourist. As they argue "understanding how the tourist experiences a precinct, and in particular the attributes, both tangible and intangible, which engender a certain quality to that experience, can produce implications for the effective planning, development, management and marketing of the precinct". They offer a new understanding of the destination and the ways in which the physical and social attributes shape the experience of the visitor. But just as important for this collection they show effective use of a phenomenological approach to explore this complex area.

Tourist consumption and its relationship with the destination also lie at the heart of the chapter by Stephenson (*The Socio-Political Implications of Rural Racism and Tourism Experiences*). In this case he explores the sensitive and under-researched area of social exclusion. *Tourism for All* is one of the bold slogans of the UK government as part of its social-inclusion strategy. But the barriers to equal access and enjoyment are often subtle and deep seated. Marcus Stephenson explores the situation in rural England. He draws our attention to how "romantic depictions of UK rural destinations have been formalised through the strategic process of *branding*, where marketers have devised and promoted nostalgic connections between particular places and famous English personalities." He offers the examples of "the tourism logos of *Shakespeare Country* (South Warwickshire), *Wordsworth's Country* (Cumbria), *Bronte Country* (West Yorkshire) and *Hardy's Wessex* (Dorset)." Stephenson emphasizes the notion of the rural idyll and demonstrates the crucial part played in its construction by classic literary works. He argues that popular representations of the countryside as an expression of Englishness and/or Britishness exclude black minorities from appreciating rural environments. It is not only marketing and literature at work here, but the practices of rural communities that create "racialised boundaries of countryside communities". Here Stephenson points to the ways in which rural communities establish a cultural sense of *insidership*, which necessarily creates a category of otherness and thereby excludes the interests of outsiders. He cites studies that have identified insidership factors such as "strong kinship ties, interactive social networks and *insider knowledge* of rural folklore and tradition". It is these kinds of ties, networks and tacit knowledge that according to Stephenson inhibit minorities from actively participating in rural tourism. Making a wider point from this, he argues, "as members of the UK, the black community do not necessarily share a national way of life, exemplified by their marginalisation from popular social activities such as countryside travel."

Many of the challenges presented by tourism, including the challenge of exclusion are placed at the doors of the policy makers, yet according to Nancy Stevenson we have scant knowledge about how policy makers reach their decisions and more importantly what they think about tourism and why. In her research presented here in the chapter *Researching the Experiences and Perspectives of Tourism Policy Makers*, she suggests that much of the previous work about tourism policy has underplayed the fact that policy making is essentially a social process "involving interactions and negotiation between individuals and groups of people". Her research addresses this by combining complexity theory and grounded theory to use the perspectives of the people involved in the process to gain better insights into process. In doing so it gains a broader perspective ... "than is provided by theory that focuses on physical manifestations such as written policies and technical processes [alone]". Here the sheer complexity and multi-faceted nature of the issues involved demand new research approaches and the chapter amply demonstrates how they can be effectively used in this area of tourism.

Included among the challenges faced by policy makers is how to ensure effective interaction between the many organisations involved in the tourism destination. Noel Scott and Chris Cooper (*Network Analysis as a Research Tool for Understanding Tourism Destinations*), by using network analysis, provide a new way of viewing these relationships and in the process also throw new light on the boundaries of destinations. They point to the fact that network analysis has a long pedigree in the social sciences but has seldom been used as an analytical framework for destinations. As they say "the organisation of tourism production has been considered previously from a systems perspective ... as derived from life cycle processes ... and through the use of concepts of collaboration and cooperation of individual stakeholders. ... The social network approach emphasizes the systemic and interaction effects between tourism organizations". By using relational rather than attribute data, this provides insights into the actual functioning of destinations with clear implications for their management and marketing. Clearly the availability of analytical and visualization software provides an important ingredient both in relation to the ability to carry out this work as well as in its effective presentation.

As indicated, these chapters represent just a small selection of the work that is being carried out in Tribe's *non-business* field of tourism. But between them they provide good indications of the ways in which this field of tourism knowledge is being populated. The work is covering new territory and introducing new perspectives, here for example, by exploring the perspectives of the tourist and examining the challenges raised by tourism, and in doing so, is drawing on a much broader range of research traditions and methodological approaches. To this extent it represents a broadening of the tourism studies. The final chapter in this section further extends the coverage by reaching from the business to the non-business field, and in a truly critical way, challenging how we perceive tourism. Here Michael Hall (*Tourism and Regional Competitiveness*) explores the whole ideological basis within which it is taken for granted that tourism development occurs. Hall recounts how the search for competitiveness is one of the major drivers in contemporary tourism and that this manifests itself at the level of destinations, businesses and even competitive institutions. Hall traces the desire for this kind of competitiveness to the power of the neoliberal project. He notes that neoliberalism promotes market-led economic and social restructuring and that an important outcome of this is an orientation of economic and social policy to the private sector's needs. Hall thereby implicates regional competitiveness as a part of a hegemonic discourse. Finally he explains why the regional competitive discourse is so dominant and notes that one reason is the unexamined situatedness of academic knowledge production. This analysis of course takes us back to the essential overlap between Tribe's two fields. It is impossible fully to understand tourism from the perspective of only one field. Hall's work brings this into the foreground.

Chapter 10

Tourists on Tourists: The Impact of Other People on Destination Experience

Cathy Guthrie and Alistair Anderson

Introduction

"No man is an island, entire of itself; every man is a piece of the continent, a part of the main." (Donne, 1624). Donne's meditation was occasioned by hearing a stranger's death knell, but it is also true that no tourist is entirely separate from either their travelling companions, or the other people they encounter in a destination. Tourists are often in couples, family groups or groups of friends, whether travelling independently or as part of an organised; even solo travellers cannot completely ignore those around them: other tourists, hosts or destination residents. Thus these interactions, within their travel party or with strangers, are part of tourists' destination experience, and may colour not only their own perceptions of the destination, but also the image they reflect to others through their holiday stories. It is therefore important that destination managers and marketers understand the impact of other people on individual destination experience in order to improve visitor management and targeted marketing messages.

Despite this, Dann and Phillips noted very little contemporary research which investigated the impact on tourists of their interactions with the destination, whether with tourism industry personnel, the resident or host community or other tourists (2001, pp. 256–257). They acknowledged investigations of the impact of tourists on the host community, but suggested that there was little which had "systematically examined the sociocultural consequences of tourists mixing with each other" (2001, p. 257). This chapter considers the literature relating to tourist interactions, suggesting that material published since 2001 continues to focus on tourist–host and tourist–resident interactions. It addresses the question of tourist–tourist interactions by reporting findings from an investigation of the impacts of tourist interactions on destination image and draws implications from these for both visitor management and destination marketing.

Tourist Interactions

Tourists interact with each other and with the host community, either directly in face-to-face encounters or indirectly by taking part in the same activity or being in the same space. These interactions form part of the overall destination experience, and are likely to influence both the tourist's perceptions of the destination and the destination image transmitted to others. However, existing research has paid little attention to these aspects of tourist interaction, focussing instead on tourist–host interactions; tourist–tourist interactions have been considered only incidentally, as secondary elements in research into leisure or heritage experience.

Tourist Host Interactions

Much existing literature on tourist–host interactions concentrates on the cultural perceptions or on the impacts of tourists on residents (Table 10.1).

McIntosh (2004, p. 2) argued that previous studies into tourist perspectives on indigenous tourism products and services had been carried out in support of a variety of different agendas, thereby giving a piecemeal understanding of demand. Moreover, in concentrating on tourists' views at or in relation to specific sites or attractions, they gave no indication of the type of experience the tourist actually sought rather than consumed because it was available. Although many tourists' expectations and prior knowledge are formed by material in guidebooks or tourist brochures, and may thus be somewhat stereotypical, McIntosh suggested that tourists' motivations and expectations play a role in their appreciation and experience of the host culture, and indeed might also determine whether they seek a spectacle, a learning experience or a deeper engagement (2004, p. 3). Similarly, it can be argued that motivation and expectations may also be important elements in tourists' interactions with each other. If a tourist wants a deep, spiritual experience in, say, a wilderness location, what might be the impact of either a group member or other, non-associated tourist talking incessantly? For some visitors, therefore, this interaction with others may play a key role in their experience.

Travel supposedly broadens the mind, leading to greater insights into other societies and cultures. These can be obtained not only from tourists' interactions with the host community,

Table 10.1: Tourist–host interactions.

Cultural perceptions	
Tourist perceptions of host culture	McIntosh (2004)
Cross cultural differences	Pizam and Sussmann (1995); Pizam and Jeong (1996); Reisinger and Turner (1997, 1998); Pizam et al. (2000)
Tourist impact on host community	
Social distance	Thyne and Zins (2003)
Residents' attitudes toward tourism	Williams and Lawson (2001)

but also through encountering tourists from other cultures whilst on vacation. However, referring to previous research suggesting that tourist experience of indigenous culture contributes to a greater understanding of that culture, and therefore changes perceptions, McIntosh cautions against viewing tourists as "amateur anthropologists" (2004, p. 13). Her findings indicate that despite expressed desire for a sincere encounter with the culture, the level of actual learning was shallow, indicating rather that tourists seek interactions with host cultures as a form of exotic encounter. Pizam and colleagues, studying tour guides' perceptions of tour groups from different countries, noted this tendency toward stereotypical assumptions about other, different cultures (Pizam & Sussmann, 1995; Pizam & Jeong, 1996). Accepting Dann's (1993) arguments relating to the problems inherent in using nationality as a marketing segmentation variable, Pizam and colleagues nevertheless found that nationality should be considered alongside the other variables (personality, lifestyle, social class, culture and tourist role), as their research indicated that tour guides perceived differences between different nationalities of groups in relation to social interaction (Pizam & Sussmann, 1995, p. 285; Pizam & Jeong, 1996, p. 915). Furthermore, Pizam and Sussman (1995, p. 916) noted that others in the destination, such as residents and other tourism employees also tended to use nationality to distinguish between tourists.

Reisinger and Turner (1997, 1998) compared the cultural differences between Indonesia and Australia, and between Mandarin-speaking tourists and their Australian hosts. They suggested that greater awareness of cultural differences and their impacts could be used to improve both service delivery and training provision, as well as to target promotional messages more effectively at these markets. They argue that the host country and its tourism providers should understand the culture of the tourists they receive, in order to minimise unintentional misunderstandings and enhance service provision by better anticipating and meeting overseas tourists' requirements. If host communities and tourism providers use such stereotypical perceptions of different nationalities to distinguish between tourists, might tourists also use them to distinguish other tourists? For example, only a few moments' reflection brings to mind some of the more entrenched stereotypical images of other nationalities within the UK: early morning German tourists using towels to claim sun loungers; Japanese tourists with their cameras; Americans on whirlwind tours "This is Tuesday, it must be Paris". Do these or other perceptions of tourists encountered during a holiday affect the overall impression carried away and transmitted to others? What impact does the presence of large numbers of other tourists have on the overall image of a destination or an attraction, and does this relate to individual expectations?

Other researchers have considered tourist–host interactions in terms of residents' perceptions of tourists and tourism. Thyne and Zins (2003) measured the social distance, or degree of sympathy and understanding, between tourists and the host community, suggesting that host community attitudes to tourists and tourist development may vary with the tourists' nationality. The more socially distant the host community from the tourists they receive, the more negative their attitude to the impacts of tourism. Williams and Lawson (2001) investigated New Zealand residents' perceptions of the impact of tourism on their community in order to identify opinion groups and describe their opinions on tourists and tourism. They found that attitudes to community-related issues were more important than opinions of tourists as such — in areas with many tourists, one resident might welcome them, perceiving little or no disruption to local services, whereas another might consider them an unwelcome intrusion, causing them to feel like strangers in their own home or creating too much noise, litter and pollution (2001, pp. 283–284). There may be a consequential impact on tourists, making them feel unwelcome, or that their money is welcome but not their presence. However, it is also possible that the same concerns in relation to crowds, noise, spoiling of the experience may be felt by one tourist in the presence of others, depending upon motivations and expectations, and may in turn affect their image of the destination.

Tourist/Tourist Interactions

Since Dann and Philips (2001) identified tourist interactions as an area requiring investigation, there have been a few studies which have considered tourist–tourist interactions. Mykletun, Crotts, and Mykletun (2001) included travel party composition among the independent variables in a study to identify the most valuable visitor segments to the Baltics. They looked specifically at the impact of visitor role in predicting whether visitors would value Bornholm as a destination and hold a positive attitude toward it. However, visitor role was defined as travel party type and trip purpose, with no discussion or investigation of the impact of that role on others in the party, and purpose of trip appeared to be the major indicator, in that one of the conclusions was that respondents travelling to Bornholm for holidays and visiting friends and relatives placed the highest value on the destination. Moreover, they did not indicate whether the presence of other tourists outside the travel party was a factor in visitors' evaluation. Fairweather and Swaffield (2001) investigated tourists' appreciation of different landscape experiences available in Kaikoura, New Zealand. Respondents were categorised into one of five different experience-seekers, two of which appeared to comment on the impact of other tourists on their experience. Several respondents identified as maritime recreational tourists appeared to be seeking escape from the pressures of everyday life; this group overall expressed dislike of commercial tourism activities which encouraged or indicated growing numbers of tourists. The second group, family coastal holiday tourists, chose images showing other recreational tourists, highlighting activities such as sharing experience of mammals and enjoying the facilities of the town, which suggests a more positive approach to the presence of other tourists and a preference for activities, which could be enjoyed by the whole family.

Research into the impact of intergroup interactions has been largely in the area of vacation choice behaviour. Gilbert and Hudson (2000), investigating constraints on participation in skiing holidays, found that interpersonal factors were significant not only in whether or not a skiing holiday was chosen, but also in the amount of skiing undertaken. These interpersonal factors included items such as other potential party members lacked the money or time to go, too many family commitments, fear of embarrassing oneself in front of friends or family members and partner not interested in skiing. Acknowledging that their research was limited to constraints on skiing participation, they suggested that similar research could be conducted into participation in other tourist activities (2000, p. 922). The findings reported here suggest that some of these interpersonal constraints or considerations can apply during the course of a holiday as well as in the decision-making process beforehand, depending upon the motivations of the individual tourist in relation to others in their party. Masberg and Silverman (1996) in their study of heritage site experience found that travel companions figured largely in the student visitors' recollections of experience, and touched briefly on the importance of significant companions in relation to the heritage visit experience, without exploring this aspect in any depth.

Existing research touching on tourist interactions, therefore, has been in relation to tourist–host interactions and their impact on host community attitudes to tourists and tourism. Findings relating to tourist–tourist interactions have been incidental to the main focus of studies of leisure participation and heritage experience. There has apparently been no work investigating either the impact of tourist–tourist interactions on destination experience or how this affects the destination image portrayed in tourists' holiday stories. Recommendations from family and friends are frequently cited as an important source of reference material in choosing a holiday (Gunn, 1972; Gartner, 1993; Baloglu & McCleary, 1999; Bigné, Sanchez, & Sanchez, 2001; Bansal & Eiselt, 2004; Guthrie, Thyne, & Anderson, 2004). Destination managers and marketers, therefore, need to understand how such tourist–tourist interactions may shape this word of mouth publicity material in order to ensure their destination is offering the most appropriate experiences and possibilities to their target market.

The Study

The overall aim of the current study was to investigate the impact of tourist interactions on destination image. The findings reported here specifically address tourist–tourist interactions, the way these are reported in tourists' stories and the implications of this for the destination image transmitted to others. The study was undertaken using a phenomenological approach to enable the richness of the tourist experience to be explored and used to illuminate the essential characteristics of destination experience. Tourists were interviewed to elicit anecdotes about their expectations, their experiences and the image of the destination they would convey to others following their visit. They were interviewed during their stay so that the researcher would be the first audience for their traveller's tales and therefore able to capture the freshness of the tourists' *lived experience* of the destination (van Manen, 1990).

Fifty-six interviews took place at three different locations each within Edinburgh (October 2004) and the Greenwich World Heritage site (May 2005). Both Edinburgh and Greenwich are marketed and recognised as destinations in their own right. Edinburgh attracted 3.96 million staying visitor trips in 2003, representing 12.99 million bed nights (VisitScotland, 2004), and Greenwich attracted 6.8 million visitors in 2003 (Greenwich Council, 2004). Interviewing in multiple locations in two destinations was considered to minimise the likelihood of the eventual key characteristics of the lived experience being either attraction or destination specific. Whilst the study also considered tourist–host, tourist–resident and tourist–attraction interactions, the key findings presented here relate to tourist–tourist interactions.

The interview transcripts were imported into QSR NVivo 2.0, a software package designed to assist qualitative data analysis (Guthrie & Thyne, 2006). The transcripts were read and re-read to uncover the key characteristics of each interviewee's experience and how they spoke of it, with examples of interactions identified and categorised as either tourist–host (official or front-line tourism provider), tourist–resident, tourist–attraction or tourist–tourist. This chapter explores the two types of tourist–tourist interaction that emerged: the impact of others within the immediate travel party, and the impact of the presence or behaviour of other tourists.

Travelling Companions

Both the physical and psychological well-being of travelling companions can influence a tourist's enjoyment of a destination, whilst the fact of being in a couple or a group can necessitate the conscious or unconscious accommodation of the interests, likes and dislikes of the other members of the travel party. Both factors may play a role in the choice of attraction visited or activity undertaken. In the present study, the majority of people interviewed (44 of 56) were travelling with other people, and the following examples illustrate ways in which this appears to have affected their destination experience.

At one extreme, two ladies in Edinburgh would have explored more of the attractions on offer, but their husbands had both had "flu and then caught a stomach bug", so they "just did the girls' things". Whilst they appeared to retain a good impression of Edinburgh, they had clearly been affected by the treatment they received in their hotel. One husband was diabetic, so needed food despite being ill, but all the hotel could provide was "toast and some butter, and I mean that was the only thing on the whole menu that they could actually offer him… it was disgusting." The offhand attitude of the staff made them feel that "I wouldn't like to come back to Hotel A"[1] and that when talking to people, "If they were going to Edinburgh, you wouldn't say 'Go to Hotel A'", although this experience will not affect their view of Edinburgh because they have enjoyed other aspects of the city, such as the Closes and the Royal Yacht Britannia. Nevertheless, their hotel experience has clearly made an impact, and it is possible they will inadvertently convey to others the impression that people in Edinburgh are offhand and unwelcoming, even if the attractions are worth visiting.

Several interviewees chose itineraries or attractions taking into account the physical limitations of their travelling companion. One lady, travelling with her mother, said:

> we're looking up all the key places to visit. Mum … she's only got one lung
> … we walk a lot of places cos that's the way to do it, but we have to be
> a bit selective. Like we can't just go three or four kilometres because she
> can't physically get there. So a lot of our trip is around making it easy
> for her.

Other Greenwich interviewees appreciated the little train, which runs between the observatory and the rest of the site, because it made it easier for their travel companion:

> My husband hasn't been well so we've really enjoyed also having that vehi-
> cle to take us…That was really worthwhile for someone who shouldn't be…
> overdoing things.

---

[1]The name of the hotel has been changed in the interests of anonymity.

There were numerous instances of interviewees placing a priority on doing things that would be enjoyed by their travel companions, even when this was not what they would necessarily have chosen. In most instances, this had ultimately enhanced their experience. Melanie, travelling with five friends, "really didn't want to go on the (London) Eye because I'm absolutely terrified of heights, but it was brilliant, absolutely brilliant". Similarly Chris, fitting sightseeing into a business trip, had come to the National Maritime Museum "because one of us wanted to see the Harrison clocks". Although these are actually in the observatory, he had nevertheless enjoyed both the Museum and discovering Greenwich. Talking to others, he would describe it as "kind of rich and warm, and… cloaked in mystery…definitely scenic" and direct anyone with an interest in history to visit it, as it "has a lot to offer in that respect". Chris and Melanie each made discoveries through falling in with the plans of others in their group; Malcolm on the other hand seemed restricted:

> *my nearest and dearest … she's half English, you see, and she's been to London so many times, and so I say, "Oh, let's go and see Buck House" and she'll say, "Oh, really, come on, that's boring, you don't want to do that, let's go to …" So I didn't see Buck House, and that's fine, you know, I don't mind.*

Having persuaded her to take a boat trip to Greenwich earlier in the week, Malcolm had returned on his own for what he described as "selfish motives" to look for traces of his ancestors, an activity he did not believe she would find interesting or enjoyable. In each of these examples, there has been some negotiation between travel party members about what to do, resulting in various forms of compromise, either one member acquiescing in the group preference, or agreeing to do jointly agreeable things one day, and independent ones another. In both cases, the end result appears to be an expanded consideration list.

Others seemed to find enhanced pleasure from their travelling companions' enjoyment. Shirley had come to Greenwich because her husband was interested in maritime attractions; she had specifically chosen to do something her husband would prefer because he had had a difficult time recently, with his father dying six months previously, and being himself newly retired:

> *…we usually do what I want to do, or what my daughters want to do, which is trundle round the shops, and this time, I knew my husband was very interested in ships.*

She found it "nice to be relaxing for a change. Being on our own." Another interviewee, Wendy, also seemed to derive added enjoyment from the fact that Greenwich offered her the opportunity to indulge her love of history whilst at the same time allowing her husband to satisfy his mechanical curiosity:

> *My husband's like the mechanical, and all that sort of thing. I love the history part of it, so we've both had a glorious day because you've managed to put them both together very nicely…. Made the mechanical things come to life, as well as me being able to say, 'Oh yes, I remember reading about…*

Similarly, Max came to Greenwich to see the Cutty Sark and the various museums primarily because his father had wanted to see them, having "been to London and around here
in World War II, so he'd been back and forth across the Atlantic a bunch of times during
the War". Having been in the US Coastguard like his father, Max was also interested in
naval things, and that shared interest seems to have enhanced his experience and appreciation of Greenwich. These findings indicate that interactions with others in the immediate
travel party do affect the tourist's destination experience: both concern for the physical or
psychological comfort of travel companions, and accommodation of their interests, can
influence impressions of the destination and choice of attractions and activities during the
visit.

Other Tourists

Tourists, as well as their travel companions, are affected by the presence of and encounters with other, unknown or stranger, tourists. Some perceive large numbers of other
tourists as positive: Pauline, visiting London from South Africa, expected and welcomed
the liveliness of a city destination, almost exulting in the hustle and bustle. She enjoyed
"just walking around. Being in the taxi cabs, the movement of the people and all the different kinds of people".

Other tourists are often seen as something to be accepted, even commented upon, but
worked around where possible. Commenting on the difference between Edinburgh at
Festival time and in October, Sara's overriding feeling was that at Festival time it was "difficult to move around, there's so many people … It's a bit claustrophobic at times".
Charles enjoyed the people-watching element of visiting cities, but "when it's the Fringe,
you're almost sated with the number of people to watch." They accepted the presence of
other tourists because of the attractions of the Fringe and the International Festival, which
was also their reason for being in the city, but employed avoidance tactics, coming to the
Castle, because "not many people come up to the Castle and round through the Park, so
you can get away from them". In the years when the James Herriott TV series boosted
tourism to the Yorkshire Dales, Mike and Sheila recalled that they were not put off by
walking holidays there "because you could still get away from them, just walking". John
and Jancis, Australians on a touring holiday in Britain, regarded the presence of other people as "part of the adventure". They felt the number of people in the main streets in
Cambridge the previous day had been "*crazy*" but had not detracted from their enjoyment
because "once we got away around the Backs, it was terrific."

Several interviewees, fearing the presence of too many other tourists would prevent
them getting the most from their visit, used a different strategy for minimising the impact
of other tourists — planning to visit outside the main tourist season. Edward and Martha,
from Tasmania, deliberately chose to come to Scotland in the low season (October) because
it was an expensive trip, and they wanted to "be able to soak up as much as we can. I mean,
I know that's a selfish reason…" Pauline, although appreciating London's busyness, would
choose the off-season to go to Rome, because she would prefer it "quieter, less frenetic."
Carla and Mark's trip to Greenwich had been fitted into a gap in work commitments, but
they too tried to go "when it's not high season… it's not as crowded, which makes it easier to get in places and do things, we're less restricted."

However, there were specific instances where the press of other tourists had prevented interviewees being able to experience attractions or places at their own pace and in their own way. Karen vividly described how her experience could be spoiled in part by the presence of other tourists, and not just in the Castle. Like others quoted above, she was pleased to have come to Edinburgh slightly out of season, because busy tourist areas mean queues: "Like in here, you come and you have to queue a long time for the café, find a place, queue for the toilets, have to queue to see everything, in fact." Queuing had a detrimental effect on Karen's experience: "When there are loads of people and you're walking behind someone, you feel that you can't stop." She preferred it when "I can take my time". When there were lots of people, she became "frustrated and irritated" because "if there are loads of people stopped to look, it stops the whole queue and you can't go anywhere. You can't walk, you have to wait … and you can't see properly because people are standing in front of you". She noted she was not alone in feeling this irritation, which seemed to affect other tourists as well, in turn increasing the general negative effect: "people tend to be tired when they queue for something, or they become very arrogant and frustrated and irritated and that kind of reflects those feelings when you start to feel irritated and tired and its just, you know, constant like, "Excuse me"."

Very few interviewees commented on the characteristics of other tourists. Edward and Martha regarded any differences as part of the experience, commenting, "they just have a different philosophy of life, I guess, from what we do." Jancis appeared to feel a mismatch between her expectations and experience, in that the large number of French tourists in London and Greenwich meant that she sometimes didn't "realise that I actually am in England, the number of French accents", while Matthew was really commenting on the skills and attitude of their Edinburgh Castle guide:

> *The amazing thing was when we started the tour, he asked everybody where they were from, he literally asked everybody, and it was amazing. We'd got people from all round the world in our little group … Poland, America, Canada, Australia... It was nice that he did that, though, it's nice to have an idea of who you're alongside.*

Comments which would support the notion that tourists hold stereotypical perceptions of other cultures or nationalities were made not in relation to other tourists, but to the differences between the tourist's own country and the residents of the one they were visiting.

All the above instances indicate the impact of the presence of unknown, or stranger, tourists. The few instances of actual encounters between interviewees and stranger tourists were usually cases of attractions or places being recommended. Kirsty had obviously chatted with other guests in her B&B (bed and breakfast), and came to the Royal Yacht Britannia "because the people next to me at breakfast this morning said 'It's fabulous'". Unless obliged to engage with them by virtue of being in a tour group, most interviewees were aware of other tourists mainly through observation. Indeed, one interviewee, having commented on the variety of other nationalities holidaying in England, said "But do we mingle? No."

There seems to be a preference for maintaining a certain distance from other tourists whilst extracting the most from the destination in terms of engaging with the atmosphere and attractions, preferably also unimpeded by the numbers of other tourists. At the same time, it is important that all members of the travel party enjoy their experience. A partner or travel companion's discomfort or lack of enjoyment can colour the tourist's experience and shape their holiday stories; similarly, the experience can be enhanced if both partners' different interests or motivations can be satisfied in the same destination, as their individual positive experience is multiplied by seeing the other person enjoy themselves as well.

Conclusions

This study demonstrates that the presence of other tourists, whether travel companions or strangers, has an impact on destination experience and supports Dann and Phillips' contention that the area of tourist–tourist interactions is worthy of further research (Dann & Phillips, 2001). Whether this impact is positive or negative depends upon the individual. Within the travel party, it is dependent upon the tourist's motivation toward their travelling companions. If tourists feel that their travel companions are, or may be, physically or emotionally uncomfortable, their own enjoyment of the destination is compromised. Although they may have positive experiences from their holiday to counterbalance the negative, any audience to whom they recount the negative incident may not have the same balancing memories; for example, they might extrapolate from Marilyn and Rachel's experience that not only are staff in that hotel unfriendly, so are people in Edinburgh. More positively, the negotiation and compromise necessitated by travelling with others appears to result in an expanded consideration list of attractions and activities. This tends to confirm that Gilbert and Hudson's interpersonal factors are indeed valid for participation in general tourist activities, and for decision making whilst on holiday as well as in destination choice (Gilbert & Hudson, 2000). Moreover, it is not only travel companions who may shape the choice of places to visit; instances of encounters with tourists outside the travel group influencing the decision to visit a particular attraction indicate the very real power of word of mouth recommendation.

On the other hand, the presence of other, stranger, tourists can be a negative factor, leading to stories about overcrowded attractions, lack of space to stop and stare, or being hustled through with no time to appreciate the attraction, artefacts or buildings, which may deter potential tourists. This study suggests that the sheer presence and number of other tourists can produce negative perceptions of a destination being crowded or too busy, but are less likely to lead to stereotypical perceptions based on nationality or culture as discussed by Pizam and colleagues (Pizam & Sussmann, 1995; Pizam & Jeong, 1996) or Reisinger and Turner (1997, 1998). Although further research is required, this study indicates that McIntosh (2004) is right to caution that tourists do not necessarily seek or appreciate a deeper insight into other societies and cultures, whether those of the host or other tourists. Moreover, the presence of too many other tourists can lead to disappointment. Overseas visitors may have had to save both money and leave allowance for some time before travelling, and therefore feel they must soak up as much of the destination as possible. If they are prevented from doing so by large numbers of other tourists, they may feel frustrated and this can become apparent through their holiday stories.

These findings carry implications for destination managers. The majority of tourists travel in groups, whether couples, families or groups of friends. At the same time as promoting a particular message to a specific market segment, it is important to signpost other options within the destination so that even if the primary aim of a holiday is to soak up culture, for example, there is the opportunity for others in the travel party to do or see other things. If a destination attracts older tourists, issues of physical comfort should be addressed. For example, the little train between the main maritime Greenwich sites was very much appreciated, as it enabled several interviewees to experience more of the destination without fearing that their partner/parent would be tired out, which would have spoilt everyone's enjoyment.

In terms of visitor management, it is clear that for a place to be crowded detracts from the experience: Pauline has noted that Greenwich is developing as a tourist destination and is glad she has visited now, "because in five or ten years' time it will be much, much busier and, to me, might have lost a bit of its appeal". This poses a challenge to destination managers. The more visitors and tourists they attract, the greater the potential income to the destination through accommodation and attraction spend. However, it seems there is likely to be a point where the destination is too crowded for tourists to enjoy their experience. Not only might this deter them from making a repeat visit, it may also deter people to whom they talk about their experiences. The difficulty, of course, is that while there are fewer tourists in the shoulder and off-season months, the lower numbers make it uneconomic for some visitor attractions and facilities to operate, meaning that those tourists who do come at that time do not have the opportunity to experience everything the destination has to offer and may feel disappointed. The answer may lie in emphasising quality of experience over variety of things to see and do during the current low season. As for the problems of crowds during the main season, destination managers will need to pay careful attention to visitor flow, identifying and finding ways to ease bottlenecks and pinch points, and perhaps increasing the use of timed entrance tickets and advance booking where capacity is limited.

In summary, this study sought to address the acknowledged lack of research into tourist–tourist interactions. Interviews with tourists during their holiday indicated that their interactions with other tourists, whether travelling companions or strangers, not only affect their perceptions of the destination but also the anecdotes with which they convey their experience to others. The implications of tourist–tourist interactions for destination managers and marketers have been highlighted, and suggestions made as to how these can be addressed. Further research in this area could usefully be extended into destinations in other countries, and particularly consider cross-cultural issues in more depth, as the interviewees in the current study were, with one or two exceptions, either British or from the English speaking, developed world.

References

Baloglu, S., & McCleary, K. W. (1999). A model of destination image formation. *Annals of Tourism Research*, 26(4), 868–897.

Bansal, H., & Eiselt, H. A. (2004). Exploratory research of tourist motivations and planning. *Tourism Management*, 25, 387–396.

Bigné, J. E., Sanchez, M. I., & Sanchez, J. (2001). Tourism image, evaluation variables and after purchase behaviour: Inter-relationship. *Tourism Management*, 22(6), 607–616.

Dann, G. (1993). Limitation in the "use of nationality" and "country of residence" variables. In: D. G. Pearce & R. W. Butler (Eds.), *Tourism research: critiques and challenges* (pp. 88–112). London: Routledge.

Dann, G., & Phillips, J. (2001). Qualitative tourism research in the late twentieth century and beyond. In: B. Faulkner, G. Moscardo, & E. Laws (Eds.), *Tourism in the 21st century*. London: Continuum.

Donne, J. (1624). Meditation 17: Now, this bell tolling softly for another says to me, thou must die. In: R. Scott (Ed.), *No man is an island: A selection from the prose of John Donne*. London: The Folio Society.

Fairweather, J. R., & Swaffield, S. R. (2001). Visitor Experiences of Kaikoura, New Zealand: An interpretative study using photographs of landscapes and Q method. *Tourism Management, 22*(3), 219.

Gartner, W. C. (1993). Image formation process. *Journal of Travel & Tourism Marketing, 2*(2/3), 191–215.

Gilbert, D., & Hudson, S. (2000). Tourism demand constraints: A skiing participation. *Annals of Tourism Research, 27*(4), 906.

Greenwich Council. (2004). *Greenwich: A place to visit*. Greenwich Council.

Gunn, C. A. (1972). *Vacationscape: Designing tourist regions* (2nd ed. (1988)). New York: Van Nostrand Reinhold.

Guthrie, C., & Thyne, M. (2006). *Understanding destination experience: Evaluating QSR NVivo 2.0 as a tool for tourism research*. Paper presented at the Cutting Edge Research in Tourism, University of Surrey.

Guthrie, C., Thyne, M., & Anderson, A. (2004). Destination image: The impact of the interaction effect between the visitor and the destination on tourist perceptions. *Tourism State of the Art II*. University of Strathclyde, Glasgow: Scottish Hotel School.

van Manen, M. (1990). Researching lived experience: Human science for an action sensitive pedagogy. New York: State University of New York Press.

Masberg, B. A., & Silverman, L. H. (1996). Visitor experiences at heritage sites: A phenomenological approach. *Journal of Travel Research, 34*(4), 20–25.

McIntosh, A. J. (2004). Tourists' appreciation of Maori culture in New Zealand. *Tourism Management, 25*(1), 1–15.

Mykletun, R. J., Crotts, J. C., & Mykletun, A. (2001). Positioning an island destination in the peripheral area of the Baltics: A flexible approach to market segmentation. *Tourism Management, 22*(5), 493.

Pizam, A., & Jeong, G. H. (1996). Cross-cultural tourist behavior. *Tourism Management, 17*(4), 277–286.

Pizam, A., & Sussmann, S. (1995). Does nationality affect tourist behavior? *Annals of Tourism Research, 22*(4), 910–917.

Pizam, A., Uriely, N., & Reichel, A. (2000). The intensity of tourist-host social relationship and its effects on satisfaction and change of attitudes. The case of working tourists in Israel. *Tourism Management, 21*, 395–406.

Reisinger, Y., & Turner, L. (1997). Cross-cultural differences in tourism: Indonesian tourists in Australia. *Tourism Management, 18*(3), 139–147.

Reisinger, Y., & Turner, L. (1998). Cultural differences between Mandarin-speaking tourists and Australian hosts and their impact on cross-cultural tourist-host interaction. *Journal of Business Research, 42*, 175–187.

Thyne, M., & Zins, A. (2003). Designing and testing a Guttman-type social distance scale for a tourism context. *Tourism Analysis, 8*(2), 129–135.

VisitScotland (November 2004). *Tourism in Edinburgh 2002–2003*. [online]. VisitScotland. Available from: http://www.scotexchange.net/edinburgh_2003-2.pdf [21 January 2005].

Williams, J., & Lawson, R. (2001). Community issues and resident opinions of tourism. *Annals of Tourism Research, 28*(2), 269.

Chapter 11

A Tale of Two Precincts

Bruce Hayllar and Tony Griffin

Introduction

Tourism has long been a feature of many major cities, but the nature of the urban tourist experience is still relatively poorly understood. In most urban destinations, tourist visitation tends to be concentrated rather than dispersed, and specific locales within cities, 'tourism precincts', become the foci of visitor activity. This study aims to build on work conducted by the authors over recent years on urban tourism in general and tourist precincts in particular (Griffin & Hayllar, 2004; Hayllar & Griffin, 2005; Griffin, Hayllar, & King, 2006).

For the purposes of this research we have defined a tourism precinct as:

> A distinctive geographic area within a larger urban area, characterised by a concentration of tourist-related land uses, activities and visitation, with fairly definable boundaries. Such precincts generally possess a distinctive character by virtue of their mixture of activities and land uses, such as restaurants, attractions and nightlife, their physical or architectural fabric, especially the dominance of historic buildings, or their connection to a particular cultural or ethnic group within the city. Such characteristics also exist in combination. (Hayllar & Griffin, 2005, p. 517)

The research on urban tourism precincts to date has been somewhat limited and narrow in scope, with a preponderance of studies examining precincts from a geographic or planning perspective (Stansfield & Rickert, 1970; Wall & Sinnott, 1980; Ashworth & de Haan, 1985; Law, 1985; Jansen-Verbeke, 1986; Meyer-Arendt, 1990; Burtenshaw, Bateman, & Ashworth, 1991; Getz, 1993a, b; Getz, Joncas, & Kelly, 1994; Pearce, 1998). The scope of precinct studies has also embraced a sociological perspective (Mullins, 1991; Chang, Milne, Fallon, & Pohlmann, 1996; Conforti, 1996). McDonnell and Darcy (1998) raised the notion of tourism precincts functioning as part of the marketing strategy of destinations, although not specifically in an urban context, while Judd (1995) developed ideas around the economic development role of precincts.

Other studies have focussed on particular types of urban tourism precincts. In the context of this study the work of Rowe and Stevenson (1994) is apposite. Rowe and Stevenson (1994, p. 181) trace the development of the 'festival market place' concept from the redevelopment of the Boston waterfront that "provided an urban tourism model for other depressed cities and urban sites to emulate, first in the United States and then around the world. Baltimore's Harborplace (sic), New York's South Street, San Francisco's Fisherman's Wharf and London's Docklands can all be seen as fashioned on the festival market place". In a series of similarly relevant studies on historic precincts, Ashworth and Tunbridge's (1990, 2000) work "attempts to define and explain the composite concept of the tourist-historic city and to outline the processes which have created and maintained it … and the planning and management of such cities" (p. 5).

Overall, the research on urban tourism precincts has been and focused on: their role in the tourism attractions mix; their physical and functional forms; their economic significance; their role as a catalyst for urban renewal; accounts of their evolution and associated development processes; and, perhaps more broadly, their role, locality and function within the context of urban planning.

In contrast, recent studies by the authors of this paper have attempted to understand the 'precinct experience' from the tourist's perspective using an approach grounded in phenomenology. This paper builds on that work using 'The Rocks' historic area and the 'Darling Harbour' festival market place, two highly significant tourism precincts in Sydney, Australia, as case studies. As we have argued elsewhere, "understanding how the tourist experiences a precinct, and in particular the attributes, both tangible and intangible, which engender a certain quality to that experience, can produce implications for the effective and appropriate planning, development, management and marketing of the precinct" (Hayllar & Griffin, 2005, p. 518).

The research undertaken for this paper was part of a project conducted under the auspices of the Australian Government's Sustainable Tourism Co-operative Research Centre.

The Study Sites

The Rocks

'The Rocks' is located on the western side of Sydney Cove, directly opposite the Sydney Opera House and adjacent to the Sydney Harbour Bridge. It is one of Sydney's most successful tourism precincts, receiving over 13 million visits from July 2005 to June 2006, of which 22% were made by international tourists (Sydney Harbour Foreshore Authority (SFHA) Fact Sheet, July 2005–June 2006). Half of all international tourists to Sydney visit The Rocks at sometime during their stay, making it the city's third most visited place behind Darling Harbour and the Opera House (SFHA Fact Sheet, March–December 2002).

The Rocks takes its name from the rocky outcrops that once dominated the western side of Sydney Cove. It is generally acknowledged as the site of the first European settlement and as such is promoted to tourists as the 'Birthplace of Australia'. The Rocks contains Australia's oldest extantsiprivate dwelling (Cadman's Cottage) and some of its earliest commercial buildings and warehouses. Tourism activities and land uses predominate, with few residents remaining, although the adjacent and largely uncommercialised area of Millers Point retains both its historic built fabric and a significant resident population.

Darling Harbour

A former wharf and railway goods marshalling area, Darling Harbour, was transformed to coincide with the bicentennial of European settlement in Australia. Formally opened by Queen Elizabeth in May 1988, it has continued to grow and develop. It now contains a range of museums, including the National Maritime Museum, and commercial attractions such as the Sydney Aquarium and IMAX. Darling Harbour also features extensive tourist shopping areas, restaurants and cafes, public open space, children's playgrounds, hotels, open air performance areas, the Sydney Convention and Exhibition Centre, and is adjacent to the Sydney Casino.

Darling Harbour is Sydney's most successful tourism precinct, hosting over 25 million visitors in July 2005–June 2006 (SFHA Fact Sheet, July 2005–June 2006). Of these, 19% were international tourists and 65% local 'Sydneysiders'. The latter highlights the important role played by the precinct as part of the urban entertainment mix for Sydney residents. Located south-west of the Harbour Bridge, it is easily accessed by boat from Circular Quay (5 minutes) or on foot from the CBD (5–10 minutes).

Precincts Together

While their history and management are intertwined, theoretically these precincts present contrasting experiences for the tourist. An historic precinct such as The Rocks perhaps implies an experience of relaxed contemplation and an enlivened curiosity toward the social and cultural tapestry of the area. Alternatively, the festival market place typified by Darling Harbour is presented as a place for action and movement, a place of attractions and interaction with others.

The paper compares and contrasts the activities of tourists in both precincts with a view to examining how the social, cultural and design aspects of a precinct conspire to shape the collective experience of its visitors.

Both Darling Harbour and The Rocks are managed by the SHFA.

Methodology

The Approach

An outline of the phenomenological approach used in these two precincts is detailed in Hayllar and Griffin (2005). However, in order to maintain the internal integrity of the current work, a brief review is provided.

To describe phenomenology and its constituent methodology is complex given that there are 'phenomenologies' to which are ascribed a variety of research and interpretive approaches. Patton (2002, p. 104) maintains that the term phenomenology has become so "popular and has been so widely embraced that its meaning has become confused and diluted". While a review of phenomenological philosophy and theory is beyond the scope of this paper, the approach adopted accords with the central tenets of phenomenology which is to explore lived experience and how individuals transform this lived experience into consciousness, both individually and as shared meaning. "This requires methodologically, carefully, and thoroughly capturing and describing how people experience some phenomenon — how they perceive it, describe it, feel about it, judge it, remember it, make sense of it, and talk about it with others" (Patton, 2002, p. 104).

Van Manen (1990, p. 36) argues that the "aim of phenomenology is to transform lived experience into a textual expression of its essence — in such a way that the effect of the text is at once a reflexive re-living and a reflective appropriation of something meaningful — a notion by which a reader is powerfully animated in his or her own lived experience". More eloquently he notes, "there is a determinate reality-appreciation in the flow of living and experiencing life's breath. Thus a lived experience has a certain essence, a 'quality' that we recognise in retrospect" (Van Manen, 1990, p. 36).

The method adopted in this study is primarily hermeneutic phenomenology. It attempts to be descriptive, to show how things look, to let things 'speak for themselves' and, in the context of the hermeneutic project, it is interpretive. While there may be, at first glance, an implicit contradiction between description and interpretation, this may be resolved, "if one acknowledges that the (phenomenological) 'facts' of lived experience are always already meaningfully (hermeneutically) experienced. Moreover, even the 'facts' of lived experience need to be captured in language (the human science text) and this is inevitably an interpretive process" (Van Manen, 1990, p. 180).

Van Manen (1990) suggests four methodological practices for hermeneutic phenomenological writing. In brief, these practices are:

Turning Toward Lived Experience   To 'do' phenomenological research requires orienting one's thinking toward the questions: what is something really like, what is the nature of the lived experience, what is it about this phenomenon that sets it apart from similar or like phenomena? In turning toward lived experience the researcher needs to 'bracket' his or her prior experience. Bracketing requires the laying aside or 'suspension' of our understandings, assumptions and previous knowledge of the experience under investigation in order to approach it with fresh insight (Husserl, 1973).

Investigating the Experience as Lived   This practice points to the use of methods appropriate to yielding data suitable for phenomenological analysis. The major source of data for these projects was a series of in-depth interviews.

Reflecting on Essential Themes   Moving from data collection to data interpretation involves a process of phenomenological reflection (Van Manen, 1990). The grasping, elucidating or explicating of the essential characteristics of an experience is the basis of the phenomenological endeavour. Reflection and interpretation are the means to that end.

Reflecting on themes and 'working' the text is a dialectical process between the text, the researcher and the writing endeavour.

Writing and Rewriting   To a large extent, the ideas of phenomenological reflection expressed above, and the writing task itself, are false dichotomies; writing and reflection are symbiotic tasks. Van Manen (1990) argues that the approach to writing should focus on maintaining an underlying sensitivity to the language, and through that, to the phenomenon being explored.

In addition to these processes of epistemological practice, Van Manen (1990) also identifies what may be considered as principles that course through each of the above practices. These are:

Maintaining a Strong and Oriented Relation   This principle is a warning to those writing phenomenology to ensure that their writing and interpretations remain oriented to the phenomenological questions under investigation.

Considering Parts and Whole   The final principle is concerned with ensuring that the interpretation is consistent with the various parts of the analysis. "At several points it is necessary to step back and look at the total, at the contextual givens and how each of the parts needs to contribute toward the total" (Van Manen, 1990, pp. 33–34).

Taken together, each of the practices and principles provide a workable methodological framework for a phenomenological study.

The Research Questions

Data collection and analysis were guided by the primary phenomenological question: what is the essence of the visitor experience to The Rocks/Darling Harbour?

Data Collection

Data were collected by in-depth interview in both precincts. To qualify for an interview at The Rocks, participants had to be either international tourists or Australian residents from outside of Sydney. Based on the earlier Rocks study, the sample for Darling Harbour was broadened to include Sydney-based residents. Given the relatively small number of Sydney (and NSW region) residents in the Darling Harbour sample, the differences between the two sites based on the impact of Sydneysiders in particular, and NSW residents in general, is likely minor.

In both precincts, data were collected at the respective visitors' centres. Visitors were encouraged to participate with the offer of two bottles of Australian wine. Volunteer respondents were informed of the time involved (up to 1 hour) and permission was sought to tape record the interview. Interviews took place over 2–3 day periods in March 2001 (The Rocks) and October 2002 (Darling Harbour).

The Samples

The Rocks sample consisted of 20 interviews involving 31 participants. Eleven participants were interviewed individually, seven in pairs and two in groups of three. At Darling Harbour, 36 interviews were conducted involving 59 participants. Fourteen were interviewed individually, 21 in pairs and one in a group of three.

In both studies, first names — for the ease of later identification on the tapes; age – in 10-year bands; and place of origin were collected. An overview of the participants in both studies is outlined in Tables 11.1 and 11.2.

Table 11.1: Age of participants.

Age band (years)	The Rocks	Darling Harbour
20–29	10	24
30–39	6	10
40–49	1	7
50–59	6	9
60 plus	8	9
Total	31	59

Table 11.2: Place of origin.

Origin	The Rocks	Darling Harbour
USA/Canada	12	5
UK/Ireland	5	17
Europe	10	10
New Zealand		3
Australia (other)	3	17
NSW — regional		1
Sydney		3
Other	1	3
Total	31	59

Approaching the Interpretation of Data

In accord with the suggestions of Van Manen (1990), Moustakas (1994) and Crotty (1996) the first 'level' of analysis undertaken was thematic. The three approaches recommended by Van Manen (1990) were used.

Analysis and Interpretation

Analysing the Data: A Thematic Approach

Developing themes implicitly implies a process of data reduction — the narrative is pulled apart, disconnected and then reassembled. The process of theme development is a dialectical process between the text, the researcher and the act of writing.

   In the context of the current work, the themes and their respective categories (or 'subthemes') have emerged from an amalgam of ideas garnered through studies of four separate precincts: The Rocks and Darling Harbour in Sydney and Federation Square and the Southbank Promenade in Melbourne. The latter two studies (Griffin et al., 2006) led to a refinement of the themes that evolved from the earlier work. Subsequent to these studies, data from The Rocks and Darling Harbour were then re-examined and refined. It should

Table 11.3: Themes and categories.

Major themes	Definitions	Categories
Physical form	Architectural and other physical features of the precinct and the extent to which such form(s) implicitly or explicitly shape activity	Setting/fabric; location; activity
Atmosphere	Overall 'feel' of the precinct, created by the dialectical interaction of the social and personal experiences of the visitor	Social experience; contrast; personal experience
Meaning	How the individual's collective experiences provide some sense of personal meaning for their visit	External; internal

be noted that the 'new' themes as outlined in Table 11.3 represent more a clarification and sharpening of language rather than fundamental shifts in our evolving understanding of the experiential character of precinct visitation.

In the following analysis, the first names of participants have been noted. Direct quotes have been placed in italics and the line numbers from the text noted: viz 'Ln.: *x*'. The line numbers provide an audit trail back to the individual texts located within the software (NVIVO) master documents.

Theme 1: Physical Form

'Physical form' refers to the architectural and other physical features of the precinct and the extent to which such form(s) implicitly or explicitly shape activity.

Setting/Fabric   The Rocks and Darling Harbour present themselves as strikingly different architectural forms. The historic yet evolved streetscape of The Rocks with its low rise, more human scale 19th and 20th century buildings is an archetypal precinct.

The architecture links Sydney to its colonial past. Amanda (Ln.: 48) thought that the *monuments and the buildings are very English,* while Angus (Ln.: 97–98) noted the cultural connections when he commented that the *architecture is quite colonial and that you notice the kind of old fashioned buildings.* May (Ln.: 111–113) noticed the changes over time: *You can see the difference. You can see the different years. I don't mean separate years but you can see where they've had a different style or they've added a building. You can see all the different parts; that's good.*

Interestingly, there was little comment on the precinct's relationship to the adjacent Sydney Harbour. Like many places of its type, The Rocks turns its back on the harbour. The setting is inward looking toward the street and its associated activity. Given its close proximity to the Harbour Bridge and Opera House this perspective likely enhances the historic 'feel' of the precinct sheltered as it is from nearby modernist icons.

Darling Harbour contrasts markedly with The Rocks in both architectural fabric and setting. The 'festival market place' style comprises a discordant mix of building types and forms. Its buildings are invariably described as modern and are arranged to take maximum advantage of the harbour-side location. Carolina (Ln.: 73–76) was effusive about the buildings, *beautiful, beautiful, beautiful … very modern … .* The mix of types was commented upon by many respondents such as Christie and Brian (Ln.: 218–219), who noted *the very different mix of buildings — quite cosmopolitan.* However, the somewhat eclectic layout did not appeal to all. Abbey and Hannah (Ln.: 189–197) noted:

> *Well you've got northern parts and then you've got the basin, the cafes and …*
> *then you've got that expensive social bit … and then you've got a children's*
> *playground, and then you've got an information bit … there's no theme as*
> *a whole harbour area.*

Barry and Margaret's comments epitomised those of many respondents who valued the harbour-side setting nearby the *beautiful harbour* (Ln.: 94–95) and *the people, the boats and the water, just love it, absolutely brilliant* (Ln.: 170–172).

Location   The location of both precincts is pivotal to the experience of visitors. The Rocks is adjacent to the main tourist hub of the city. Coach companies, harbour tour operators, major hotels and the city metro are within easy walking distance. The Rocks is also close to the CBD and its offices and shopping areas. It is surrounded by vibrant inner city life and tourist activity. Indeed its relative quietness, its change of pace and its scale are in sharp contrast to its surrounds.

Like The Rocks, Darling Harbour's location appears central to defining its character and the experience of visitors. Unlike The Rocks, it is open space in the city and oriented to the water. The open-water views of sailing and other recreational craft, the working-harbour activity and the northern suburbs of Sydney hugging the distant shoreline, position Darling Harbour as a window to a quintessential Sydney experience. Ian (Ln.: 147–151) notes that *it fits in with the rest of Sydney, it's sitting on the harbour which is one of the main attractions … I think it fits with the rest of the city.* Jill (Ln.: 152–154) also commented that, w*ater's a very big part of Sydney* a point reinforced by Sally and Rob (Ln.: 703–772) who argued that people *just want to be near water. I don't know why it is, I don't know whether people like the sound and the lapping of waves …* Yvette too (Ln.: 99–101) sees the water in the context of its location: *You don't feel obviously it's like being in the city, no. I think a lot of that's got to do with the water 'cause everything's worked around the water.*

Activity   The level and type of activity is a substantial point of contrast between the two precincts. The Rocks is a more 'urbanised' experience. For many visitors, The Rocks is a place to meet, eat, drink and purchase goods — the latter with a specifically Australian identity.

In contrast to the more organic activity in The Rocks, 'Play it your way' is the SHFA developed theme for Darling Harbour. There are numerous tourist attractions, ongoing themed events (such as the Spanish inspired 'Fiesta'), open-air concerts, children's play areas and open space for 'promenading' along the waterfront — all in addition to the ubiquitous restaurants and cafés. The responses highlight the diverse nature of activity in Darling Harbour:

> *It is a big entertainment centre* (Andy and Christian, Ln.: 126).

> *There is so much to see* (Barry and Margaret, Ln.: 22–25).

> *It's all leisure. People sort of passing through, sort of strolling through …* (Bob and April, Ln.: 238–241).

Theme 2: Atmosphere

The 'atmosphere' refers to the overall 'feel' of the precinct created by the dialectical inter-action of the social and personal experiences of the visitor.

Social Experience   Like other forms of leisure behaviour, visiting a precinct is inherently a social experience. The Rocks visitors acknowledge the social aspects of their experience in general terms but in particular note the social context of their experience. The Rocks is an urban melting pot of international tourists, domestic tourists, local residents, office workers and Sydney residents 'in town' for the day. Joyce (Ln.: 454–455) recognised the 'living' Rocks which is *like a community, not just like packed up when people leave at night; it doesn't just shut down.* The living community gives The Rocks a unique charac-ter *where people are walking here and there, going to work and then you have people who are just strolling around* (Darlene, Ln.: 235).

Unlike The Rocks, the social aspects of Darling Harbour were less context focussed. The prevailing theme here was concerned with the social nature of the precinct. A place for meeting; a place for families; a place to 'do' things together. *It's a people place* (Bob and April, Ln.: 272–275). While the image of the 'living community' is not as marked as in The Rocks, Darling Harbour nevertheless conveys the image that it is part of the city, not apart from the city. Michael and Nancy encapsulated the ideas of many others when they noted that *if you want to go to a tourist resort you go to a tourist place but this is a city so you expect to see normal people doing normal things* (Ln.: 114–116).

Contrast   Contrast refers to the extent to which the atmosphere is shaped by the juxtapo-sition of the precinct with its surrounds. In both precincts, visitors expressed ideas con-cerning the difference of the precinct with the remainder of the city. In The Rocks, the contrast is one of scale, pace and style — smaller buildings, a slower more relaxed pace and an old world style. Nierke (Ln.: 87–89) eloquently captures the sentiment in what she called *its more human measure.*

In Darling Harbour the dominant theme is one of space and openness — a place where you can take things more slowly and not walk into people. *It's out of the city but it's in the city. Its got its own little atmosphere* (Gloria and Graham, Ln.: 116–118). The type of space is also a point of contrast. The adjacent harbour creates a sense of space and contrast, as do the park areas with grass and gardens. Like The Rocks there is humanness to space in contrast to the backdrop of the city. As Maureen and Alf argue *I think it's important to have a wee bit of space in a city, it makes it feel better* (Ln.: 257–258).

Personal Experience   The final category in this theme, personal experience, relates to how visitors described their general feelings and level of engagement with the precincts.

There were similarities in both. Being in a city but being withdrawn from its postmodern sensibilities provides individuals with feelings of relaxation and peacefulness, albeit ascribed from different social and physical characteristics. The Rocks' narrow streets, its living precinct character and human interactions convey a particular type of experience, in part a sense of timelessness. While ostensibly a place of activity, Darling Harbour also radiates a type of calmness *because you come down here and you've got the water there and it's a bit more laid back and a bit more, kind of 'ahh', a bit more relaxing. You can sit down and take a breath ... .*(Sally and Rob, Ln.: 81–85)

A notable point of contrast is the younger 'feel' of Darling Harbour. Older respondents recognised that the changing pace of the precinct in the evening made it a place for young people to come out and enjoy themselves. While they feel safe and secure in the precinct there is also a sense that they know when to disengage.

Overall, there is a resonance in the language of positive feelings toward both precincts. These are areas of different character and style from which visitors draw personally meaningful experience. This sense of meaning is developed further in the following section.

Theme 3: Meaning

The final theme is concerned with how an individual's cumulative experiences and level of engagement provide some sense of personal meaning to their visit. In the sense described here, meaning is examined at two levels. The first is concerned with the meaning the precinct gives to the 'host' city itself; as a marker for Sydney as a destination. This category we have labelled as external. The second relates to the more inward-looking, or internal meaning, attributed to the individual by their experience.

External   In both precincts there is an unambiguous sense that visitors are experiencing 'Sydney' but in manifestly different ways. Both are measures of distinctiveness. At The Rocks, visitors recognise they are moving in the environs of old Sydney and do not appear to be concerned with what might be considered the imposition of the modern or 'inauthentic'. Indeed Wang's notion of 'existential authenticity' (cited in Ashworth & Tunbridge, 2000, p. 17), where authenticity lies in the experience not the object, is relevant to this group of visitors.

Darling Harbour provides a different marker. Its design, and particularly its location, mark it as quintessentially Sydney, ergo post-modern Australian city — informal, relaxed and open — a place of light, colour, space and movement. As Tanya notes, *I mean it is comparatively similar to an equal city in the US and so, but when I go, when I come here I feel like I'm in Sydney, I feel like I am somewhere else* (Ln.: 138–141).

Internal   Respondents at both sites expressed positive 'feelings' toward their experience. They felt 'safe', 'comfortable', 'less stressed' and 'not hassled'. However, these expressions were more marked in reference to The Rocks. It could be that the greater 'depth' and complexity of the environment in The Rocks provided a richer experiential foundation for meaningful reflection. Indeed support for this observation is provided in our Melbourne precinct studies (Griffin et al., 2006).

Phenomenological Reflection: The Essence of Experience

The analysis now moves toward a more phenomenological explication of the data; an engagement with the essence of experience.

The themes developed above primarily reflect the experiential structures of precincts. However, essences are not particular actions, interactions or components within the physical and social environment. Rather an essence is a 'construct' that arises from the individual interaction with those components, i.e. how the phenomenon is experienced (the experience of experience). Thus developing essences is a reconstructive or constructive act (Denzin, 1989).

Moving from the experiential structures to essence involved a process of reading and reworking the ideas expressed within the texts to explicate the inherent 'whatness' of the identified themes. Questions such as the following guided this reflective process. Is there embedded within the precinct experience a phenomenon that links and flows through the experience? Is there an essence without which the experience of the precincts (as understood by the participants in this study) would cease to exist? In responding to these rhetorical questions we engaged in a process of thinking through the phenomenological character of the work to date. Further, we engaged in a discursive process of data analysis and discussion between co-researchers.

In the context of The Rocks, emerging from these dialectical processes was a sense of the contested notion of 'place' (see Relph, 1976; Agnew, 1987; Massey, 1994), as previously reported (Hayllar & Griffin, 2005). However, our revisiting of the data in the course of the current study has confirmed the original analysis. What then of Darling Harbour? Again, we would argue that 'place' is the essence of that experience.

In the context of Darling Harbour (and The Rocks) 'place' encapsulates the affective domain of experience through the thematic notion of Atmosphere; 'place' is psychologically experienced through the dialectical interactions with self, others and the precinct space. A further affective dimension emerges within the theme of Meaning. As recognised within the thematic categories, there is a type of phenomenological dualism between 'place' as the experiential 'marker' of a city (external) and 'place' as an experience (internal) of the precinct, i.e. what it means to the individual visitor.

'Place' also resonates with the affective, cognitive and psychomotor domains in consideration of the human interaction with the 'physical form'. In so doing, questions such as: how do I make sense of this form; what does the physical form convey about the precinct; how does the physical form impact upon my experience; and what opportunities for personal action does the physical form imply, are sub-consciously dealt with and acted upon in the course of the experience.

Taken together, the differing physical form, atmosphere and meaning offered by both precincts produce a similar phenomenological experience — a sense of place.

Discussion

Theorising Place

The phenomenon of place emerged somewhat unexpectedly for Darling Harbour, given that precincts of this type are often referred to pejoratively. For example, Huxley (1991 cited in Craig-Smith, 1995) noted the similarities between the Baltimore Inner Harbor (sic) Area and Darling Harbour complaining that these developments were becoming clones of one another. In a similar vein, Rowe and Stevenson (1994, p. 181) argued that "festival marketplaces involve the calculated packaging of time and space, seeking to satisfy tourists' expectations of an authentic experience of place by constructing often decontextualised and sanitised simulations of urban landscapes", and further that these types of precincts resonate with the "urbanism of universal equivalence so that anywhere can now be everywhere." However, our findings suggest that visitor experiences of Darling Harbour run counter to this 'conventional wisdom'. It is not 'anywhere' or simply a carnival like atmosphere with its implied superficiality and depthlessness — it is somewhere! Some possible explanations of this phenomenon will now be explored.

In theorising *place* within The Rocks (Hayllar & Griffin, 2005), we invoked the work of the phenomenologist Alfred Schutz (1973). Using Schutz's notions of 'finite provinces of meaning' and 'paramount and non-paramount realities', we maintained that the characteristics of the historic precinct provided a meaningful architectural and cultural counterpoint to the adjacent city while the experience itself effectively engaged the visitor to suspend their disbelief. As Schutz (1970, p. 252) argued, it is the "meaning of our experiences, and not the ontological structure of objects, which constitutes reality". The maintenance of this experiential reality rests on the extent to which the precinct itself sustains its non-paramount character. For example, a clash of architectural form, the intrusion of external noise, or 'out of character' social action may challenge the phenomenon being experienced. While Schutz's ideas have meaning within this discussion, in particular those on the nature of reality, the Darling Harbour experience might be alternatively theorised from the phenomenological ideas of the influential Norberg-Schulz (1963, 1980).

Norberg-Schulz was one of the key theorists of the concept of *genius loci* from which the ideas of 'sense of place' evolved. According to Jackson (1994 cited in Jiven and Larkham, 2003, p. 68) 'sense of place' is an "awkward and ambiguous translation of the Latin term *genius loci*." While the interpretation of the term has moved over time "we now use the current version to describe the 'atmosphere' to a place, the quality of its environment ... we recognise that certain localities have an attraction which gives us a certain indefinable sense of well-being ..."

Norberg-Schulz (1980) was influenced by both Husserl and Heidegger. However, it is Heidegger, and his ideas on pre-industrial life and landscape that appear formative. In Norberg-Schulz's conceptualisation of *genius loci*, four thematic levels are recognised (see Jiven & Larkham, 2003, p. 70):

- the topography of the earth's surface;
- the cosmological light conditions and the sky as natural conditions;

- buildings;
- symbolic and existential meanings in the cultural landscape.

This conceptualisation has particular relevance to Darling Harbour as it implicitly acknowledges the interplay of topography, light, architecture and the cultural landscape in formulating an inter-subjective sense of place. Thus, while place is socially constructed (Knox, 2005), Norberg-Schulz's work acknowledges the centrality of the natural aesthetic in formulating this construct — an aesthetic recognisable within the experience of visitors to Darling Harbour.

Accordingly, we contend that while a sense of place is maintained by a type of inward looking 'cohesive reality' within The Rocks, for Darling Harbour, place manifests itself from a more outward looking, dialectical association with its setting and cultural meanings as conceptualised in the ideas of *genius loci*.

Conclusion

In this paper we have compared and contrasted the experience of visitors in two contrasting precincts using a phenomenological analysis. Our analysis and interpretation highlight the ways in which the physical and social attributes of a precinct shape the experience of visitors. Importantly, we contend that while precincts may be outwardly dissimilar, such differences do not by themselves produce a different phenomenological outcome.

Our theorising on place, and the types of experiences, interactions, environments and design characteristics that manifest themselves in the phenomenon remains a work in progress. A more complete understanding should emerge as further precincts are investigated and the experiences of visitors better understood. Indeed, understanding the experience of visitors in all forms of precincts has both theoretical and practical implications.

References

Agnew, J. A. (1987). *Place and politics: The geographical mediation of state and society*. Boston: Allen and Unwin.

Ashworth, G. J., & de Haan, T. Z. (1985). *The tourist-historic city: A Model and initial application in Norwich, U.K.* Field Studies Series no. 8. Geographical Institute, University of Groningen, Netherlands.

Ashworth, G. J., & Tunbridge, J. E. (1990). *The tourist historic city*. London: Belhaven Press.

Ashworth, G. J., & Tunbridge, J. E. (2000). *The tourist historic city: Retrospect and prospect of managing the heritage city*. Oxford: Pergamon.

Burtenshaw, D., Bateman, M., & Ashworth, G. (1991). *The European city*. London: David Fulton Publishers.

Chang, C., Milne, T. S., Fallon, D., & Pohlmann, C. (1996). Urban heritage tourism: The global-local nexus. *Annals of Tourism Research, 23*(2), 284–305.

Conforti, J. M. (1996). Ghettos as tourism attractions. *Annals of Tourism Research, 23*(4), 830–842.

Craig-Smith, S. J. (1995). The role of tourism in inner-harbor redevelopment: A multinational perspective. In: S. J. Craig-Smith & M. Fagence (Eds.) *Recreation and Tourism as a catalyst for urban waterfront redevelopment: An international survey* (pp. 15–35). Westport, CT: Praeger.

Crotty, M. (1996). *Phenomenology and nursing research*. Melbourne: Churchill Livingstone.

Denzin, N. K. (1989). *Interpretive interactionism*. Newbury Park, CA: Sage.

Getz, D. (1993a). Planning for tourism business districts. *Annals of Tourism Research, 20*(1), 58–60.

Getz, D. (1993b). Tourist shopping villages: Development and planning strategies. *Tourism Management, 14*(1), 15–26.

Getz, D., Joncas, D., & Kelly, M. (1994). Tourist shopping villages in the calgary region. *Journal of Tourism Studies, 5*(1), 2–15.

Griffin, T., & Hayllar, B. (2004). *The essence of place: An evaluation of the tourist experience of Darling Harbour, Sydney*. Presented at Networking and Partnerships in Destination Development and Management: 11th International ATLAS Conference, Naples, Italy, 4–6 April.

Griffin, T., Hayllar, B., & King, B. (2006). *City spaces, tourist places? An examination of tourist experiences in Melbourne's riverside precincts*. Proceedings of the Council of Australian Tourism and Hospitality Educators Annual Conference, Melbourne, Australia, February 6–9.

Hayllar, B., & Griffin, T. (2005). The precinct experience: A phenomenological approach. *Tourism Management, 26*(4), 517–528.

Husserl, E. (1973). *The idea of phenomenology*. The Hague: Martinus Nijhoff.

Jansen-Verbeke, M. (1986). Inner city tourism: Resources, tourists, promoters. *Annals of Tourism Research, 13*(1), 79–100.

Jiven, G., & Larkham, P. (2003). Sense of place, authenticity and character: A commentary. *Journal of Urban Design, 8*(1), 67–83.

Judd, D. R. (1995). Promoting tourism in US cities. *Tourism Management, 16*(3), 175–187.

Knox, P. L. (2005). Creating ordinary places: Slow cities in a fast world. *Journal of Urban Design, 10*(1), 1–11.

Law, C. M. (1985). *Urban tourism: selected British case studies*. Urban Tourism Project Working Paper No. 1, Department of Geography, University of Salford, Salford, UK.

Massey, D. (1994). *Space, place and gender*. Cambridge: Polity.

McDonnell, I., & Darcy, S. (1998). Tourism precincts: A factor in Bali's rise in fortune and Fiji's fall from favour — An Australian perspective. *Journal of Vacation Marketing, 4*(4), 353–367.

Meyer-Arendt, K. (1990). Recreational business districts in the gulf of Mexico seaside resorts. *Journal of Cultural Geography, 11*, 39–55.

Moustakas, C. (1994). *Phenomenological research methods*. Thousand Oaks, CA: Sage.

Mullins, P. (1991). Tourism urbanization. *International Journal of Urban and Regional Research, 15*(3), 326–342.

Norberg-Schulz, C. (1963). *Intentions in architecture*. Oslo: Universitetsforlaget.

Norberg-Schulz, C. (1980). *Genius loci: Towards a phenomenology of architecture*. New York: Rizzoli.

Patton, M. Q. (2002). *Qualitative research and evaluation methods*. Thousand Oaks, CA: Sage.

Pearce, D. (1998). Tourist districts in Paris: Structure and functions. *Tourism Management, 19*(1), 49–66.

Relph, E. (1976). *Place and placelessness*. London: Pion.

Rowe, D., & Stevenson, D. (1994). "Provincial Paradise": Urban tourism and city imaging outside the metropolis. *Australian and New Zealand Journal of Sociology, 30*(2), 178–193.

Schutz, A. (1970). *On phenomenology and social relations*. Chicago: University of Chicago Press.

Schutz, A. (1973). *Collected Papers I: The problem of social reality*. The Hague: Martinus Nijhoff.

Stansfield, C., & Rickert, J. (1970). The recreational business district. *Journal of Leisure Research*, 2(2), 209–225.

Van Manen, M. (1990). *Researching lived experience*. London, Ontario: State University of New York Press.

Wall, G., & Sinnott, J. (1980). Urban recreational and cultural facilities as tourist attractions. *Canadian Geographer*, 24(1), 50–59.

Chapter 12

The Socio-Political Implications of Rural Racism and Tourism Experiences

Marcus L. Stephenson

Introduction

For the purpose of this paper, the term 'black' commonly refers to individuals of African origin and recent Caribbean descent, sometimes referred to as 'Afro-Caribbean' or 'black Caribbean'. Importantly, 'black' represents a state of political consciousness and a 'positive source of identity' (Pilkington, 2003, p. 37), and is arguably a more appropriate form of expression than the conceptual application of 'black British'. The prevailing need for first- and second-generation populations to connect and/or reconnect with the ancestral home-land is indicative of people's reluctance to identify with British and/or English attributes of identity (Stephenson, 2002, 2004). Despite recent conceptual movements toward locating 'black Britishness' as a significant appellation for Britain's black community (Owusu, 2000), this chapter deliberately avoids using this term as a possible descriptor because of the ideological and cultural implications associated with racialised dimensions of a 'British identity'.

The forthcoming discussion emphasises the point that members of the UK black com-munity do not necessarily share a national way of life, exemplified by their marginalisation from popular social activities such as countryside travel. Their self- and collective-identities are not necessarily adaptable or biddable as the (relatively new) 'black British' concept implies. Popular representations of the countryside as an expression of Englishness and/or Britishness have the desired effect of disenfranchising black minorities from appreciating rural environments. Attempts personally to reconstruct or renegotiate a sense of black Britishness would thus imply that individuals are capable of adopting some form of dou-ble consciousness during their countryside visits. However, the debate draws attention to how British/English forms of ethnic identification appear to be inconsequential because of the degree to which racialised countryside experiences prevent black individuals from empathising with the national experience.

Developments in Tourism Research
Copyright © 2007 by Elsevier Ltd.
All rights of reproduction in any form reserved.
ISBN: 978-0-080-45328-6

Racism is often defined as a process by which individuals and groups stereotype members of another race on the basis of possessing inherent (physical) characteristics (e.g., pigmentation) (Yeboah, 1988). This categorisation works on the belief that some races are naturally superior to other races. However, racism is arguably a social construct, relating to the ways in which powerful ethnic groups develop racialised categories and stereotypical representations of those perceived to be socially and culturally inferior. These constructs have the effect of producing what Balibar (1991, p. 18) terms — the 'stigmata of otherness', i.e., a social disposition which has implications beyond biological determinism.

Racism arguably celebrates not only biological supremacy but also cultural difference and social superiority (Barker, 1981; Gilroy, 1987). Barker (1981) maintains that nationalist discourses often construct definitions of the 'British Nation' on the basis of socio-biological beliefs, appropriated by the dominant ethnic group in an endeavour to preserve its status and position in society. Racism thus functions on the assumption that it is not natural for people from different cultural and ethnic backgrounds to be part of a 'bounded community' or a 'nation' (1981, p. 21). It can transpire through territorial claims and acts of physical exclusion, which effectively impede the socio-political rights of those classified as 'outsiders'. As the chapter illustrates, racial abuse toward black minorities and their physical disenfranchisement from the civilised enjoyment of rural (white-populated) domains seriously questions the extent to which black minorities are perceived as UK citizens, possessing the necessary citizenship entitlements as their white counterparts; particularly rights to social and cultural forms of citizenship.

National culture has been defined and redefined through the gradual development of racial boundaries, which exclude those individuals who are perceived to be a threat to the cultural values of the nation. English nationalism is arguably one of the most potent determinants of racial exclusion because it operates through the political and ideological role of the British state. As Gilroy (1993, p. 75) reminds us, the British state can exist without a need for a unique British culture because English nationalism has an all-defining capacity to construct and dictate the 'cultural content' of 'authentic' national life. Popular representations of the English countryside pertinently illustrate how national life is presented and constructed, where countryside ideals and pastoral myths reinforce Anglo-centric notions of identity and tradition; an issue that will be discussed at length in the forthcoming discussion.

Members of the black community frequently experience difficulties in attaining equal opportunities and benefits of British citizenship. Evidence suggests that racial inequality is prevalent within the housing and education sectors (Pilkington, 2003). The denial of equal opportunities and benefits of citizenship has the effect of disenfranchising significant sections of the community from society, whether as a consequence of intentional or unintentional racial practices. Critical inquiries have profiled the range of racial problems that black communities face: economic exploitation (Rex & Tomlinson, 1979), racial violence (Keith, 1995) and racial surveillance (Lyon, 2003). Such problems are thought to prevail within urban (multi-racial) communities, where racism affects socially excluded and economically marginal (inner city) societies. Racism is thus commonly perceived as an urban concern, based on the assumption that 'racism only spatially occurs where black people live' (Watt, 1998, p. 688). This perspective is being challenged through 'growing recognition of the existence of racism in new spatial contexts' (Watt, 1998, pp. 689–690). Enquiries have seriously addressed the role of racism in countryside environments (Agyeman & Spooner, 1997; Neal,

2002; Chakraborti & Garland, 2004). Nevertheless, despite several initial observations (Stephenson, 2004; Stephenson & Hughes, 2005; Prieto Arranz, 2006), analysts have not significantly embraced the study of countryside tourism and racism.

A critical appreciation of the problems of rural racism perhaps illustrates that racism is not a 'monolithic' construct, but something, which operates uniquely in 'differing local, geographic, social, economic contexts' (Neal, 2002, p. 456). Nevertheless, there are underlying political ramifications associated with the way in which power-bound relations lead to the social exclusion of 'black others' from rural spaces and places. This observation encourages ontological-based debates concerning the 'right to travel', 'citizenship rights' and 'multi-racial forms of mobility'. The discussion generally emphasises that, although ethnic minority movements can be perceived as elements of risk because of the social and geo-political threats that such groups seemingly pose to ethnic majority communities, relations of power ensure that minority groups are marginalised from the countryside. Importantly, this paper suggests ways in which tourism researchers can approach the study of tourism, racism and the countryside.

The 'English'/'British' Countryside: Racial Prejudice and Notions of 'Insidership'

Non-white minorities, visiting or considering visiting rural environments, potentially anticipate or encounter racial prejudice. People's personal experiences suggest that the countryside can generate uncomfortable feelings for black visitors. The novelist, Andrea Levy, explains her feelings of visiting countryside environments:

> As soon as I step outside a major city, I feel self-conscious and it's unpleasant. It has made me feel vulnerable. I've had unpleasant experiences in pubs, comments made. When people look at me they look at me as different. That comes into my head like a Pavlovian reaction. You just want to blend in and fear that you won't (Guardian, 2004a).

Watt's (1998) study, concerning opinions of 'out-of-town' visits and places in southeast England, illustrates that non-urban (white) places are often perceived by non-white groups as places which harbour significant levels of racial conflict. One of his research informants, for instance, expressed his opinion of a nearby commuter village, commenting:

> ...I don't feel safe to walk around there...that place is so racist, they don't like black people up there...yeah, white area, up there if you spot a black man up there walking, that's it, you've got about one or two black people up there (Watt, 1998, p. 698).

It is difficult to quantify the extent to which ethnic minority groups travel to the UK countryside, particularly as government bodies and rural organisations have not significantly monitored the ethnic backgrounds of countryside users. Only recently have the

Ramblers' Association and the National Trust recognised the importance of ethnic monitoring (Guardian, 2004a). Nevertheless, compared to white suburbanites/urbanites, black
(and Asian) minorities are far less likely to travel into the countryside because of increased
levels of racial violence. Trevor Phillips, Chair of the Commission for Racial Equality,
announced that the countryside sustains a 'passive apartheid', by claiming a 'gradual shift
toward a difficult situation in which people from ethnic minorities feel uncomfortable'
(Guardian, 2004b).

Based on the number of racially recorded incidents in comparison to the size of local
ethnic minority populations, it was estimated that racial violence is ten times more likely to
occur in rural areas than in urban areas (Observer, 2001). Yet rural incidents have more than
doubled since 2001 (Rayner, 2005), a possible outcome of the intensification of racism and
xenophobia in the aftermath of the 11 September, 2001 incident. Although Cumbria is now
ranked as the most racist region in England and Wales, other 'danger areas' are Cornwall and
Devon, most of Wales, Cleveland, Durham and Norfolk. However, the southwest region has
attracted significant attention from the regional press, where headlined stories have reported
on the range of racialised incidents occurring in such popular tourist destinations as Bodmin
(Cornwall) (Western Morning News, 2004a), Exeter (Devon) (Western Morning News,
2004b) and Torquay (Devon) (Torbay Herald Express, 2004).

In addition to racial motivation and intent, other factors responsible for limiting black
people's opportunities to travel to the countryside have been identified: lack of free time
and limited disposable income (Agyeman & Spooner, 1997), inadequate (and overly traditional) publicity material concerning countryside recreation (Prieto Arranz, 2006) and limited cultural familiarity with a rural life (Stephenson & Hughes, 1995). Accordingly,
countryside communities naturally establish their own cultural sense of 'insidership', which
excludes the interests of outsiders. Rural-based studies have identified factors enabling village communities to distinguish themselves from the world outside: strong kinship ties,
interactive social networks and 'insider knowledge' of rural folklore and tradition (see
Cohen, 1982). For individuals to appreciate countryside life and experience hospitable
environments, they may have to acquire deep-seated knowledge of local social systems
and cultural processes. This indeed is an arduous undertaking for black (urban) minorities
as they do not necessarily have strong kinship connections and regular social contact with
rural communities.

Pahl (1968) highlights the complex 'social mix' of rural residents: large (traditional)
property owners, middle-class professionals, former (retired) urban workers, commuters
who work in urban areas and local workers who work beyond their environments. Yet it
would be naive to claim that socio-cultural distinctions between rural communities and
urban societies are always significantly distinctive, particularly as the physical boundaries
between the two locales are becoming less spatially demarcated as suburban and rural spaces
are increasingly appropriated by migrating urban (middle-class) populations (Phillips, 1993),
or what Jedrej and Nuttall (1996) appropriately term — the 'white settlers'. Nevertheless, the
social constitution of village life inadvertently elevates the racialised differences between
white middle-class inhabitants and ethnic minority populations, especially in places where the
former group seek to define, redefine and/or uphold the socio-cultural conventions of village
life (Tyler, 2003). Despite the social changes affecting rural societies, black minorities still
predominantly reside in spatially distinct areas of the inner city.

Countryside Representations: National Values and Ideals

Although lack of contact and limited familiarity with the rural way of life may explain why members of this community have little opportunity fully to appreciate countryside environments, it could be that media representations (e.g., countryside magazines, television programmes and brochures) and popular perceptions of rurality indirectly safeguard the racialised boundaries of countryside communities; creating an impression of the countryside as a domain exclusive to the interests of (white) English populations. Even if it is no longer appropriate to perceive rural environments as having a distinctive way of life based on consensually shared interests, harmonised socio-cultural systems and strong community values, they are popularly represented as 'homogeneous', 'timeless', 'idyllic', 'uniform' and 'natural'. The 'countryside milieu', constructed through authentic notions of 'Englishness', powerfully signifies national values and customs.

The rural idyll has a crucial role to play in classic literary works (e.g., Thomas Hardy's (1974), 'Tess of the D'Urbervilles'), autobiographies (e.g., Hannah Hauxwell's (1990), 'Seasons of My Life: Story of a Solitary Daleswoman') and radio soaps (e.g., 'The Archers'); as well as television soap operas (e.g., 'Heartbeat'), comedies (e.g., 'The Good Life'), dramas (e.g., 'All Creatures Great and Small') and films (e.g., 'Cider with Rosie'). Cider with Rosie, a dramatisation of Laurie Lee's (1959) novel concerning his childhood experiences in a secluded Cotswold valley, recalls the halcyon days of 'flower-fill meadows', 'church outings' and 'home-made wines'. It presents the rural idyll through the eyes of a child who fails to appreciate the hardships of rural life. Tess of the D'Urbervilles also reinforces the pastoral and romantic images of an agrarian (Wessex) lifestyle, with the image of Tess and her village friends dancing together in white dresses on the village green. In a subtle manner the novel implicates the external effects that industrialism and urban life can have on rural life, with a passionate message conveying that rural life ought to be firmly protected from external threats.

Place marketers have cultivated the image of the countryside as a bucolic idyll, rich in heritage and tradition. Romantic depictions of the UK rural destinations have been formalised through the strategic process of 'branding', where marketers have devised and promoted nostalgic connections between particular places and famous English personalities. This is illustrated through the tourism logos of 'Shakespeare Country' (south Warwickshire), 'Wordsworth's Country' (Cumbria), 'Bronte Country' (west Yorkshire) and 'Hardy's Wessex' (Dorset).

In his book 'England: An Elegy', right-wing philosopher Roger Scruton (2000) plaintively accounts for ways in which English virtues and conventions have been threatened by the ill effects of modernisation: urban expansion, industrial pollution and social entropy. He laments over the demise of country houses and the uprooting of hedgerows. The hedgerow, a consequence of the rapid enclosure of land in the late eighteenth century, purposefully protected livestock and those who lived and worked within its borders. The hedge was a 'symbol of Englishness' and a 'reminder to the English that the thing which defines them — the land itself — is also being removed from them' (2000, p. 242). Scruton's (2000) work suggests that the 'enchanting' and 'sacred' nature of rural environments should inspire inhabitants with a sense of confidence and social purpose; so as to ensure that remaining areas and landscapes are clearly preserved. The countryside should be 'fought for before all lesser things' (2000, pp. 41–42).

Nevertheless, Scruton's (2000, pp. 234–243) account of the English countryside is overly sentimental, lacking critical appraisal of the rural realities of social division, racial exclusion, ethnic dominance and intercultural discord. His discussion concerning the key attributes of Englishness pays little attention to socio-political constructions of English ethnicity and ways in which Englishness historically reflects a hybrid race (see Young, 2005).

The national project, manifested in the cultural attributes of rural life and romanticised perceptions of the countryside, is synonymously reinforced through conceptions of rural areas as 'safe havens' for white communities. The projection (and protection) of the 'English way of life' has an affect in making the countryside less accessible to black visitors. However, black minorities are not only being denied access to countryside environments but 'symbolic access to the icons of nationhood' (Kinsman, 1995, p. 301). Neal (2002, pp. 444–445) draws attention to the racial implications of presenting the countryside as a symbol of national identity, stating:

> In contemporary Britain the deployment of rurality as a symbol of national identity is at odds with its multi-ethnic composition because nostalgic notions of rurality re-inscribe and treasure hyper-whitened and thereby exclusive versions of Englishness.

Unsurprisingly, the countryside has been targeted by the British National Party (BNP) in an endeavour to raise its share of the public vote. This intention reinforces the BNP's wider socio-political ambitions for the maintenance and expansion of multi-cultural free zones. This political organisation has recently campaigned in such places as Dorchester (Dorset), Malmesbury (Wiltshire), Newlyn (Cornwall) and Penzance (Cornwall) (Cornish Guardian, 2004; Guardian, 2004c; Western Daily Press, 2004).

There are clear historical associations between ethnic minorities and the countryside, which have been disregarded from national heritage representations. Neal (2002), for instance, acknowledges the historical link between ethnic minorities and the English countryside, illustrating that some of England's stately homes were built from capital generated by the transatlantic slave trade. She also asserts that the prevalence of village public houses with such names as 'Jamaica Inn' and 'Indian Queens', and one might also add 'Black Boy', authenticates the countryside's colonial legacy (2002, p. 445). There are various examples of situations where non-white persons either occupied or frequented the British countryside. Agyeman (1995) describes how soldiers from North Africa were used to protect Hadrian's Wall during the Roman Empire, while Brown (1998) acknowledges the presence of Sikh pedlars in the Scottish Highlands in the early 20th century. Regrettably, countryside heritage is popularly imagined through mono-cultural and mono-ethnic narratives of rural life.

Social and Cultural Perceptions of 'Black Others'

The mass production of spurious images of black communities may also influence the establishment of social divisions between black visitors and white hosts, as well as negatively impacting the way in which 'black others' are viewed in public places and spaces. The social construction of popular myths of black criminality, i.e., black people as 'drug pushers', 'thieves' and 'muggers', illustrates ways in which black societies are stereotypically portrayed, socially perceived and culturally construed (Hall, Critcher, Jefferson, Clarke, & Roberts, 1978). Poet Benjamin Zephaniah's experience illustrates the degree to which black individuals are instantaneously perceived as a threat or danger to the rural community. He recalls:

> I was in Essex on a friend's farm and went for a long jog. Never left his land. When I got back to his house, the place was surrounded by police, a helicopter circling above. 'We have had reports of a suspicious jogger', the police said. My friend was outraged (Guardian, 2004a).

The perceived threat that 'black others' pose to local lifestyles and the cultural mores of the community depends on the extent to which they are commonly viewed as sources of cultural pollution and social danger. Although these constructs are widely addressed in anthropological enquiries concerning cultural manifestations of the human body (Douglas, 1984), their application to the study of inter-ethnic relations in host environments could help to explain reasons why racialised encounters and exchanges develop. They importantly indicate why symbolic frames of expression and communication (e.g., verbal insults, intense staring and physical provocation) are directed at those considered to be ethnically and racially different from the expected norm.

In his ethnographic study of tourism and travel experiences by first- and second-generation members of Manchester's black community, Stephenson (1997) highlights occasions where individuals experienced direct racial provocation during countryside visits. Stephenson's research confederate, Junior, drew attention to one incident when he and several (black) colleagues were 'car chased' from a Shropshire village, commenting:

> They were closely behind hasslin' us. It wasn't as if we were not familiar with this sort of thing… I wasn't taking any risk. When we stopped I got hold of two pieces of brick, cos' you never know! … I was terrified and very worried. Fortunately, we must have lost them… I like the countryside…the scenery mainly, but you can be vulnerable. You know what we say in Jamaica, 'Trouble doesn't settle like rain'. Wherever you go, you are always thinking of what's around the corner… I wouldn't go back to that place again (1997, p. 139).

Continual awareness and anticipation of risk encounters in countryside environments is of fundamental importance to members of the black community, especially in terms of self-preservation and personal protection. The restriction and control of black people's access to white spaces signifies how 'blackness' is perceived to pollute 'whiteness', and how there are subsequent attempts by the dominant group to 'purify' the primary space. Scruton (2000, p. 50) emphasises that 'physical existence exposes you to a danger of contamination. Strangers must remain strangers, lest they pollute you with their intimacy'. His justification for this claim relates to his observation concerning the English entitlement of privacy, where the home and the land were valued social gifts. He further claims:

> To the English there was no more valued freedom than the freedom to close a door. The Englishman's home was not just a castle, but an island of 'mine' in

an ocean of 'ours'. The English saw their country as home and the land as their entitlement; hence they could not be content without a piece of it (Scruton, 2000, p. 51).

Gardens, lawns and floral borders were symbolic of people's desire to affirm an 'inalienable right of possession to the plot of land that was theirs' (Scruton, 2000, p. 52). Nonetheless, the need to maintain physical distance relates to the fear of exposure to those polluting elements associated with social encroachment and cultural intrusion, rather than the sole need to protect commercial interests and the values associated with private ownership and land entitlement. However, as members of the black community are popularly perceived to belong to the urban domain, the perception of 'blackness' as a source of pollution ought to be contextualised within an analytical framework that accounts for socio-spatial representations of black (urban) societies. Conceptions of urban domains are often guided by popular images of social decay and environmental contamination. The functional myths and representations of the rural idyll symbolise a contrast to the dysfunctional images of the inner city as a place of chaos and squalor. According to Agyeman and Spooner:

> In the white imagination people of colour are confined to town and cities, representing an urban, 'alien' environment, and the white landscape of rurality is aligned with 'nativeness' and the absence of evil or danger (1997, p. 199).

Black populated areas of inner cities have not attracted considerable attention of the 'tourist gaze', nor have they been significantly selected by tourism marketers as sites for 'visual consumption' (Urry, 1992, p. 19). The perception of the inner city as a source of social pollution seemingly discourages mass interest. Yet the supposed inherent 'whiteness' of rural spaces is often the subtext for concerns over the housing and accommodation of asylum seekers, where such people (immigrants/non-whites) are assumed not to be 'suited' to rural life and to be located 'elsewhere', i.e., in the inner city. Accordingly, resident and community groups have firmly opposed government proposals to construct asylum centres and hostels in such rural areas as Bichester (Oxfordshire), Over Stowey (Somerset) and Throckmorton (Worcestershire) (Guardian, 2000, 2002, 2003). Lowe, Murdoch and Cox (1995) claim that:

> ...in recent times, as the countryside has become of increasing value as a 'positional good', tied to the cultural construction of 'Anglo-centricity', the need to exclude undesirable, multi-ethnic 'others' has become of increasing concern to both rural residents and the central state...the 'urban' must be kept at bay (1995, p. 66).

The representational disconnections between rural and urban locales suggests that the view emphasising that people from all social backgrounds are becoming increasingly exposed to the lifestyles and private spaces of others (Urry, 2002) and that different cultures and societies are becoming more interdependent (Rojek, 1993), is not necessarily productive in explaining social distances between those who live in rural communities and minorities who live in urban societies. These distances are created as a consequence of the complex interplay between ideologically informed representations of rurality, ideologies of local and national identity, social constructions and perceptions of black cultures and societies and relations of power.

Power-Bound Relationships, Citizenship Rights and Identity Issues

Cheong and Miller (2000, p. 383) maintain that it is important to acknowledge the extent to which tourists and visitors can be perceived as 'primary objects' of the 'local gaze', especially as their physical, cultural and economic presence can instigate intense local surveillance and suspicion. Thus locals can be antagonistic toward tourists by acting 'as agents in power relations by galvanizing (active or passive) resistance to tourists' (2000, p. 382). If this perspective seriously accounted for the ethnic and racial status of tourists/visitors, it would apply more directly to an understanding of the ways in which black tourists/ visitors are received in rural (host) environments than to tourists per se, especially as such visitors are seemingly more subjected to power-bound relationships than their white (tourist) counterparts. If white tourists do encounter displays of aggression in non-white (host) communities, then this may be partly understood as a reaction to their economic superiority and racial status. The racially imperious nature of tourist quests and encounters is a dominant concern in provocative critiques of Western forms of travel/tourism (Kincaid, 1988; Dunn, 2004). Dunn (2004, pp. 483–496), for instance, examines ways in which Africa has been constructed and consumed by the 'Western tourist gaze', with the undesired affect of fixing 'African otherness' as well as freezing 'de-evolving' and 'primitive' images of Africa.

The claim that tourists can be perceived as 'targets of power' (Cheong & Miller, 2000, pp. 380–382) should be reevaluated once issues of racial dominance and inequality are considered. Studies concerning power-bound relationships in tourism should thus account for racialised encounters and inequalities that transpire between (and within) different cultures, societies and ethnic groups.

For members of the black community, the desire or need for secure and safe encounters may be a more important personal priority than the need to indulge in chance encounters and experimental experiences. Consequently, black people's aspirations and perceptions do not seemingly conform to post-modernist theories concerning tourists' sensibilities, particularly the increasing desire independently to explore isolated destinations and new territories. This aspiration apparently belongs to the 'post- (mass) tourist', i.e., someone who is prepared to take chances and experience challenging situations (Feifer, 1985, p. 259). Individuals may actually aspire to travel to destinations that limit their exposure to socially dislocated experiences and the consequent threat of racialised encounters. Accordingly, travel could be less threatening in places where there is a significant presence of 'black others'. The homelands of the Caribbean are likely destinations for the UK black Caribbean visitors to feel a sense of safety and comfort, especially as racialised encounters are expected to be nominal (Stephenson, 2002). This form of travel is likely to encourage individuals to undergo a process of ethnic and cultural familiarisation, contributing to a clear understanding of the multi-cultural (and multi-racial) dynamics of travel and mobility.

Confrontational encounters occurring between black visitors and white locals are politically problematic because black citizens supposedly have legal rights associated with British citizenship, i.e., the right to live and work in any area of the UK. Therefore, racially inspired reactions and hostile encounters politically restrict people's socio-physical access to public spaces. These constraining and threatening elements, which hinder the rights and freedoms of ethnic minority nationals to establish, express or extrude citizenship entitlements, actually reflect a continuation of the experiences and encounters of the black (African–Caribbean) diaspora: incarceration, relocation, containment, deportation and enforcement (see Clifford, 1997).

Marshall (1950, 1963), who wrote a series of thought provoking essays on the nature of citizenship in post-World War II Britain, suggests that a civilised society ought to acknowledge people's right to 'live the life of a civilised being according to standards set in society' and their right to 'share to the full in the social heritage' of the nation (1963, p. 74). Although Marshall's view has deep nationalist undertones, with implications that citizenship ought to be achieved through cultural assimilation and social obligation, the underlying message suggests that some kind of 'social citizenship' ought to exist on the basis of acknowledging the social rights and roles of all individuals within a civilised society. Nonetheless, members of the UK black community are arguably denied full status as 'social citizens' because of their limited ability to experience complete participation in the valued activities of the wider community. Restricted access to such socially oriented activities as countryside tourism indicates that sections of the national community are deprived of certain social citizenship entitlements, especially if it is to be accepted that countryside recreation is an important social (and cultural) entitlement in post-industrial societies.

Increased access to the countryside could be viewed as a movement toward the reclamation of citizenship rights, particularly if rights of citizenship are to be interpreted along social lines. Attempts to gain access to the countryside are not just an issue of challenging forms of British racism but an attempt to make black Britishness and perhaps black Englishness no longer oxymoronic. In this context, the view of black people from 'elsewhere' (i.e., 'foreign lands'), together with the belief that the countryside is a signifier of white Britishness/Englishness, could be disrupted and partially dissolved. For this situation to take effect rural communities would need to undergo a process of 'de-racialisation'. The prevailing socio-political climate of rural communities would make this task difficult to achieve, ambitiously entailing a complete delimitation of boundaries of ethnicity, race and nationality — not forgetting social class.

Nevertheless, if individuals are restricted from entering countryside environments then they are seemingly prevented from attaining rights to full cultural participation, particularly if they are denied rights to 'symbolic presence and visibility', 'dignifying representation', 'propagation of identity' and 'maintenance of lifestyle' (Pakulski, 1997, p. 80). Consequently, we are not only just dealing with elements of social citizenship but also aspects of 'cultural citizenship'. These two aspects of citizenship clearly illustrate that the right to travel is a politically important objective in achieving societal-based equality, despite the fact that black minorities arguably have a legitimate and legal right to British citizenship.

Conclusion and Research Implications

Racial prejudice inhibits minorities from actively participating in rural tourism. It can thus be assumed that individuals are restricted from experiencing the social benefits of countryside recreation. Countryside destinations are perceived to harbour racial resentment and host communities are thought to negate opportunities for productive forms of social exchange. Although racialised rural experiences represent social conflict and racial interaction existing between black and white groups within the wider societal (urban) context, rural racism has unique features in that it targets individuals and/or small groups as opposed to physically immobile and geographically static (minority) communities.

The black visitor can become an 'element of spectacle' in white communities and destinations — viewed and censored by the prevailing power of the 'white gaze'. Although the 'white gaze' may not always be founded on hypercritical perceptions and harmful images of 'black others', it does have a unifying ability to provoke feelings of desolation in white areas. It may be difficult to convince members of the black community that public perceptions are not always racially motivated. Past experiences of racism, whether encountered personally or encountered by 'significant others' (e.g., friends and family members), would explain why individuals may be overly suspicious of the 'white gaze'; whether or not it is racially intended. Unlike post-tourists, who are often provided with the opportunity to seek out 'new places to visit and capture' (Urry, 1992, p. 5), it could be the case that members of the black community are compelled to travel to known destinations which personify familiarity and offer a sense of security.

Black visitors are seemingly viewed as a threat to the social order and norms of (white) rural communities. Their association with the urban environment reinforces their 'outsider' status, especially as popular representations of urban life endorse the need to retain rural societies as domains where white communities feel safe and secure. Racial representations of 'black others', together with ethnic representations of Englishness and the rural idyll, strengthen the racialised boundaries that pre-exist between black visitors and white hosts. Therefore, racial boundaries and divisions potentially reinforce black people's self- and collective-identities, especially as racialised experiences and encounters contribute to the fortification of an identification process that venerates a sense of being black but at the same time denigrates any sense of being British.

Nonetheless, black people's increased access to rural space would represent a challenge to the countryside's national iconographic status. The de-territorialisation of white space could enable members of the black community to rethink the configuration of their own identities, particularly as increased representation in white-dominated spaces and places could confirm black people's permanency in British society and national life.

As this paper indicates that it is a citizenship entitlement to enjoy the benefits of countryside travel without prejudice or discrimination, it would also be useful for future studies to seriously address the socio-political (and cultural) rights of ethnic minorities to travel to places unrestricted by the actions and/or reactions of others; specifically focusing on the socio-political ramifications of power-bound relations pre-existing in white (host) environments (see Stephenson, 2006). Consequent strategies for achieving mutual exchanges, constructive experiences and positive encounters may then develop to the socio-cultural advantage of ethnic minority groups. Immediate attention ought to be drawn to the range of ethnic minorities groups experiencing racism in rural areas in ways that reflect ethnic, religious and gendered diversities, thereby enabling enquiries to acknowledge the complexities of power-bound relations inherent in multi-racial forms of mobility.

An important research feature would be to examine differences in perceptions and experiences between minority ethnic tourists and 'fixed' minority ethnic rural households, contributing to a clearer understanding of the problems associated with 'tourism racism'. It would also be appropriate for enquiries to consider the fragmented constitution of white ethnic identities in rural England, especially in terms of geographical location and social class. This line of enquiry would help produce multi-dimensional perspectives concerning ways in which differing social compositions of inhabitants perceive 'racialised others'. It is imperative, however, that racialised perceptions are fervently challenged. Consequently, it is of fundamental importance to remove the 'white gaze' as being the only or dominant way to observe and make sense of the world.

References

Agyeman, J. (1995). Environment, heritage and multiculturalism. *Interpretation: A Journal of Heritage and Environmental Interpretation, 1*(1), 5–6.

Agyeman, J., & Spooner, R. (1997). Ethnicity and the rural environment. In: P. Cloke, & J. Little (Eds.), *Contested countryside cultures: Otherness, marginalisation and rurality* (pp. 197–217). London: Routledge.

Balibar, E. (1991). Is there a neo-racism? In: E. Balibar, & I. Wallerstein (Eds.), *Race, nation, class: Ambiguous identities* (pp. 17–28). London: Verso.

Barker, M. (1981). *The new racism.* London: Junction Books.

Brown, M. (1998). The unheard cries. *Connections: A CRE Publication,* Summer, 8–9.

Chakraborti, N., & Garland, J. (Eds.), (2004). *Rural racism.* Devon: Willan Publishing.

Cheong, S.M., & Miller, M. L. (2000). Power and tourism: A Foucauldian observation. *Annals of Tourism Research, 27*(2), 371–390.

Clifford, J. (1997). *Routes: Travel and translation in the late twentieth century.* Cambridge, MA: Harvard University Press.

Cohen, A. P. (1982). *Belonging: Identity and social organisation in British rural cultures.* Manchester: Manchester University Press.

Cornish Guardian. (2004). BNP not welcome says MP as members visit Penzance, 12 February.

Douglas, M. (1984). *Purity and danger: An analysis of the concepts of pollution and taboo* (2nd ed.). London: Routledge and Kegan Paul.

Dunn, K. C. (2004). Fear of a black planet: Anarchy anxieties and postcolonial travel to Africa. *Third World Quarterly, 25*(3), 483–499.

Feifer, M. (1985). *Going places: The ways of the tourist from imperial rome to the present day.* London: Macmillan.

Gilroy, P. (1987). *There ain't no Black in the Union Jack: The cultural politics of race and nation.* London: Unwin Hyman.

Gilroy, P. (1993). *Small acts: Thoughts on the politics of Black cultures.* London: Serpent's Tail.

Guardian. (2000). Rural revolt over asylum seekers' hostel (Gibbs, G.), 17 June.

Guardian. (2002). Protesters rally at asylum centre site (Dodd, V.), 8 July.

Guardian. (2003). Stitch-up over rural asylum centre (Hall, S.), 20 August.

Guardian. (2004a). Countryside retreat (Prasad, R.), 28 January.

Guardian. (2004b). Villagers bristle at accusation of rural prejudice (Smith, L.), 9 August.

Guardian. (2004c). BNP trawls for votes in quiet Cornish port (Taylor, M.), 25 February.

Hall, S., Critcher, C., Jefferson, T., Clarke, J., & Roberts, B. (1978). *Policing the crisis: Mugging, the state and law and order.* London: Macmillan.

Hardy, T. (1974). *Tess of the D'Urbervilles.* London: Macmillan (first published 1891).

Hauxwell, H., & Cockcroft, B. (1990). *Seasons of my life: Story of a solitary daleswoman*. London: Arrow Books Ltd.

Jedrej, C., & Nuttall, M. (1996). *White settlers: The impact on rural repopulation in Scotland*. Luxemburg: Harwood.

Keith, M. (1995). Making the street visible: Placing racial violence in context. *New Community, 21*(4), 551–565.

Kincaid, J. (1988). *A small place*. London: Virago Press.

Kinsman, P. (1995). Landscape, race and national identity: The photography of Ingrid Pollard. *Area, 27*(4), 300–310.

Lee, L. (1959). *Cider with Rosie*. London: Penguin Books Ltd.

Lowe, P., Murdoch, J., & Cox, G. (1995). A civilised retreat? Anti-urbanism, rurality and the making of an anglo-centric culture. In: P. Healey, S. Cameron, S. Davoudi, S. Graham, & A. Madani-Pour (Eds.), *Managing cities: The new urban context* (pp. 63–82). London: Wiley.

Lyon, D. (2003). *Surveillance after September 11*. London: Polity.

Marshall, T. H. (1950). *Citizenship and social class and other essays*. Cambridge: Cambridge University Press.

Marshall, T. H. (1963). *Sociology at the crossroads and other essays*. London: Heinemann.

Neal, S. (2002). Rural landscapes, representations and racism: Examining multicultural citizenship and policy making in the English countryside. *Ethnic and Racial Studies, 25*(3), 442–461.

Observer. (2001). Race attacks risk is higher outside cities (Rayner, J.), 18 February, p. 2.

Owusu, K. (2000). *Black British culture and society*. London: Routledge.

Pahl, R. (1968). The Rural-urban continuum. In: R. Pahl (Ed.), *Readings in urban sociology* (pp. 263–305). Oxford: Pergamon.

Pakulski, J. (1997). Cultural citizenship. *Citizenship Studies, 1*, 73–86.

Phillips, M. (1993). Rural gentrification and the process of class colonialisation. *Journal of Rural Studies, 28*(9), 123–140.

Pilkington, A. (2003). *Racial Disadvantage and Ethnic Diversity in Britain*. Basingstoke: Palgrave Macmillan.

Prieto Arranz, J. I. (2006). Rural, White and straight: The ETC's vision of England. *Journal of Tourism and Cultural Change, 4*(1), 19–52.

Rayner, J. (2005). Racist attacks on the rise in rural Britain. *Observer*, 27 March, p. 1, 16.

Rex, J., & Tomlinson, S. (1979). *Colonial immigrants in a British city: A class analysis*. London: Routledge and Kegan Paul.

Rojek, C. (1993). *Ways of escape: Modern transformations in leisure and travel*. Basingstoke: Macmillan.

Scruton, R. (2000). *England: An elegy*. London: Chattoo and Windus.

Stephenson, M. L. (1997). Tourism, race and ethnicity. Unpublished doctoral dissertation, Manchester Metropolitan University, Manchester.

Stephenson, M. L. (2002). Travelling to the ancestral homelands: The aspirations and experiences of a UK Caribbean community. *Current Issues in Tourism, 5*(5), 378–425.

Stephenson, M. L. (2004). Tourism, racism and the UK Afro-Caribbean diaspora. In: T. Coles, & D. J. Timothy (Eds.), *Tourism, Diasporas and Space* (pp. 62–77). London: Routledge.

Stephenson, M. L. (2006). Travel and the 'freedom of movement': Racialised encounters and experiences amongst ethnic minority tourists in the EU. *Mobilities, 1*(2), 285–306.

Stephenson, M. L., & Hughes, H. L. (1995). Holidays and the UK Afro-Caribbean community. *Tourism Management, 16*(6), 429–435.

Stephenson, M. L., & Hughes, H. L. (2005). Racialised boundaries in tourism and travel: A case study of the UK Black Caribbean Community. *Leisure Studies, 24*(3), 137–160.

Torbay Herald Express. (2004). Racial Abuse Youth's Booze Night Shame, 25 February.

Tyler, K. (2003). The racialised and classed constitution of English village life. *ETHNOS*, *68*(3), 391–421.

Urry, J. (1992). The tourist gaze and the environment. *Theory Culture and Society*, *9*(3), 1–26.

Urry, J. (2002). The tourist gaze: Leisure and travel in contemporary societies (2nd ed.). London: Sage (first published in 1990).

Watt, P. (1998). Going out of town: Youth, 'race', and place in the South East of England. *Environment and Planning D: Society and Space*, *16*(6), 687–703.

Western Daily Press. (2004). Fury as British National Party targets West's market towns, 20 February.

Western Morning News. (2004a). Racism in the shadows (Young, N.), 14 February.

Western Morning News. (2004b). Drunken woman's race tirade at doc, 23 February.

Yeboah, S. K. (1988). *The ideology of racism*. London: Hansib Publishing Limited.

Young, R. J. (2005). *The idea of English ethnicity*. Oxford: Blackwell.

Chapter 13

Researching the Experiences and Perspectives of Tourism Policy Makers

Nancy Stevenson

Introduction

Tourism policy making is essentially a social process, involving interactions and negotiation between individuals and groups of people. These interactions are influenced by a wide range of factors and circumstances that occur within the wider policy environment. The social nature of the policy process is underplayed in much tourism policy and planning research, which tends to draw attention to the technical exercises and more tangible elements of policy. In order to develop and deepen understanding about tourism policy making, and to connect policy making to its wider societal context, research is required to consider policy making from the perceptions of the policy makers themselves.

This chapter discusses the development of a research strategy to investigate the practice of tourism policy making using the perspectives of people involved in that process. It is designed to acknowledge the array of contextual factors affecting tourism policy in the 'real world'. It has been developed in the belief that thinking about complex phenomena should be supported by a research strategy that is capable of taking account of complexity and multiple perspectives. The strategy draws from grounded theory on the basis that it has a methodological 'fit' with questions about policy context and has the potential to generate a richness of data to enhance knowledge from a ground level perspective.

Background

The researcher undertook a survey of English local authorities in 2000 (Stevenson & Lovatt, 2001), which relied on a questionnaire as a research instrument and was developed within the quantitative/positivist tradition. This survey focussed the tangible elements of policy making in English local authorities including the structures, policies, research and budgets and provided descriptive statistical information. Analysis of this material highlighted a number of paradoxes, inconsistencies and a complex array of contextual issues affecting tourism policy and planning (Stevenson, 2002).

This study presented an interesting but incomplete picture of the tourism policy process. The methods adopted did not enable investigation into inconsistencies and paradoxes in the data that appeared to arise as a result of contextual factors, communications and a range of human behaviours. The perceived limitations of this survey provided the impetus for a qualitative study to try to develop an understanding of tourism policy making from the perspective of policy makers.

Theory and Discussion Underpinning the Research Strategy

Phillimore and Goodson (2004) suggest that tourism researchers need to move beyond the idea of qualitative research as "a set of methods" and towards a deeper understanding in terms of "a set of thinking tools which enable researchers to consider different ways of approaching research and uncovering new ways of knowing" (2004, p. 15). At the early stages of developing this research strategy, alternative methodological approaches and wider policy research were investigated to determine the best way to develop understanding of a range of complex factors from the perspective of a variety of people. The aim was to develop a study that was 'naturalistic' and 'emergent', exploring issues and data as they unfolded in the 'real world' (Patton, 2002; Phillimore & Goodson, 2004). Grounded theory was selected to underpin the research strategy because it offered a methodology with 'positivist rigour' and enabled the researcher to build theory from the 'bottom-up'. However, a growing interest in the contribution and insights from complexity theory led to some departures from a strict adherence to the grounded methodology.

Complexity Theory

In wider management and policy literature, theorists (such as Sanderson, 2000; Byrne, 2001; Flyvbjerg, 2001; Haynes, 2001; Medd, 2001; Tsoukas & Hatch, 2001; Fonseca, 2002; Mitleton Kelly & Subhan, 2002; Shaw, 2002; Stacey, 2003) are engaged in a debate about whether and how key concepts from complexity 'science' can be applied to human or social interactions. They question the application of scientific approaches to social or human phenomena and consider ways to develop the 'art' of complexity theory and theorising. These authors identify the importance of complexity theory in terms of expanding ways of thinking about change within complex environments. They argue that complex social phenomena are affected by a range of factors, many of which are not tangible, and have developed qualitative approaches to their studies to try to describe and interpret these phenomena.

The work by these authors indicates that the understanding of complex phenomena within social or human systems requires a research methodology that can encompass the inter-relationships, interactions and interconnectivity within complex social environments. This implies the rejection of models and methods that focus our attention on systems or parts of systems and that are 'reductionist', simplifying processes and systems in order to understand them. They argue that a range of tangible and intangible factors affect complex social phenomena. These authors have developed qualitative approaches to focus attention on people who influence those phenomena and interpret their experiences taking account of their complexity.

In the tourism literature Farrell and Twining-Ward (2004), McKercher (1999), Miller and Ritchie (2003), Russell and Faulkner (1999) and Twining Ward (2002), have investigated the application of chaos and complexity theory in tourism. They have started to develop ideas from chaos and complexity theory and have questioned models and conceptual frameworks that reduce and simplify the world in order to try and understand it. In particular McKercher (1999) and Russell and Faulkner (1999) criticise the emphasis of much tourism research on the ordered, and more easily defined aspects of tourism systems, avoiding the more turbulent, complex and human aspects. This work has been developed and carried forward by the development of new theories such as Faulkner's (2001) disaster framework and a wealth of case study research on crises and disaster management (Faulkner & Vikulov, 2001; Coles, 2003; Miller & Ritchie, 2003; Prideaux, 2003).

The contribution of chaos and complexity theory to tourism phenomena is significant but limited. Its significance arises from its role in questioning the rationalism that is dominant in tourism literature. Chaos and complexity theory provide an opportunity for researchers to re-examine the nature of tourism, taking into account the complex interplay between actors or elements in a system. In particular chaos theory is used to identify and research the less predictable and controllable elements of tourism. However chaos and complexity theory have been applied to a comparatively narrow range of tourism issues by relatively few researchers. These studies are largely underpinned by chaos theory and are predominantly grouped around chaotic events or crisis management in tourism (McKercher, 1999; Faulkner & Vikulov, 2001; Miller & Ritchie, 2003) the roles, power and tensions between individuals in the process of destination development (Russell & Faulkner, 1999); and as a way of progressing sustainability research in tourism (Twining-Ward, 2002; Farrell & Twining-Ward, 2004; Miller & Twining-Ward, 2005).

The work of these researchers has brought chaos and complexity theory into tourism literature and has resulted in a shift or progression of thinking at a conceptual level. However, the tourism literature does not investigate the *complexity* of complexity science and the variety of views and interpretations that exist in the complexity literature. These researchers do not clearly identify the debates between different groups of theorists about the chaos and complexity theory (e.g. the Sante Fe group and the Brussels group) and they do not articulate which approach they have adopted.

The tourism literature has not engaged in an explicit discussion about the methodological implications of complexity, which is evident in other fields including strategic management, organisational analysis (Mitleton Kelly & Subhan, 2001; Tsoukas & Hatch, 2001; Fonesca, 2002; Shaw, 2002; Stacey, 2003) and public/social policy analysis (Sanderson, 2000; Byrne, 2001; Flyvbjerg, 2001; Haynes, 2001; Medd, 2001). The implication of lack of debate about methodology in the tourism literature is evidenced by the continued reliance on models that exhibit the same reductionist tendencies as the 'Newtonian' linear models they seek to replace. Examples include McKercher's (1999) chaos model of tourism that explains tourism in terms of complex inter-relationships between nine major elements and Russell and Faulkner's (1999) highly polarised and simplified model to contrast the inclinations of chaos makers and regulators. There is a contradiction between conceptualising tourism using complexity theory and then using a simplified framework or model to explain complex phenomena. This type of theorising is clearly within the positivist frame and is at odds with complexity.

The research strategy outlined in this chapter has been developed to encompass complexity at a methodological level, reflecting the debates and discussion about methodology that are occurring in other areas of policy and organisational research. These debates have influenced the development of a research strategy to research complex human phenomena in a way that captures and takes account of their complexity.

Grounded Theory

The research strategy discussed here has been influenced by grounded theory, a methodological approach developed by Glaser and Strauss in the 1960s, which aims to "bridge the gap between theoretically 'uninformed' empirical research and empirically 'uninformed' theory by grounding theory in data" (Goulding, 2002, p. 41). It provides a systematic procedure for collecting and analysing qualitative data and guides the researcher towards theory building, from description through abstraction to conceptual categorisation. It seeks to predict, explain and provide a perspective on the actions, words and behaviour of those under study (Glaser & Strauss, 1968; Goulding, 2002).

Grounded theory emphasises theory development and building that is "true to the data" (Goulding, 2002, p. 45). Theorists challenge positivist perceptions of theory as "the formulation of some discovered aspect of a pre-existing reality ..." and take the view that "truth is enacted and theories are interpretations made from given perspectives" (2002, p. 43).

Grounded theory is based upon a belief in:

- "the need to get out in the field if one wants to understand what is going on
- the importance of theory grounded in reality
- the nature of experience in the field for the subjects and researcher as continually evolving
- the active role of persons in shaping the worlds they live in through the process of symbolic interaction
- an emphasis on change and process and the variability and complexity of life, and
- the interrelationship between meaning in the perception of subjects and their action" (Glaser, 1992, p. 16).

Grounded theorists engage in debates about method and process with a clarity that is unusual in qualitative method. They establish a collection of rules and procedures for collecting evidence which include:

- the need to study phenomena using the perspectives or voice of those studied;
- the need to collect and analyse data simultaneously and to revisit, add to and refine theory. This includes clear advice on what should happen at different stages of interpretation, including the process of identifying concepts, categories and developing theories;
- the need to collect a range of data including policy documents, secondary data and even statistics providing the information has relevance to the study (Glaser & Strauss, 1968).

Grounded theory is not a tightly integrated theoretical school. The main theorists, Glaser and Strauss initially worked together and then developed their own separate paths to building and refining the theory. Strauss and Corbin (1998) refined grounded theory by introducing a new coding process emphasising conditions, context, action/interaction strategies and consequences. They developed frameworks, matrices and conceptual diagrams as a method to show the relationships between concepts and "to conceptualise beyond the immediate field of study" (Goulding, 2002, p. 45). The main differences between the two approaches are:

> "On the one hand Glaser stresses the interpretive, contextual and emergent nature of theory development, while, on the other the late Strauss appeared to have emphasised highly complex and systematic coding techniques" (Goulding, 2002, p. 47).

Goulding (2002) identifies a number of researchers who have criticised Strauss and Corbin's approach including Coyle (1997) who is critical of the way in which they break down or fragment the idea of theoretical sampling, and proposes that this confuses the issue, and Melia (1996) who argues that the formulistic nature of their work is oriented to description, leads to the over-conceptualisation of single incidents and lacks attention to activities which are associated with theory building.

The most significant critic of the approach advocated by Strauss and Corbin is Glaser who argues that theory should "only explain the phenomena under study" (Goulding, 2002, p. 45) and that their methods propose "so many rules, strictures, dictums and models to follow one can only get lost in trying to figure it all out" (Glaser, 1992, p. 104). Glaser (1992) claims that Strauss's overemphasis on the mechanics of research reduces the degree of theoretical sensitivity and insightful meaning. He is particularly critical of the use of pre-defined matrices, which he claims forces preconceptions on the data and undermines their relevance.

Grounded theory has most frequently been used to investigate behaviour and a wealth of case study material is available on its applications in consumer behaviour/marketing (i.e. Goulding, 2002) and health/medicine (i.e. Coyle, 1997). Much of this research focuses on peoples' motivations and personal experiences and considers the characteristics of individuals and the way that this impacts on their behaviour. The focus of these studies is the individual and the factors that affect human behaviour or motivations in specific settings.

Phillimore and Goodson (2004) suggest that tourism researchers have rarely used the "full grounded theory". They identify a range of tourism research that is influenced by grounded theory including Miller's use of the Delphi technique in 2001 to structure group communication in respect of the development of indicators for sustainable tourism and Burns and Sancho's use of grounded theory in 2003 principles to present and theme oral data from interviews. It is interesting to note that both of these studies are outside the traditional 'behavioural' frame of grounded theory in that they focus on individual's perceptions of ideas or processes rather than their behaviours or motivations.

Grounded theory has not been directly applied to tourism policy research but a number of writers (including Hall & Jenkins, 1995; Elliott, 1997; Hall, Jenkins, & Kearsley, 1997; Bramwell & Sharman, 1999; Hall, 2000; Tyler & Dinan, 2001a, 2001b) have developed work that focuses on the more human and intangible aspect of policy.

The use of grounded theory and concepts from complexity science provides a research strategy that focuses on the context, communications and human behaviours that shape the process rather than the things that have to be done to create written policies. After careful consideration of the aims and nature of the study the decision was made to develop a research strategy drawing from the work of Glaser and Strauss (1968) and the subsequent refinements and clarifications advocated by Glaser (1978, 1992, 1993, 1998). The appeal of this approach is the emphasis on letting the data tell its own story with the focus on the interpretive, contextual and emergent nature of theory.

The Research Process the Theory

The Interview

With grounded theory the most common form of interview is the unstructured or semi-structured conversational interview. These methods are favoured because they have the potential to generate rich and detailed accounts of experience from the perspective of the individual (Goulding, 2002). Unstructured interviewing engenders flexibility and is designed so that questions flow from context. The advantage of this approach is its responsiveness, and the potential it offers for actors to define interests and issues. Difficulties with this approach include the time and number of interviews required before themes emerge, the difficulties in analysing the diversity of material collected and the possibility of 'interviewer effects' such as bias, preconceived ideas and leading questions (Patton, 2002).

In the semi-structured approach, the interviewer identifies subject areas and these are explored with the interviewee. This gives the freedom to develop conversations within the subject areas. It has the advantage that it provides a degree of focus and structure to the interviews and makes the best use of limited time. This approach is more systematic, delimiting in advance issues to be explored (Patton, 2002).

Both the unstructured and the semi-structured interview techniques require the interviewer to play an active role in the research process and to develop qualities of self-awareness and reflexivity (Patton, 2002). Strauss and Corbin (1998) identify 'self' as an instrument of data collection, and highlight the importance of attributes such as authenticity, credibility, intuitiveness, receptivity, reciprocity and sensitivity. Leedy and Ormarod (2001) discuss the role of researcher as a research instrument during interviews highlighting the need for "a rigorous spirit of self awareness and self criticism, as well as openness to new ideas" (2001, p. 147).

Developing Theory

Grounded theory evolves during the process of field research, and is produced by the continuous interplay between data collection and analysis (Glaser & Strauss, 1968; Glaser, 1978; Strauss & Corbin, 1998; Goulding, 2002). A grounded approach involves the collection and analysis of data at the same time. Glaser says, "the process of data collection is 'controlled' by emerging theory" (1978, p. 38) which means that the nature of the study changes over the research period on the basis of the emerging data.

Grounded theorists and researchers have adopted different approaches to conceptualising and operationalising the grounded method and in this sense the method has been rewritten and evolved over time. Goulding (2002) identifies several 'constants' in the methodology as it has evolved including,

> "the constant comparison of data to develop concepts and categories;
> the gradual abstraction of data from the descriptive level to higher order

theoretical categories … the use of theoretical sampling as opposed to pur-
posive sampling, the writing of theoretical memos which help track the
process and provide a sense of reorientation and the saturation of data"
requiring the researcher to "stay in the field until no new evidence emerges"
(2002, p. 46).

Goulding (2002) identifies the use of memos throughout the research process as a central
part of grounded theory method. Memos provide a 'bank of ideas' (2002, p. 65) that have
been noted during data collection and create a way of mapping these ideas to illustrate the
journey toward the emergence of theory. Memos can be used to help the researcher to identify concepts, refine those concepts and generate relationships using the data. They also
provide a useful way of noting ideas outside of the data and identifying how these are used
to clarify relationships or provide direction to the coding process.

Coding Strategies

In grounded theory coding strategies are adopted as a way of breaking down interviews
and other appropriate data into "distinct units of meaning" (Goulding, 2002, p. 74). The
first stage of this process, called open coding, aims to open up the interview data. Open
coding fragments data, identifies concepts and uses constant comparison to scrutinise the
data for every meaning (Glaser, 1992).

"Open coding is the process of breaking down the data into distinct units of
meaning. It is the product of early analysis and describes what is happening in the data. Open codes may comprise key words, phrases or sentences"
(Goulding, 2002, p. 170).

Goulding (2002, p.169) defines constant comparison as "the exploration of similarities and
differences across incidents in data". Glaser (1992) says that this part of the coding process
is a fundamental part of the method and is where incidents are coded for properties and
categories that connect them together. These initial codes are labelled "to generate concepts"
which are "clustered into descriptive categories" (Goulding, 2002, p. 74). Once concepts
have been identified they are analysed in more depth and are grouped under more abstracted
'higher order' concepts. At this stage incidents are compared within the data and between
the data to incidents recalled from experience or from the literature. This process of
'systematic comparison' sensitises the researcher to properties and dimensions in the data
that might have been overlooked (Strauss & Corbin, 1998).

Axial coding is described by Goulding (2002, p. 169) as "a more sophisticated method
of coding data which seeks to identify incidents which have a relationship to each other"
and to reassemble data "that were fractured during open coding" (Strauss & Corbin, 1998,
p. 124). Axial coding is an important method to achieve a higher level of abstraction that
aims to lead to an appreciation of dynamic interrelationships between concepts (Glaser,
1992; Goulding, 2002). At this stage the descriptive codes become subsumed into a higher
order category, which unites "the theoretical concepts to offer an explanation or theory of
the phenomenon" (Goulding, 2002, p. 169).

Writing Up

Glaser (1978) advises that in grounded theory the style of writing should follow the conventions of the 'sociological monograph' with an introduction outlining the general problem, the methodology, a prose outline of the substantive theory and then the theory. He advises that the introduction should not derive the problem from a general perspective or from a literature search but should be derived from the grounded theory that has been generated in the research. Glaser suggests that by the writing up stage, the researcher has captured the meaning of the data through extensive 'sorting' of memo's and this stage is merely writing up piles of sorted memos. He refers to the need to 'funnel down' to the core relevance and highlights the need to "*write conceptually* by making theoretical statements about the relationship between concepts, rather than writing descriptive statements about people" (1978, p. 133).

A number of complexity theorists including Stacey (2003) Mitleton Kelly and Subhan (2002) develop 'narratives' as a way of bringing together themes using the experience, definitions and understanding of those involved in the policy process. A narrative is "… a story line linked by reflections, comments upon and categorisations of, elements of the story line" (Stacey, 2003, p. 350). Narratives provide a way of creating "… meanings by bringing things into relation, by making connections, by drawing attention in one way or another so as to create a pathway in time, a train of events" (Flyvbjerg, 2001, p. 27). They are "accounts which contain transformation (change over time) … they have an overall plot and are a central means with which people connect together past and present, self and other" (Lawler, 2002, p. 242).

Tsoukas and Hatch (2001) contend that narratives allow the reader to explore some material first hand and let the story unfold but give the narrator a clear role in linking, reflecting upon and categorising elements of the story. In developing a narrative the researcher becomes involved in the story rather than trying to stand outside and observe what happens in a scientific way. Narratives provide a way for the narrator to become involved in the process, a way of 'dissolving' categories and of recognising and of accepting the paradoxes inevitably created in complex social environments (Shaw, 2002). Narratives work from the premise that "individuals and groups interpret the social world and their place within it" (Lawler, 2002, p. 243). They allow the story to unfold from multiple perspectives of the people involved which are diverse, complex and sometimes conflicting and attempt to capture the depth and richness of the experience (Flyvbjerg, 2001; Mitleton Kelly & Subhan, 2002).

From Theory to Practice — Developing and Implementing the Research Strategy

The first issue that arose in developing a 'pure' grounded approach was the researcher's prior knowledge and experience of tourism policy making. Glaser says,

> "The first step in grounded theory is to enter the substantive field for research without knowing the problem" (1998, p. 122).

The researcher's degree of familiarity with policy theories and practical experience in the field meant that she had some awareness and preconceptions of the problem. It was the prior experience and research that had led to her adopting a social conceptualisation of the policy process and the impetus for a study focussed on practice from the perspectives of policy makers. This led to the exploration of theories and methodologies in the search for a methodology that could encompass the societal context, multiple perspectives and complexity of tourism policy making. Whilst it could be argued that the researcher was moving beyond the boundaries of her existing knowledge by researching policy making in a different way, it was difficult completely to suspend prior knowledge.

The researcher endeavoured to approach this study with openness and with a willingness to challenge her pre-conceptions. She attempted to limit the impact of her existing knowledge in the field and during the interviews she was careful not to ask leading questions. She also made the decision not to develop a formal literature review until the codes and themes had been developed and the emerging theory had some substance. In practice the narratives were used to explore the relationships between concepts, to identify themes and to present the substance of the emerging theory to the reader. After the narratives were written a formal literature review took place, drawing on existing ideas and refining the emerging theory further.

The Interviews

The research strategy involved the adoption of a series of semi-structured interviews around a series of broad topics. The interviewees were asked to identify the issues and interactions influencing the tourism policy process in their experience. Their responses usually led to reflections about key people, the place of tourism within local authority policy making, the political will to make tourism policy, the networks and joint arrangements to deliver tourism policies but where they did not cover all of these areas the interviewer made a broad inquiry into that aspect. At the end of each interview the interviewee was asked if there were any other important issues that had not been discussed. This gave them the scope to broaden out the frame of reference and introduce new themes.

Interviews were carried out in three phases, the first two in geographically distinct areas and the third as a follow up in one of the study areas. The third phase was developed a year after the first. It aimed to clarify and elaborate ideas discussed at first meeting and to identify new issues and themes that had emerged during the year. It was loosely structured around the researcher's conceptualisation of themes identified in the first and second stage interviews. Interviewees were invited to discuss and comment on the themes and other interpretations arising from these interviews. This enabled reflection between the researcher and interviewee and provided opportunities to revise interpretations. This constant checking meant that interpretation of data was an ongoing and two way process.

The rolling programme of interviews was designed towards thick description and the approach adopted enabled the researcher to move back and forth between inductive open-ended encounters with interviewees to more deductive attempts to theme ideas. The inductive approach was used to ascertain the dimensions of the study but after each stage of interviewing a more deductive approach was used to theme ideas and "solidify ideas that emerge from those more open-ended experiences..." (Patton, 2002, p. 253).

The first interview was not taped in accordance with advice from Glaser (1998) that taping interviews slows down coding and analysing, edits the truth and generates superficial responses. Notes were taken during the interview and were written up immediately after.

The researcher noted that it was extremely difficult to develop sufficient rapport or engagement with the interviewee whilst trying to write detailed and useful notes. The researcher was concerned that she was not sufficiently skilled to take objective and accurate notes whilst trying to maintain the conventions of a conversation, such as eye contact, responding to facial expressions and humour. Also she was concerned that her listening and note taking might be more intense when the interviewee said things she expected to hear.

After the first interview, the decision was made to tape the remainder of the interviews so that a verbal record of the full interview was available and the researcher could revisit this information during the research process. The decision to tape had a number of advantages including the ability to engage and converse with interviewees, to establish rapport, and to probe and clarify issues as they emerged in the conversation. The act of transcribing led to direct engagement with the interview and enabled thoughts and concepts to develop about the material. Memos were written to capture these thoughts. At the end of the transcription process data were held in several forms, written data was used to code in a formalised way and taped data provided conversational nuances and helped to clarify the meaning of comments within interviews.

Method of Analysis

The research strategy called for manual analysis on the basis that the study topic and methodology required the researcher to immerse herself in the data. This immersion meant repeatedly revisiting the data and ideas throughout the research process, reconsidering them and recoding to capture patterns or themes as they emerged. Data collection and analysis happened concurrently and knowledge was drawn from outside of the text of the transcribed interviews by personal reflections in the memos. After the findings had been written up in two narratives, a literature review was developed to draw in wider knowledge to the analytical process.

The analysis process started from full transcription of the first phase interviews, and segments of text were colour coded by hand. Then line-by-line analysis was used to identify key words or phrases connecting the account to the experience under investigation. This process enabled the creation of a basic set of coding categories developed from the content of the interviews. Once a basic preliminary coding had taken place the transcripts were re-read and the tapes listened to again. During this process memos were written to document impressions and codes and categories were generated and reviewed. This process led to the broad codes being modified to take account of reflection and consideration of incidents across the interviews.

The coding was used to identify patterns and recurring events in the data and to compare data from each respondent across the case study area. In considering the interpretations by respondents, similarities were noted in the way their experiences were shared and expressed about the tourism policy and its context. Through this process of coding, conceptualising and theming a number of core variables were identified and these were used as a structure for subsequent interviews. The second and third phase interviews were then transcribed and analysed in the same way and patterns or themes started to emerge. Open coding was used to break down data into distinct units of meaning and these units were then labelled to generate concepts. Axial coding was used to cluster concepts into groups that seem to indicate a relationship that said something about the phenomena under study (Glaser, 1992; Goulding, 2002).

Constant comparative analysis enabled the researcher to develop the codes further as the process continued which directed further data collection. The process involved a mixture of induction and deduction, allowing for flexibility through the research process and focussed on what was happening in the field rather than what should be happening (Glaser, 1978; Coyle, 1997; Strauss & Corbin, 1998; Goulding, 2002).

In developing a style for writing memos, initially a mixture of informal jottings and a formal structure was used, and comparisons between the two methods were made. Memos were not standardised but an attempt was made to title them. Memos were reviewed in terms of their content and reflexivity after each batch of interviews, after the findings had been written up and again during the literature review.

Writing Up

The narrative approach was favoured as it enabled the study of the dynamic of the policy process in a way that acknowledged its complexity, its environment and the multiple voices of the interviewees. In developing a narrative approach it was intended to reflect the social context of policy making, and create meaning and connection. The narrative approach enabled the researcher to discuss her findings and ideas within the context of multiple interpretations of data, rather than presenting consensus around her ideas.

This represented a slight departure from the grounded approach advocated by Glaser (1978, 1992, 1993, 1998) and Glaser and Strauss (1968) on the basis that the narratives presented 'emerging' theory derived directly from the fieldwork data. This approach was adopted to illustrate the multiple voices of the policy makers and complexity underlying the emerging theory. Once the narratives had been written, the literature review was undertaken and was used conceptually to connect the emerging theory from the policy makers to existing theory in the field. The decision to present the emerging theory was based on the researcher's aspiration to present the process of theory development with as much transparency as possible. She also wanted to make a clear distinction to the reader between the theory that was derived from the data and the refined theory that connected into existing policy theory.

Conclusion

The research strategy outlined in this chapter has been developed in the belief that thinking about complex phenomena should be supported by a methodology that is capable of taking account of complexity and multiple perspectives. It is designed to encompass complexity at a methodological level reflecting the debates and discussion in other areas of policy and organisational research. It is intended to generate a richness of data, to enhance knowledge from a ground level perspective and encourage thinking outside the positivist frame (by taking account of complexity and context). It represents an attempt to gain a broader perspective of tourism policy making than is provided by theory that focuses on physical manifestations such as written policies and technical processes.

The conceptualisation of policy as something that emerges from human action and interaction rather than as procedures, techniques or tangible policies, has implications on the design of research strategy. The conceptualisation of tourism policy making as a complex phenomenon, which is embedded within a wide range of social processes adds a further dimension to the study. Grounded theory has been chosen to underpin the research and offers a way to theorise about tourism policy from the experiences and perceptions of policy makers' perceptions. Attention has been given to contributions from complexity theory and in portraying complex issues in their complex or multi-faceted form (in this study from the multiple perspectives of those people involved in the tourism policy process).

The intention in developing this strategy is to develop and deepen understanding of the relationship between tourism policy and its context stemming from actors perceptions of issues and processes. The study is concerned with documenting and analysing the 'realities' of the relationship from the perspectives of the practitioner and developing understanding from the 'bottom-up'. The research strategy underpins a study into what happens from the practitioner's perspective and through the coding, concept analysis, theming and writing up, leads to the development of theory.

Acknowledgements

To David Airey and Graham Miller who supervised my Ph.D. and provided invaluable advice and to Maria Di Domenico, for providing guidance at the early stages of this research.

References

Bramwell, B., & Sharman, A. (1999). Collaboration in local tourism policymaking. *Annals of Tourism Research, 26*(2), 392–415.
Byrne, D. (2001). Complexity science and transformation in social policy. *Social Issues, 1*(2) http:/www.whb.co.uk/socialissues/db.htm (last accessed on 24th November 2006).
Coles, T. (2003). A local reading of a global disaster: Some lessons on tourism management from an annus horribilis. *Journal of Travel and Tourism Marketing, 15*(2–4), 173–198.
Coyle, I. T. (1997). Sampling in qualitative research: Purposeful and theoretical sampling: Merging or clear boundaries? *Journal of Advanced Nursing, 26*(3), 623–630.
Elliott, J. (1997). *Tourism: Politics and public sector management*. London: Routledge.
Farrell, B., & Twining-Ward, L. (2004). Reconceptualizing tourism. *Annals of Tourism Research, 21*(2), 274–295.
Faulkner, B. (2001). Towards a framework for tourism disaster management. *Tourism Management, 22*(2), 135–147.
Faulkner, B., & Vikulov, S. (2001). Katherine washed out one day, back on track the next: A post mortem of a tourism disaster. *Tourism Management, 22*(4), 331–344.
Flyvbjerg, B. (2001). *Making social science matter*. Cambridge: Cambridge University Press.
Fonseca, J. (2002). *Complexity and innovation in organisations*. London: Routledge.
Glaser, B. (1978). *Theoretical sensitivity*. Mill Valley, CA: Sociology Press.
Glaser, B. (1992). *Basics of grounded theory analysis: Emergence vs. forcing*. Mill Valley, CA: Sociology Press.
Glaser, B. (1993). *Examples of grounded theory: A reader*. Mill Valley, CA: Sociology Press.
Glaser, B. (1998). *Doing grounded theory: Issues and discussions*. Mill Valley, CA: Sociology Press.
Glaser, B., & Strauss, A. (1968). *The discovery of grounded theory: Strategies for qualitative research*. London: Weidenfeld and Nicholson.

Goulding, C. (2002). *Grounded theory: A practical guide for management, business and market researchers*. London: Sage.

Hall, C. M. (2000). *Tourism planning: Politics, process and relationships*. Harlow: Prentice Hall.

Hall, C. M., & Jenkins, J. (1995). *Tourism and public policy*. London: Routledge.

Hall, C. M., Jenkins, J., & Kearsley, G. (1997). *Tourism planning and policy in Australia and New Zealand*. Sydney: Irwin.

Haynes, P. (2001). Complexity, quantification and research for the management of policy. *Social Issues, 1*(2). http:/www.whb.co.uk/socialissues/ph.htm (last accessed on 24th November 2006).

Lawler, S. (2002). Narrative in social research. In: T. May (Ed.), *Qualitative research in action* (pp. 242–258). London: Sage.

Leedy, P., & Ormarod, J. (2001). *Practical research planning and design* (7th ed.). Upper Saddle River: Prentice Hall.

McKercher, R. (1999). A chaos approach to tourism. *Tourism Management, 20*(3), 425–434.

Medd, W. (2001). Complexity and the policy process. *Social Issues, 1*(2). http:/www.whb.co.uk/socialissues/wm.htm (last accessed on 24th November 2006).

Melia, K. M. (1996). Rediscovering Glaser. *Qualitative Health Research, 6*(3), 368–378.

Miller, G., & Ritchie, B. (2003). A farming crises or a tourism disaster? An analysis of the foot and mouth disease in the U.K. *Current Issues in Tourism, 5*(3/4), 1–22.

Miller, G., & Twining-Ward, L. (2005). *Monitoring for a sustainable tourism transition*. Wallingford: CABI.

Mitleton Kelly, E., & Subhan, N. (2002). *Experiencing complexity thinking in practice (a narrative)*. London: LSE Complexity Research Programme.

Patton, M. Q. (2002). *Qualitative research and evaluation methods* (3rd ed.). Thousand Oaks California. London: Sage.

Phillimore, J., & Goodson, L. (Eds.) (2004). *Qualitative research in tourism: Ontologies, epistemologies and methodologies*. London: Routledge.

Prideaux, B. (2003). The need to use disaster planning frameworks to respond to major tourism disasters: Analysis of Australia's response to tourism disasters in 2001. *Journal of Travel and Tourism Marketing, 15*(4), 281–298.

Russell, R., & Faulkner, B. (1999). Movers and shakers: Chaos makers in tourism development. *Tourism Management, 20*(3), 411–423.

Sanderson, I. (2000). Evaluation in complex policy systems. *Evaluation, 6*(4), 433–454.

Shaw, P. (2002). *Changing conversations in organisations: A complexity approach to change*. London: Routledge.

Stacey, R. (2003). *Strategic management and organisational dynamics — The challenge of complexity*. Harlow: Prentice Hall.

Stevenson, N. (2002). The role of English local authorities in tourism. *Insights ETC, 4*, A107.

Stevenson, N., & Lovatt, S. (2001). *The role of English local authorities in tourism survey 2000*. Unpublished research report. University of Westminster, London.

Strauss, A., & Corbin, J. (1998). *Basics of qualitative research — Techniques and procedures for developing grounded theory* (2nd ed.). Thousand Oaks, CA; London: Sage.

Tsoukas, H., & Hatch, M. (2001). Complex thinking, complex practice: The case for a narrative approach to organisational complexity. *Human Relations, 54*(8), 979.

Twining-Ward, L. (2002). *Monitoring sustainable tourism development: A comprehensive, stakeholder-driven, adaptive approach*. Unpublished doctoral dissertation. University of Surrey, Guildford.

Tyler, D., & Dinan, C. (2001a). The role of interested groups in England's emerging tourism policy network. *Current Issues in Tourism, 4*(2–4), 210–253.

Tyler, D., & Dinan, C. (2001b). Trade and associated groups in the English tourism policy arena. *International Journal of Tourism Research, 3*, 459–467.

Chapter 14

Network Analysis as a Research Tool for Understanding Tourism Destinations

Noel Scott and Chris Cooper

Introduction

This paper reports on research into the inter-organizational network connecting key tourism organizations in tourism regions of Australia. In this study, social network analysis techniques (Mitchell, 1969; Burt & Minor, 1983; Knoke, 1993; Wassermann & Faust, 1994; Scott, 2002) were used to examine the relationship between key members of Regional Tourism Organizations (RTOs). The research reported here is part of a larger study funded by Tourism Queensland and the Cooperative Research Centre for Sustainable Tourism.

Tourism involves the joint production of a 'product' through the interaction of organizations including attractions, hotels, transport, national park agencies, and others. This interaction highlights the importance of being able to describe and analyze the organization of tourism in a region and a number of approaches have been used. The organization of tourism production has been considered previously from a systems perspective (Leiper, 1989), as derived from life-cycle processes and subject to modification due to post-stagnation effects (Agarwal, 2002) and through the use of concepts of collaboration and cooperation of individual stakeholders among other approaches (Selin & Chavez, 1995; Hall, 1999; Bramwell & Lane, 2000; Selin, 2000; Pavlovich, 2001, 2003a). The social network approach emphasizes the systemic and interaction effects between tourism organizations.

The analysis of networks of social entities (*viz.* social network analysis) dates back to the sociological writings of Simmel (1908); the social anthropological work of Radcliffe Brown (1935); and more recently Barnes' (1952) work on the sociology of a Norwegian island parish is credited with the post-war resurgence of the approach. These writers share a structural view of social interaction highlighting the importance of social organizations, relationships and interactions in influencing individual decisions, beliefs and behaviour (Scott, 2000). Here, network structures are seen as recurring patterns of social relationships rather than focusing on the attributes and actions of single individuals or organizations (Brinton Milward & Provan, 1998). Social network analysis identifies and measures

Developments in Tourism Research
Copyright © 2007 by Elsevier Ltd.
All rights of reproduction in any form reserved.
ISBN: 978-0-080-45328-6

the causal pressures that are inherent in social structures and is therefore ideally suited to the analysis of tourism destinations (Tremblay, 1998).

While the tourism sector is appropriate for the study of the structure of inter-organizational relationships, there has been little use of social network analysis techniques. Despite the concept of networks being discussed in the tourism literature (Copp & Ivy, 2001; Halme, 2001; Tinsley & Lynch, 2001; Tyler & Dinan, 2001), few studies have used formal social network analysis techniques. An exception is the use of social network analysis to study planning decision making in the Northern Territory of Australia (Pforr, 2002b).

In analyzing these systems of organizations as networks, there are three basic elements of interest: actors, relationships and resources (Knoke & Kuklinski, 1991). Firstly, actors perform activities in relationship with other actors and control network resources. These actors can be of different sizes and are generally considered as highly diverse. Secondly, relationships may be considered as transactions between actors involving the transformation of resources. Such relationships are the building blocks of network analysis. Indeed, a network is generally defined by a specific type of relation linking a defined set of persons, objects or events (Mitchell, 1969). The resources that are exchanged among actors represent the third element of a network. These resources may include knowledge or money. Together these three elements define an actor network where the actor is linked together with all of its influencing factors to produce the network.

Networks and Destinations

Network analysis can therefore deliver a number of useful outcomes for the analysis of tourism destinations. It provides a means of visualizing complex sets of relationships and simplifying them, and so can be useful in promoting effective collaboration within a destination actor set. It also allows the identification of critical junctures in destination networks that cross functional, hierarchical or geographic boundaries (Cross, Borgatti, & Parker, 2002). Finally, the use of standard network-analysis methods enables the comparative study of the evolution and overall efficiency of destination networks.

For tourism, Tremblay (1999) identifies three types of network. The first of these is an innovative milieu where organizations share complementary assets such as the destination-based coordination of suppliers. This will include organizations holding similar technological capabilities but servicing different markets and in different destinations including airline alliances and hotel consortia. Secondly, organizations may share marketing knowledge of specific customer segments and so cross-functional coordination is achieved to deliver the product. Here, tourism examples include the vertical and horizontal integration strategies of larger companies. The third type is a networks coordinating complementary assets at the destination level. This includes destination marketing alliances and promotion (a common approach in the past) and the more recent approach of jointly shaping new products and innovation. These local destination-based networks are critical in balancing the interests of various stakeholders and boost destination competitiveness by linking the myriad fragmented elements of the destination. Tourism businesses then strategically position themselves within the network to leverage from innovation and future organizational configurations.

Elements of Destination Networks

Nodes   The nodes of any destination network can be thought of as stakeholders, of varying size, cooperating to compete, as a direct response to an externally turbulent environment (Tremblay, 1999; Wilkinson, Mattsson, & Easton, 2000). Here the strategy of an organization embedding within a destination network delivers security as stakeholders develop and maintain effective relationships with the other destination organizations upon which they depend. These relationships display varying degrees of formality and complexity ranging from close, cooperative relationships to the more distant (Pavlovich, 2003b). The nature of stakeholder relationships also influences the overall efficiency of the network. For example, an overemphasis on either competitors or complementary stakeholders reduces network efficiency.

A stakeholder's position within a destination network depends upon the number of its relationships and its role in the network (Wilkinson et al., 2000). Stakeholders gain power from their position within a network, and, the more centrally located the stakeholder, the stronger the power and influence of that organization within the destination (Pavlovich, 2003a). In turn, weaker organizations can develop ties with central ones to leverage benefits.

Relationships   The topology of a network suggests that events closer in space and time to the actor are more influential than distant ones, and so there is a separation of scales and process. Pavlovich (2003a) conceptualizes this by viewing the links between stakeholders as either weak or strong. According to Pavlovich (2003a), strong ties encourage conformity, acceptable action and inclusion and so they encourage destination network cohesion. Weak ties on the other hand, can exclude other stakeholders and tend to act as bridges to those stakeholders who are external to the network. As such, they play an important role in importing new information into the network and therefore underpin innovation. An optimally efficient network comprises both weak and strong ties, although a dominance of either type will weaken a network (Welch, Welch, Young, & Wilkinson, 1998). Pavlovich (2003a) uses the example of Waitomo Caves in New Zealand to show how weak relational ties within a destination lead to limited resource and information flows, but that stakeholders can transform networks as they evolve and improve strong ties. For weak ties, the geographical location of the destination network also influences its ability to build effective external relationships (Wilkinson et al., 2000). This can be aided by the presence of international organizations (such as hotel chains) within a network, where other stakeholders can benefit from links to external networks.

Network Analysis for Destinations

While network analysis has a long pedigree in the social sciences, it has seldom been used as an analytical framework for destinations, with the notable exceptions of Pavlovich (2001, 2003a, 2003b), Pforr (2002a) and Tremblay (1999). Yet, the approach is highly appropriate as an analytical tool for destinations for a number of reasons. Firstly, tourism more than most economic sectors, involves the development of formal and informal collaboration, partnerships and networks (Selin & Chavez, 1995; Hall, 1999; Bramwell & Lane, 2000; Selin, 2000; Copp & Ivy, 2001; Halme, 2001; Tinsley & Lynch, 2001; Tyler & Dinan, 2001). In other words, destinations can be viewed as loosely articulated groups of independent suppliers who link together to deliver the overall product. Here, network analysis can provide useful insights on the structure and behaviour of destinations and can be used to recommend strengthening of links and coordination between destination organizations.

Secondly, network analysis delivers a flexible tool with which to analyze the dynamics of destinations as they operate within a turbulent and shifting system. Destinations represent networks of cooperative and competitive linkages and are fashioned by both their internal capabilities and those of the external environment (Tremblay, 1999). Tremblay sees this as a 'proto-commodity' and argues that it characterizes tourism at a stage in evolution, which will lead eventually to a more coordinated and integrated industrialized sector.

Thirdly, network analysis provides insights into the behaviour of destinations. Networks themselves have loose governance systems, which, at the destination level, act as an alterative to the public sector. The behaviour of destination networks acts to encourage cooperative ventures and to avoid cut-throat competition, allowing stakeholders to find a balance between competition and innovation. For tourism destinations, an important notion is that of networks having their own embedded macro-culture, with the behaviour of suppliers reflecting the branding, symbols and images of the destination environment (Pavlovich, 2001). Network analysis can therefore assist in the understanding of complex stakeholder tourism environments and their governance, as outlined below.

Fourthly, network analysis provides insights as to how a destination network can become more efficient in terms of linkage and coordination. For destination networks, policy can be effective in increasing the efficiency of the overall network through strengthening links, reducing barriers and encouraging stakeholders to share information (Wilkinson et al., 2000). Policy formation in this area tends to draw heavily on policies devised for research and development where innovation and knowledge sharing is encouraged, in this case across a network of organizations. Effectively, efficient networks, which deliver competitive destinations, become the outcomes of policy (Welch et al., 1998).

Finally, network analysis neatly sidesteps the problem of defining the spatial boundaries of destinations (Framke, 2002). Network analysis provides an alternative view to that of the 'bounded' destination, as the extent of the network links defines the spatial extent of the destination, supporting Thrift's (1996) contention that regions, or destinations, are not places but instead, settings for interactions.

Method

The fundamental difference between social network analysis and more traditional methods for understanding organizational networks is that it depends on relational rather than attribute data. The presence and nature of a relationship between actors is the focus, rather than the characteristics of each individual actor. Before collecting data, a network researcher must decide the most relevant type of social organization to be studied and the units within that social organization that will comprise the network nodes. Possible social organizations for study include individuals, aggregates of individuals, organizations, classes and strata, communities and nations.

A network researcher also needs to specify the transactional content of the interaction to be studied. Transactional content refers to what is exchanged when two actors are linked. Different types of transactional contents can be distinguished such as exchange of affect (liking, friendship), exchange of influence or power, exchange of information, and exchange of resources goods or services. Szarka (1990), for example, discusses three types of network linkages among small business based on social interaction, business communication and transactional exchange.

The nature of the linkages between pairs of individuals can be described in several ways such as intensity or reciprocity. Intensity is the strength of the relation as indicated by the degree to which individuals honour obligations or forego personal costs to carry out obligations (Mitchell, 1969), or by the number of contacts in a unit of time. Reciprocity is the degree to which individuals report the same (or similar) intensities with each other for a content area. In a classic study Granovetter (1973) discussed the strength of weak ties, highlighting the importance of social relationships in addition to formal business ties.

The structural characteristics studied may be at a number of levels of analysis. The total network involves study of a given a set of actors that make up the network and the ways they are linked. Alternatively an ego network may be studied to define the set of links between one node and all the others to which it is joined. Between these is the study of clusters (groups of closely linked actors), coalitions (temporary alliance of actors who come together for a limited purpose) and cliques (more permanent informal associations and exist for a broader range of purposes).

In developing a social network analysis it is important to ensure the scope of the investigation is delimited by specification of system boundaries (Thatcher, 1998). Determining a boundary for a network study may be done by alternatively focusing on the organizations, their relations (Knoke, 1993) or critical policy events (Pforr, 2002b). Thus we may focus on actors sharing a common goal or use actors located within geographical limits (Laumann, Galaskiewicz, & Marsden, 1978, p. 460). The idea of focusing on actors within a geographical area is related to the study of clusters or industrial districts as these also have a geographical basis.

Within this boundary the actors to be interviewed must be identified. It may be that all actors within a specified boundary are interviewed but resource limitations usually mean that certain section rules are used. One common method is to distinguish between actors on the basis of their degree of influence and leads to the use of key stakeholders. Various methods and approaches have been used to identify key stakeholders, for example, position approach, reputation method and decision method or participation/relational methods (Tichy, Tushman, & Fombrum, 1979; Knoke & Kuklinski, 1991; Thatcher, 1998). Each of these approaches has strengths and weaknesses as discussed in Tichy et al. (1979).

Once a domain and sample have been identified, data collection can proceed. The data sources that may be used for social network analysis are as diverse as in other areas of social research. One tourism study used archival analysis to identify respondents followed by a mail questionnaire (Pforr, 2002b). Problems with data collection are also similar to those in other areas of the social sciences although particular problems may be experienced in quantification of relationships and also different types of relationships may be intertwined (Thatcher, 1998).

In this study, the frequency of contact between organizations was used as a first operationalization of the relationship between organizations. The survey collected information on the relationships among these respondents by asking with which other of the key tourist organizations identified did they exchange information.

Data Collection

The sampling of organizations for this study was based on identification of key tourism sector stakeholders using the reputation method. Based on initial discussions with staff from state tourism organizations and further snowball sampling, key organizations were identified and interviewed. This method allows prioritisation of key stakeholders for contact based on the number of times each is mentioned. It also allows the number of interviews in each region to be reduced to a manageable number. Efforts were made to obtain comments from each of these organizations about the other organizations as well as other organizations were considered to be important. In addition, during the study, organizations from outside the region were identified but not interviewed. While these numbers are small, these respondents were perceived as the key stakeholders in the region. A telephone contact method was used to collect data from a random sample of tourism operators selected from the members of the regional tourism organization.

While it may be argued that the sample is not statistically significant, this is not particularly relevant to the study conducted here. The aim of the study is to find those organizations that make a difference in tourism region. The owner or manager of each organization was interviewed face to face with the interviews taking around one hour. A written questionnaire was used and respondents were asked a series of semi-structured questions concerning the organizations they had relationships with, the frequency of interaction and the type of interaction (i.e., planning, marketing, special projects). Data was collected using predetermined code frames.

Visualizing Social Network Data

In analysing network data, techniques are used to establish the network position of stakeholders and the relationships between them using indicators such as intensity of communication, reputation or resources (Thatcher, 1998, p. 399). One approach to analysis is visualization (Brandes, Kenis, Raab, Schneider, & Wagner, 1999) Graphical displays are particularly attractive since they efficiently display the relevant actors in a network and how the actors relate to each other. Relationships may be reciprocal or directed, in which case, an arrow is used to indicate the direction of a relationship.

A number of different techniques may be used to display data from the use of hand-drawn relational 'maps' to diagrams derived using sophisticated statistical techniques. One conceptually simple heuristic for displaying relationships is the Spring Embedder technique (Eades, 1984). This is a heuristic for laying out arbitrary kinds of networks with the idea being to consider the nodes of the network to be repelling rings. Those linked are joined by a spring and a positioning with the lowest forces exerted on the rings is sought. The resultant diagram is interpreted visually. A number of computer software packages are available to map relational data (Scott, 1996).

Analysis of the coded data files was made using the relationship network programs, Ucinet 6 (Borgatti, Everett, & Freeman, 1999) and Pajek. These programs require data to be presented as a list of all the relationships reported between organizations. Thus, if organization A reports relationships to organizations B and C; the data would be entered as AB and AC. These social network analysis software programs then are used to show all these relationships as a network. The results of the analysis may be illustrated as a series of network diagrams that show the key organizations as nodes and the relationships between them as lines. These network patterns may be subject to both visual and statistical analysis.

The result is a graph (i.e., Figure 14.1) showing a number of nodes representing the organizations interviewed in this study. Each node is connected to one or more other nodes by lines representing reported frequency of communication between those two organizations for tourism purposes. These graphs are produced with no intervention by the analyst. The position of each organization is derived from the number of links and those of the other organizations to which it has links. The figure produced provides a picture of the social relationship network between organizations interviewed in the region.

Relationships Between Tourism Organizations in Victorian Destinations

The Victorian study shows how network analysis provides insights into the functioning of tourism destinations. In Victoria, sectoral organizations appear to play an important role in tourism networks. Tourism in Victoria, and especially in rural Victoria, started earlier than in most other states. As a result, organizations involved in tourism are well established and

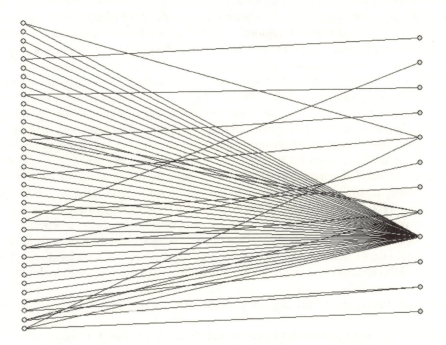

Figure 14.1: Social networks reported in Geelong-Otway Shire.

include camping and caravan parks, automobile-related tourism, hotels and other traditional components of tourism. Similarly, local government has been aware of, and has been involved in tourism for the economic development of the area for many years. This means that the more recent development of integrated tourism management across regions of Victoria is politically and organizationally difficult, as this is being imposed upon an already functioning network structure. For example, whilst the study unsurprisingly found the peak tourism body in planning, marketing and promotion to be the state tourism organization, Tourism Victoria, it also showed that the Automobile Association in Victoria has a strong central role in the network. The study also examined vertical relationships in the network between organizations operating at a regional level (operators and RTOs) and the state-wide organizations (such as Tourism Victoria or sectoral organizations). The results highlighted two network issues. Firstly, the central importance of state-wide bodies such as the Royal Automobile Club of Victoria for regional operators in addition to the expected importance of Tourism Victoria. Secondly, the analysis highlighted the fact that few of the state-wide sectoral organizations had any links to RTOs. Indeed, some of the sectoral organizations had regional organizations of their own (e.g., The Australian Hotels Association). Generally, where there were links between sectoral organizations and RTOs it was limited to particular locations. This failure in the network has led to difficulties in the ability to strategically manage tourism across the state and resulted in a series of common issues across organizations (Table 14.1).

At the shire level, it is evident that there are differences between shires in the organization of marketing and planning contacts. This means that some regions of Victoria have been able to implement strong regional tourism marketing and management, due to innovative organization across three separate shires. For example, the Geelong-Otway Shire has a very structured and highly organized network built around the RTO (Geelong-Otway Tourism) and developed in response to a regional initiative to market the region using the Great Ocean Road as the central coordinating feature and is illustrated by the focus of the bipartite network on one organization (Figure 14.1). In Figures 14.1 and 14.2, the organizations indicated as nodes on the left are operators and on the right are destination-management organizations. Effectively this network demonstrates the notion of self-governance of destination networks and is an example of Tremblay's (1999) coordination of complementary assets in a network. On the other hand, the interaction between tourism stakeholders in the Bright and Wangaratta Shires (Figure 14.2) demonstrates a more decentralized structure, in which more than one organization assumes the role of coordination. Interviews with the stakeholders demonstrated that, in contrast to Geelong-Otway Shire, these two shires are geographically and politically dissimilar and there is little incentive for the organizations to link together through the RTO. Further, the lack of social interaction between these shires due to their geographical positions discourages the formation of weak ties that may help mitigate this lack of formal organization (Granovetter, 1973). The analysis suggests that the more centralized network in the Great Ocean Road region (Geelong-Otway Shires) is associated with a more developed RTO structure and highlights the enhanced coordination provided in this region.

Clusters of Destination Organizations in Townsville, Queensland

The Townsville results demonstrate two distinct clusters (or cliques) of organizations in the network (Figure 14.3). These two clusters are linked by Townsville Enterprise (the RTO)

Table 14.1: Common problems across organizations.

	Funding	Integration with industry	Organization only partly involved in tourism	Tourism marketing/ sales core business
Aboriginal Tourism Australia	■	■	■	
Aboriginal Tourism Marketing Association (ATMA)	■	■	■	
Accommodation Getaways Victoria				■
ATEC — VIC/TAS				■
Australian Hotels Association				
Boating Industry Association of Victoria Inc.		■	■	
Camping Association of Victoria			■	
Caravan Industry Australia			■	
Cultural Tourism Industry Group	■	■	■	
Melbourne Convention & Marketing Bureau (MCVB)				■
Museums Australia (Victoria)			■	
Restaurant & Catering Association of Victoria Service		■	■	
The Professional Tour Guide Association	■	■		
Victorian Tourism Alliance Ltd	■	■		
Victorian Tourism Industry Council	■	■		
Victorian Wine Industry Council			■	

Use of ■ indicates that an organization referred to this problem.

Figure 14.2: Social networks reported in the Legends Region.

and to a lesser extent Tourism Queensland (the state tourism organization). The first cluster comprises private sector tourism operators and lies close to and above the RTO. This cluster of commercial tourism operators located above the RTO demonstrates a close grouping due to their many relationships with each other based upon mutual interest in terms of the value chain and marketing. These nodes are all major hotels or accommodation providers in the region that form a value-creation system (Parolini, 1999). The second cluster lies below the RTO and is comprised primarily of public sector organizations. This cluster is more diffuse and made up of organizations primarily involved in planning and projects, or organizations that provide access to other sectoral clusters (such as mining).

The Townsville network demonstrates interconnections between the separate public and private sector networks, and indicates the significance of the issue of the relationship of tourism to other economic sectors. Here, there appear to be important links between the structure of regional industry clusters and that of the tourism cluster (Figure 14.4). The North Queensland region is one where the contribution of tourism to the local economy is, and is perceived by key stakeholders to be, much less that other industry sectors such as mining, government, military, and general business. In planning for tourism in North Queensland, tourism is therefore seen as but one of a number of sectors (or clusters of organizations). In comparative terms, tourism is not a major player in Townsville and therefore finds it difficult to get a seat at the regional planning table. As a result, developing links with other industry sectors is an important task for the RTO and for Tourism Queensland.

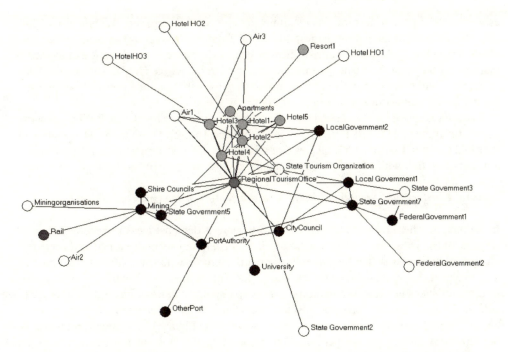

Figure 14.3: Communication interaction for organizations interviewed in Townsville.

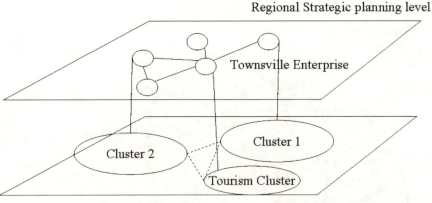

Figure 14.4: Indicative relationship between clusters of sectoral organizations and Townsville enterprise in planning.

Network Structural Divides in the Gold Coast, Queensland

The network analysis for the Gold Coast clearly demonstrates a structural divide between the Gold Coast itself and the hinterland areas (Figure 14.5). This appears to relate to geography as well as the main markets for organizations in these two sub-regions. The hinterland cluster is linked both to the nearby largest city RTO (Brisbane Marketing) as well as the Gold Coast RTO (The Gold Coast Tourism Bureau) as might be expected from the dual source markets for this area. Tourism Queensland is central to the whole Gold Coast cluster. Such structural divides are common in tourism due to causes that include political boundaries, geographical features or organization conflict.

The integration of tourism operators in the hinterland into the Gold Coast RTO is primarily a function of the Gold Coast Tourism Bureau rather that Tourism Queensland. The position of the Gold Coast in Figure 14.5 indicates that it is addressing this structural divide performing a linking function while Tourism Queensland, is more strongly linked to the coastal area.

Sectoral Clusters and Structural Divides in the Southern Downs, Queensland

In the rural Southern Downs region, the network analysis demonstrates clear sectoral clusters (Figure 14.6). These are firstly, a wine tourism cluster, and secondly a bed and breakfast cluster. It is interesting that the wine cluster overlaps more with (or contributes to) the bed and breakfast cluster than the wider tourism sector. This is most likely explained by the need to forge alliances between the two types of complementary tourism businesses in order to deliver the wine tourism product. Instead, the wine cluster is represented in the tourism cluster through a number of key industry organizations (Figure 14.7). Such representative organizations have a gatekeeper function, facilitating the flow of information between

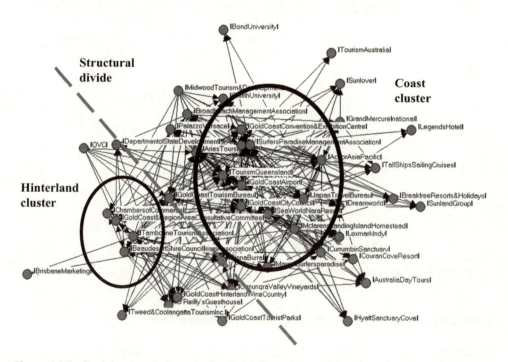

Figure 14.5: Social network diagram for Gold Coast key stakeholders showing sub-clusters.

different clusters. As gatekeepers, these organizations acquire the ability to influence the issues and activities within the destination.

There is also a structural divide between organizations based on the political boundary of the two shires of Stanthorpe and Warwick (Figure 14.7). This appears to relate to

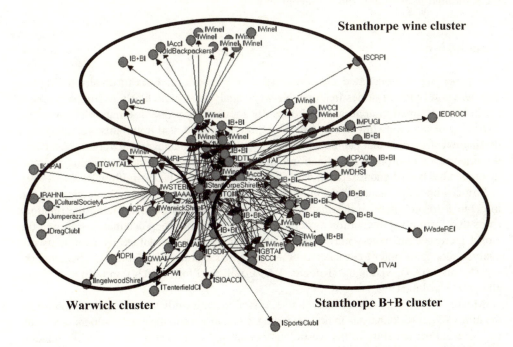

Figure 14.6: Social network analysis diagram for Southern Downs showing sub-clusters.

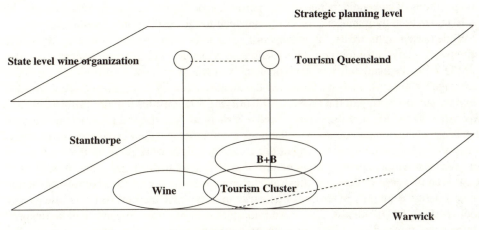

Figure 14.7: Idealized structural diagram for Southern Downs.

differences in the economies of these areas. The bed and breakfast and wine clusters are focused on the Stanthorpe area. This area is further from the capital city markets and operates as a weekend break destination. In contrast, Warwick Shire is more focused on agricultural production. The RTO (The Southern Downs Tourist Association) links these two areas through its planning and management role.

Conclusion

This paper has demonstrated the contribution of network analysis to understanding the structure and function of destinations. Network analysis is particularly useful as it adopts a whole of destination approach and does not focus on any one destination element. By analyzing destination structure and linkages, the approach also highlights weaknesses in destination structures that can be addressed by policy and management approaches. Here, the importance of proactive destination management through enhanced planning and collaboration has been demonstrated in many locations (Cooper & Jackson, 1989; Ritchie, 1999). A further important managerial implication is that the network approach underscores the imperative for competitive destinations to be collaborative, by emphasizing the relationships that form a value-creation system. As competition between destinations around the world increases, managers may improve their competitive advantage by using network analysis alongside other tools such as branding (Laws, Scott, & Parfitt, 2002), benchmarking (Kozak, 2004), visioning (Ritchie, 1999), policy (Pforr, 2002a) and value network analysis (Parolini, 1999).

Moving from theory to practice, the five Australian case studies individually demonstrate the utility of network analysis in understanding destinations and their stakeholders. The studies dissected the structure of the Australian tourism industry in two states and five regions, allowing a number of structural features such as cliques, product clusters, structural divides and central organizations to be identified. The visualization of the relationships and structural positions of stakeholders makes the approach especially useful as the structures can be easily understood by managers and communicated to the destination stakeholders.

While these results are useful, much work needs to be done to develop a research agenda for network analysis for tourism. This focuses on two areas. Firstly, from a methodological point of view, the availability of analytical and visualization software proves to be a major advantage for network analysts. However, the identification of destination stakeholders, and the 'data-hungry' nature of the process of identifying relationships remains problematic and expensive. Secondly, it is important to relate structural patterns and relationships to their effects on destination coordination, collaborative outcomes and their evolution. For example, in the area of knowledge management there has been little work done on the relationship between destination network architecture and information diffusion (Cowan & Jonard, 2004). The five case studies also illustrate differences in the organization of tourism across the destinations, not only in terms of their structures, but also their evolution (Butler, 1980; Cooper, 1990, 1997; Buhalis, 2000). An important area of future research will be to simulate past and future destination networks, based upon their current characteristics. Studies across national boundaries are also needed to examine the effect of culture upon destination organizations and structure.

Acknowledgement

The authors are grateful for the funding provided by the Sustainable Tourism Cooperative Research Centre for a part of this project.

References

Agarwal, S. J. (2002). Restructuring seaside tourism. *Annals of Tourism Research*, *29*(1), 25–55.

Barnes, J. A. (1952). Class and committees in the Norwegian Island Parish. *Human Relations*, *7*, 39–58.

Borgatti, S. P., Everett, M. P., & Freeman, L. C. (1999). UCINET 6.0 (Version 1.00). [Computer software]. Natick, MA: Analytic Technologies.

Bramwell, B., & Lane, B. (2000). Collaboration and partnerships in tourism planning. In: B. Bramwell & B. Lane (Eds.), *Tourism collaboration and partnerships: Politics, practice and sustainability* (pp. 1–19). Sydney: Channel View Publications.

Brandes, U., Kenis, P., Raab, J., Schneider, V., & Wagner, D. (1999). Explorations into the visualization of policy networks. *Journal of Theoretical Politics*, *11*(1), 75–106.

Brinton Milward, H., & Provan, K. G. (1998). Measuring network structure. *Public Administration*, *76*, 387–407.

Buhalis, D. (2000). Marketing the competitive destination of the future. *Tourism Management*, *21*(1), 97–116.

Burt, R. L., & Minor, M. (Eds.). (1983). *Applied network analysis*. London: Sage Publications.

Butler, R. W. (1980). The concept of a tourist area cycle of evolution: Implications for management of resources. *Canadian Geographer*, *24*(1), 7–14.

Cooper, C. (1990). Resorts in decline: The management response. *Tourism Management*, *11*(1), 63–67.

Cooper, C. (1997). Parameters and indicators of the decline of the British seaside resort. In: A. P. Williams & G. Shaw (Eds.), *The rise and fall of British coastal resorts* (pp. 79–101). London: Cassell.

Cooper, C., & Jackson, S. (1989). Destination life cycle: The Isle of Man case study. *Annals of Tourism Research*, *16*(3), 377–398.

Copp, C. B., & Ivy, R. (2001). Networking trends in small tourism businesses in post-socialist Slovakia. *Journal of Small Business Management*, *39*(4), 345–353.

Cowan, R., & Jonard, N. (2004). Network structure and the diffusion of knowledge. *Journal of Economic Dynamics and Control*, *28*, 1557–1575.

Cross, R., Borgatti, S. P., & Parker, A. (2002). Making invisible work visible: Using social network analysis to support strategic collaboration. *California Management Review*, *44*(2), 25–46.

Eades, P. (1984). A heuristic for graph drawing. *Congressus Numerantium*, *42*, 149–160.

Framke, W. (2002). The destination as a concept: A discussion of the business-related perspective versus the socio-cultural approach in tourism theory. *Scandinavian Journal of Hospitality and Tourism*, *2*(2), 92–108.

Granovetter, M. (1973). The strength of weak ties. *American Journal of Sociology*, *78*(6), 1360–1380.

Hall, C. M. (1999). Rethinking collaboration and partnership: A public policy perspective. *Journal of Sustainable Tourism*, *7*(3/4), 274–289.

Halme, M. (2001). Learning for sustainable development in tourism networks. *Business Strategy and the Environment*, *10*, 100–114.

Knoke, D. (1993). Networks of elite structure and decision making. *Sociological Methods and Research*, *22*(1), 23–45.

Knoke, D., & Kuklinski, J. H. (1991). Network analysis: Basic concepts. In: G. Thompson, J. Frances, R. Levacic, & J. Mitchell (Eds.), *Markets, hierarchies and networks* (pp. 173–182). London: Sage.

Kozak, M. (2004). *Destination benchmarking: Concepts, practices and operations*. Wallingford, UK: CABI.

Laumann, E., Galaskiewicz, J., & Marsden, D. (1978). Community structure as interorganizational linkages. *Annual Review of Sociology*, *4*, 455–484.

Laws, E., Scott, N., & Parfitt, N. (2002). Synergies in destination image management: A case study and conceptualisation. *International Journal of Tourism Research*, *4*(1), 39–55.

Leiper, N. (1989). *Tourism and Tourism Systems* (Vol. Occasional Paper No. 1). Department of Management Systems, Massey University, Palmerston North, New Zealand.

Mitchell, J. C. (1969). The concept and use of social networks. In: J. C. Mitchell (Ed.), *Social networks in urban situations* (pp. 1–50). Manchester: University of Manchester Press.

Parolini, C. (1999). *The value net: A tool for competitive strategy*. New York: John Wiley.

Pavlovich, K. (2001). The twin landscapes of Waitomo: Tourism network and sustainability through the Landcare Group. *Journal of Sustainable Tourism*, *9*(6), 491–504.

Pavlovich, K. (2003a). The evolution and transformation of a tourism destination network: The Waitomo Caves, New Zealand. *Tourism Management*, *24*(2), 203–216.

Pavlovich, K. (2003b). Pyramids, pubs and piazzas: An interpretation of tourism network structures. *Tourism Culture and Communication*, *4*, 41–48.

Pforr, C. (2002a). *The 'makers and shapers' of tourism policy in the Northern Territory of Australia: A policy network analysis of actors and their relational constellations*. Paper presented at the 12th International Research Conference on the Council for Australian University Tourism and Hospitality Education (CAUTHE) Fremantle, Western Australia.

Pforr, C. (2002b). The 'makers and shapers' of tourism policy in the Northern Territory of Australia: A policy network analysis of actors and their relational constellations. *Journal of Hospitality and Tourism Research*, *9*(2), 134–151.

Radcliffe-Brown, A. R. (1935). On the concept of function in social science. *American Anthropologist*, *37*(3), 394–402.

Ritchie, J. R. B. (1999). Crafting a value-driven vision for a national tourism treasure. *Tourism Management*, *20*(3), 273–282.

Scott, J. (1996). Software review: A toolkit for social network analysis. *Acta Sociologica*, *39*, 211–216.

Scott, J. (2000). *Social network analysis: A handbook* (2nd ed.). London: Sage.

Scott, J. (Ed.). (2002). *Social networks: Critical concepts in sociology* (Vol. 1). London: Routledge.

Selin, S. W. (2000). Developing a typology of sustainable tourism partnerships. In: B. Bramwell & B. Lane (Eds.), *Tourism collaboration and partnerships: Politics, practice and sustainability* (pp. 129–142). Clevedon: Channel View Publications.

Selin, S. W., & Chavez, D. (1995). Developing an evolutionary tourism partnership model. *Annals of Tourism Research*, *22*(4), 814–856.

Simmel, G. (1908). *Soziologie* (1968 edition). Berlin: Dunker and Humblot.

Szarka, J. (1990). Networking and small firms. *International Small Business Journal*, *8*(2), 10–21.

Thatcher, M. (1998). The development of policy network analyses from modest origins to overarching frameworks. *Journal of Theoretical Politics*, *10*(4), 389–416.

Thrift, N. (1996). *Spatial formations*. London: Sage.

Tichy, N. M., Tushman, M. L., & Fombrum, C. (1979). Social network analysis for organizations. *Academy of Management Review*, *4*(4), 507–519.

Tinsley, R., & Lynch, P. (2001). Small tourism business networks and destination development. *Hospitality Management*, *20*(4), 367–378.

Tremblay, P. (1998). The economic organization of tourism. *Annals of Tourism Research, 24*(4), 837–859.

Tremblay, P. (1999). *An empirical investigation of tourism business relationships in Australia's Top End.* Paper presented at the conference on Tourism & hospitality: Delighting the senses, Canberra.

Tyler, D., & Dinan, C. (2001). The role of interested groups in England's emerging tourism policy network. *Current Issues in Tourism, 4*(2–4), 210–252.

Wassermann, S., & Faust, K. (1994). *Social network analysis. Methods and applications.* Cambridge, MA.: Cambridge University Press.

Welch, D. E., Welch, L. S., Young, L. C., & Wilkinson, I. F. (1998). The importance of networks in export promotion: Policy issues. *Journal of International Marketing, 6*(4), 66–82.

Wilkinson, I. F., Mattsson, L. G., & Easton, G. (2000). International competitiveness and trade promotion policy from a network perspective. *Journal of World Business, 35*(3), 275–299.

Chapter 15

Tourism and Regional Competitiveness

C. Michael Hall

Introduction

The search for competitiveness is one of the major themes in contemporary tourism studies
whether one is examining competitive destinations and businesses, or even competitive institutions. Although it is not usually acknowledged in the mainstream business and tourism
literature, the desire for such competitiveness emerges from within the neo-liberal project.
Neo-liberalism promotes market-led economic and social restructuring which produces,
among other things, a more general orientation of economic and social policy to the private
sector's 'needs'. The chapter discusses the hegemonic discourse of regional competitiveness
but notes a number of weaknesses in the notion that regional or destination competitiveness can be treated in the same way as firm competitiveness. Five reasons are provided as to
why the regional-competitive discourse is so dominant with the final reason focusing on the
situatedness of academic knowledge production.

Regional Competitiveness

The notion of regional competitiveness is one of the key concepts in contemporary business
studies and increasingly so in the study of tourism in the form of destination competitiveness
(e.g. Buhalis, 1999, 2000; Crouch & Ritchie, 1999; Faulkner, Oppermann, & Fredline, 1999;
Kozak & Rimmington 1999; Go & Govers, 2000; Hassan, 2000; Mihalic, 2000; Ritchie &
Crouch, 2000, 2003; Dwyer & Kim 2003; Dwyer, Mellor, Liviac, Edwards, & Kim, 2004;
Gooroochurn & Sugiyarto, 2004; Hawkins, 2004; Enright & Newton, 2005). However,
despite the influence of the concept on tourism policies of the national and local state the concept has been subject to relatively little critique, nor has there been a substantive discussion
of the philosophical and ideological underpinnings of such a concept. Instead, competition,
whether it be as a tourism destination or in a wider sense of regional competitiveness, is
usually portrayed as a 'given' and what places 'must' do. For example, according to some

Developments in Tourism Research
Copyright © 2007 by Elsevier Ltd.
All rights of reproduction in any form reserved.
ISBN: 978-0-080-45328-6

economic analysts, 'the critical issue for regional-economic development practitioners to grasp is that the creation of competitive advantage is the most important activity they can pursue' (Barclays, 2002 cited in Bristow, 2005). Moreover, peak tourism organizations such as the World Tourism Organization (UNWTO) and the World Travel and Tourism Council (WTTC) have embraced the competitiveness concept through a number of their programmes. For example, the UNWTO states interest in 'competitive tourism education systems' and 'competitive destinations', while the WTTC operates a competitiveness monitor on its website that 'indicates to what extent a country offers a competitive environment for Travel & Tourism development'. Such is the language of competitiveness in government, industry and academic conceptualizations of regions, places and destinations that it presents a 'hegemonic discourse' that constitutes 'the only valid currency of argument' (Schoenberger, 1998, p. 12). Hegemony incorporates more than the ideology of a dominant elite and the beliefs and values that it disseminates. It also refers to the manner in which those beliefs and interests are sedimented into everyday practice and institutional arrangements and become taken-for-granted and natural. As Williams (1977, p. 110) stated, 'a lived system of meaning and values — constitutive and constituting — which as they are experienced as practices appear as reciprocally confirming'. Or, as Turner (2001, p. 40) noted with respect to the language of competitiveness, it 'provides a rosy glow of shared endeavour and shared enemies which can unit captains of industry and representatives of the shop floor in the same big tent'. More particularly in relation to meta-political narratives, competitiveness is a discourse that 'provides some shared sense of meaning and a means of legitimizing neo-liberalism rather than a material focus on the actual improvements of economic welfare' (Bristow, 2005, p. 300).

Why is place competitiveness hegemonic? Because many policies at different levels of the state, as well as policy documents from industry present the concept of competitiveness in an unproblematic manner as an unambiguously beneficial attribute of a regional economy or of a destination. As Bristow (2005, p. 285) observes, 'Competitiveness is portrayed as the means by which regional economies are externally validated in an era of globalization, such that there can be no principled objection to policies and strategies deemed to be competitiveness enhancing, whatever their indirect consequences'.

The focus on competitiveness has emerged out of the belief that globalization has created a world of intense place competition. For example, according to Kotler, Haider, and Rein (1993, p. 346) one of the leading texts of place competition, 'In a borderless economy, [places] will emerge as the new actors on the world scene'. According to Kotler et al. (1993) we are living in a time of 'place wars' in which places are competing for their economic survival with other places and regions not only in their own country but throughout the world. 'All places are in trouble now, or will be in the near future. The globalization of the world's economy and the accelerating pace of technological changes are two forces that require all places to learn how to compete. Places must learn how to think more like businesses, developing products, markets, and customers' (Kotler et al., 1993, p. 346). The identification of competitiveness as a significant policy goal has led to the development by academics, policy-makers and practitioners of a range of indicators that model and measure competitiveness. Thereby, identifying which places are winning in the annual 'Premier League' of place competition (e.g. Huggins, 2003; various reports of the World Economic Forum Global Competitiveness Network). Nevertheless, while all this is being done there is still substantial confusion 'as to what the concept actually means and how it can be effectively operationalised… policy acceptance of the existence of regional competitiveness and its measurement appears to have run ahead of a number of fundamental theoretical and empirical questions' (Bristow, 2005, p. 286). It is, as Markusen (1999, p. 870) would say a relatively 'fuzzy concept': 'characterizations lacking conceptual clarity and difficult to operationalize. In some cases, no attempt is made to offer evidence at all. Elsewhere, evidence marshaled is highly selective. Methodology is little discussed'. Nevertheless, more often than not, it is accepted.

The discourse of regional and destination competitiveness is problematic on several fronts. In the first instance there are the difficulties of transferring a concept that is usually used to describe firm performance to a regional or place scale. Firm competitive discourse comes from two primary sources: the discourse of economics and the discourse of the business community. Within economics 'the market is the impartial and ultimate arbiter of right behaviour in the economy and competitiveness simply describes the result of responding correctly to market signals' (Schoenberger, 1998, p. 3). A neo-classical economic perspective arguably posits a neo-Darwinian survival of the fittest approach with respect to the firm in which the driver is profit maximization. For example, one can provide the following example from Milton Friedman (1953, p. 22): '[G]iven natural selection, acceptance of the hypothesis [of maximization of returns] can be based largely on the assumption that it summarizes appropriately the conditions for survival'. Within business community discourse competitiveness 'represents the fundamental external validation of a firm's ability to survive, compete and grow in markets subject to international competition' (Bristow, 2005, p. 287) and therefore is used to explain firm behaviour. In other words a firm 'must do X in order to be competitive' (Schoenberger, 1998). Therefore, at the firm level there is a reasonably clear meaning for competitiveness that relates to a common unit — the firm — engaged in comparable activities — competing (surviving and growing) in a market, which therefore allows competitiveness to be conceived of in output related indicators and metrics (Malecki, 2004; Bristow, 2005). Indeed, for Porter (1985, 1990) firm competitiveness is a proxy for productivity. Perhaps more significantly for the discourse on regional competitiveness Porter (2002, p. 3) has also argued that regional competitiveness and productivity are equivalent terms: 'A region's standard of living (wealth) is determined by the *productivity* with which it uses its human, capital, and natural resources. The appropriate definition of competitiveness is *productivity*'.

Porter's role is important because of the extent to which he 'has successfully branded, transformed and exported his diagnosis of how regions may improve their competitiveness to development agencies and governments all over the world' (Bristow, 2005, p. 288). Porter, along with others (e.g. Kotler et al., 1993) contributed to the idea that places are equivalent to firms in competing for various forms of capital as well as market share in an increasingly competitive global economy. Porter argued that government creates the market conditions that allows firms to exploit each regional economy's competitive advantage with productivity in a region being a reflection of what firms 'choose to do in that location' (Porter, 2002, p. 3), with competitiveness ultimately depending on 'improving the microeconomic foundations of competition' (Porter, 2002, p. 5). Four sets of factors were identified as interrelated elements of the micro-economic business environments contribution to productivity: demand conditions, including local demand; the context for firm strategy and rivalry, particularly local conditions that contribute to open local competition, efficiency and investment; factor (input) conditions, which refers to high quality, specialized inputs available to firms; and related and supporting industries in the form of local suppliers and clusters (Porter, 2002, p. 6). Given the focus of Porter and others who espouse the 'New Regionalism' the starting point of which, 'is almost always the concept of regional competitiveness' (Webb & Collis, 2000, p. 858) it is therefore not surprising that 'the region' has become a focal point of economic policy as well as being regarded as a crucible of economic development and wealth generation. Nevertheless, there are differences. For example, Storper (1997, p. 264) defines regional competitiveness as 'the capability of a region to attract and keep firms with stable or increasing market shares in an activity, while maintaining stable or increasing standards of living for those who participate in it'. Although this approach is related to the same global competitiveness perspective of Porter and others, it is also strongly influenced by national and international policy discourses (Bristow, 2005; Gibson & Klockner, 2005; Malecki, 2004). Importantly, it is differentiated from Porter in that it asserts that regional competitiveness and regional prosperity are interdependent rather than equivalent notions and avoids equating regional competitiveness with productivity. As Huggins (2003, p. 89) observes:

> Although low labour costs may initially contribute to the attraction of business investment to an area, such costs are in many ways a 'double-edged sword', resulting in employees working for lower wages than their counterparts in other localities and regions. Therefore, it can be argued that true local and regional competitiveness occurs only when sustainable growth is achieved at labour rates that enhance overall standards of living.

In other words, a region is 'competitive' when it has the factors that enable it to raise its standard of living in a sustained fashion. Therefore, micro-economic productivity is regarded as a necessary but not sufficient condition for improved regional macro-economic performance.

Significantly, the confusion as to what constitutes competitiveness in the business and regional-development literature are mirrored in the policy sphere. As Bristow (2005) notes policy makers have tended to prefer approaches to competitiveness that equates it with regional prosperity and which focus on endogenous factors in influencing firm competitiveness — a situation that is further complicated by the addition of 'regional productivity' along with a range of associated indicators to the lexicon of regional policy, particularly in the UK. In summary, although the notion of regional competitiveness is embedded in regional development policy it is a somewhat 'chaotic discourse' (Bristow 2005, p. 291) as:

- regional competitiveness can be defined in different ways so that it is not entirely clear when a situation of competitiveness has been achieved;
- there is confusion as to what concrete activities constitute competitiveness; and
- how micro-level competitiveness translates into macro-level prosperity

Indeed, 'equating competitiveness with productivity is to invite tautology and ontological confusion: is a region more competitive because it is more productive, or is it more productive because it is more competitive' (Martin & Sunley, 2003, p. 15). There is, nevertheless, a central tenet of competitiveness policy discourse that regional competitiveness is firm-based (micro-level), output-related and strongly influenced by the micro-economic business environment including a stable economic framework (the macro-level) as well as system of supporting, sector specific and specialized institutions and targeted policies (the meso-level) (Lovering, 1999; Malecki, 2004; Bristow, 2005). However, such an axiom has developed even though the discourse 'is based on relatively thinly developed and narrow conceptions of how regions compete, prosper and grow in economic terms' (Bristow, 2005, p. 291). For example, with reference to the key question of what are the determinants of place competitiveness Deas and Giordano (2001) argued that the literature tends to offer a one-size fits all or 'checklist' approach to identifying the relevant determinants of competitiveness, even though inadequate empirical research has been conducted as to the relative significance of such factors. A comment that could very well be made of the literature on destination competitiveness. Similarly, Malecki (2002, p. 941) commented with respect to city competitiveness, 'all of the issues that have risen to the top of the research agenda over the past 30 years are relevant — indeed, essential…having only *some* of these conditions in good order is not enough'.

The above discussion indicates that there are a number of grounds for questioning both the universality and strength of the nexus between regional and firm competitiveness (Bristow, 2005). For example, the basis for competitiveness might lie outside of the region altogether in terms of such factors as global networks as sources of knowledge in shaping firm competitiveness (Malecki, 2002) or destination competitiveness, e.g. through transnational diasporic networks; while firm-level factors clearly remain important, and in some cases far more important than external factors (Sternberg & Arndt, 2001; Todtling & Kaufman, 2001). In addition, the notion of the 'region' or 'destination' used in competitiveness discourse is quite abstract and it is not always clear how this relates to the actual regions, destinations, places and locations where people live, particularly as to how spatial delimitations may then influence what both constitutes and influences competitive advantage (Lovering, 1999). Importantly, there is typically a failure to recognize that place is contingent in that, 'in practice, the region's influence may vary depending on the particular industrial structure and context, the balance of globally- and locally-oriented firms, and the degree to which the region constitutes an internally cohesive, homogenous economic space' (Bristow, 2005, p. 293). Moreover, in other literatures, for example, those concerned with transnational networks and mobilities (Hall & Müller, 2004; Coles, Hall, & Duval, 2005; Hall, 2005), regions are conceived of as open, discontinuous 'spaces of flows' that are constituted by a variety of economic, social and political relationships (Doel & Hubbard, 2002). Such a relational perspective emphasizes relations of power and control over space in which activities in one location clearly impacts upon development in other regions whereby core regions tend to occupy dominant positions and peripheral regions more marginal ones. This lies in stark contrast to the competitive discourse that focuses on building capacity within regions rather than considering the relationships between regions. Finally, we can note that the prevailing competitiveness discourse is output related and pays 'little or no attention to the broader non-tradeable modalities of competitive behaviour which may characterize regions' (Bristow, 2005, p. 295). Or as Hewison (1991, p. 175) put it, 'You cannot get a whole way of life into a Tesco's trolley or a V & A Enterprises shopping bag'. Therefore, the discourse of competitiveness needs to be interrogated in terms of its capacity to provide sustainable and desirable outcomes that may arise, or not, out of improved firm competitiveness.

All of this is not to deny the significance of regions and places. Far from it. The problem is the relatively simplistic way in which the region or the destination is usually conceptualized within the regional-competitiveness discourse which means that 'regions are conceived as independent, collective entities competing in directly commensurable terms in a manner directly equivalent to firms. Regions are treated as clearly defined, internally coherent, atomistic and bounded spatial entities with quantifiable attributes that are in their exclusive possession' (Bristow, 2005, p. 296). Rather than being conceptualized as territorially defined social, political, economic and environmental aggregations, with different structures and sets of localized variables. Sheppard (2000), for example, recognized several dimensions that means some regions are favoured over others. First, its embeddedness in national- and regional-regulatory systems and institutions. Second, its 'geographical trajectory' as a result of history and location within the political and economic system. Third, the fact that the policies of the higher levels of the state can have a range of intended or unintended consequences in terms of how policy outcomes may favour one region over another. Perhaps, just as importantly, the regional-competitiveness discourse is not grounded in sufficient empirical research that outlines not only how places win but also why they lose, as in every competition not everyone can be a winner.

The Low Road to Regional Competitiveness

The fact that not everyone can win does not mean that competition is without value. Rather it is to suggest that there are both benefits and problems inherent in such place competition, within which tourism is clearly embedded. However, it is significant that within regional development, tourism is primarily seen as part of an imitative 'low-road' policy in contrast to 'high-road' knowledge based policies. With Malecki (2004, p. 1103) noting that 'The disadvantages of competition mainly concern the perils that low-road strategies build so that no strengths can prevail over the long-term, which presents particular difficulties for regions trying to catch up in the context of territorial competition based on knowledge'. Low-road strategies are regarded as being focused on 'traditional' location factors such as land, labour, capital, infrastructure and location, more intangible factors, such as intellectual capital and institutional capacity are secondary. Such low-road strategies of regional competitiveness are bound up with the property-oriented growth machines that focus on the packaging of the place product, re-imaging strategies and the gaining of media attention. With respect to urban place competition, for example, investment in infrastructure is 'similar from city to city' with respect to meetings and conventions, sports, events, entertainment and shopping because they are aimed at the same markets with few cities being able to 'forgo competition in each of these sectors' (Judd, 2003, p. 14). Leading to what may be described as the serial replication of homogeneity or the serial monotony of the festival marketplace, heritage precinct, art gallery, museum, casino, marina and shopping centre (Boyer, 1988; Harvey, 1990; Hall, 1997). Such factors were described by Harvey (1989, p. 12) as being a part of urban entrepreneurialism:

> Many of the innovations and investments designed to make particular cities more attractive as cultural and consumer centers have quickly been imitated

elsewhere, thus rendering any competitive advantage within a system of cities ephemeral. ...Local coalitions have no option, given the coercive laws of competition, except to keep ahead of the game thus engendering leap-frogging innovations in life styles, cultural forms, products and service mixes, even institutional and political forms if they are to survive.

More recently, the fusion of urban entrepreneurialism with the neo-liberal political agenda has provided the ideological justification for place competitive re-imaging strategies including the hosting of mega-events (Peck, 2001; Peck & Tickell, 2002). Neo-liberalism promotes market-led economic and social restructuring which produces, among other things, a more general orientation of economic and social policy to the private sector's 'needs' (Jessop, 2002). In the case of regional development this has typically meant the development of structures and powers of governance that are opaque and unaccountable to public stakeholders and participation (Owen, 2002). Neo-liberalism therefore structures ideas about and the objectives set for community development, definitions of the public good, and definitions of citizenship that 'create wider distinctions than ever before between the "citizen" and the "consumer" and which of these ought to be the focal point of urban public life' (Lowes, 2004, p. 71).

Yet the sustainability of place competitive strategies, let alone their real benefits are increasingly questionable. Swyngedouw (1992) noted that the 'frenzied' and 'unbridled' competition for cultural capital results in over accumulation and the threat of devaluation. Even Kotler et al. (1993), who provide the standard case text for place marketing, acknowledged that 'the escalating competition... for business attraction has the marks of a zero-sum game or worse, a negative-sum game, in that the winner ultimately becomes the loser' (1993, p. 15). The desire to host sport mega-events and the requirements of having to constantly develop new and upgrade existing sports and visitor infrastructure has meant that cities 'face the possibility of being caught in a vicious cycle of have to provide larger subsidies to finance projects that deliver even fewer public benefits' (Leitner & Garner, 1993, p. 72). Indeed, as this chapter was being written it was announced that the cost of the London Olympic Games was to rise dramatically by £2 billion in order to make the East London site viable after 2012 (Mathiason, 2006). Yet even in such situations where corporate interests clearly benefit more than the public such is the strength of the discourse of competitiveness and the 'necessity' to become a place in which capital 'sticks' that the desirability to host sports mega-events by urban growth coalitions seems likely to remain unconstrained. Indeed, all this begs the question of how entrepreneurial is regional or urban entrepreneurialism.

Harvey (1989, p. 8) regarded it as entrepreneurial because it was speculative, whereas Lovering (1995) argued that such serial reproduction of similar forms of development was commodification, as entrepreneurship implies that a product is new or innovative. Indeed, Harvey also acknowledged that the 'search to procure investment capital confines innovation to a very narrow path' (1989, p. 11). Nevertheless, despite the zero-sum or negative sum prospects of speculation and places serialisation, particularly given the inability to predict what form of redevelopment package will succeed in attracting mobile production and consumption flows into a particular space for a period of time (Malecki, 2004) this strategy is still dominant with respect to tourism's role in regional competitiveness. In fact, as the experience of sporting events such as the Olympic Games illustrates, to criticize the hosting of mega-events as an economic and social development mechanism one is to be doubly damned. For not only does one contend with the neo-liberal discourse of competition and the relentless pursuit of regeneration but also the mythologies of the social benefits of sport. Sport is extremely hard to argue against. The inherent belief of many that sport is good for you, makes for better citizens, creates pride in the community, and generates a positive image is hard to overcome (Hall, 2004). This belief and a relative lack of criticism of it means that in terms of urban and regional regeneration many large-scale sport infrastructure projects and mega-events are going to continue to be funded as it provides opportunities not only for the furtherance of corporate and real estate interests but also for politicians to be seen to be 'doing something' in light of the global competition that communities face within the neo-liberal view of the world. As Hall (2004) has noted investment in accessible and affordable education, health and communications technology, along with a diversified job creation strategy is far more likely to have far more long-term benefits for urban economic and social well being than investment in elite mega-sports events and infrastructure. But given the hegemony of neo-liberal discourse in the construction of place perhaps it is just much easier to avoid these issues and just watch the World Cup finals instead.

The High Road

In contrast to the low road approach of the homogenization of the place product through serial reproduction Malecki (2004) argues that a high-road approach of genuine entrepreneurship and innovation through the development of learning regions is possible although it is a much more difficult path to follow. Cooke (2002), for example, emphasizes the case for regional innovation and knowledge economies that utilize agglomeration economies, institutional learning, associative governance, proximity capital and interactive innovation. Required regional infrastructure is regarded as requiring both hard (communications, transport, finance) and soft (knowledge, intellectual capital, trustful labour relations, mentoring, worker-welfare orientation) infrastructures in order to encourage innovation as opposed to adaptation (Malecki, 2004), or the seductive repackaging of neo-liberal urban and regional policy orthodoxies under the rubric of the 'creative class' and the 'creative city' (Gibson & Klockner, 2005; Peck, 2005). However, the soft infrastructure of learning, knowledge and interaction is difficult to control and measure, while the cognitive aspects of a regional-innovation system are also particularly difficult to influence (Grabher, 1993; Maillat, 1995). This therefore raises substantial political problems for political elites and growth coalitions who are often geared towards demonstrating competitive success in relation to election cycles. Yet, the higher road with its focus on the construction of 'territorially rooted immobile assets' (Brenner, 1998, pp. 15–16) takes considerably longer to achieve than a 3–5-year election cycle. Indeed, it is often much easier to build an innovation centre or a science park as symbols of local innovation than it actually is to create an intense bundle of communication and interaction between firms and institutions. Therefore, those places that do not attain high-road competitiveness quickly are then in danger of shifting back to low-road strategies of regional competitiveness (Leitner & Sheppard, 1998).

This is not to say that tourism does not have a part to play in high road strategies. It certainly does as high-road strategies emphasise connectivity, through transport and aviation as well as communication linkages, and high levels of amenity that may also attract visitors as well as be important for residents. In addition, high road approaches tend to place value on cultural diversity including the role of diasporic networks. However, these are the strategies of tourism as a subsidiary element of a knowledge-based economy rather than as a strategy of adaptivity and reproduction. Indeed, tourism in this sense is clearly seen as a subset of a broader understanding of human mobilities. Indeed, as Doel and Hubbard (2002, p. 263) argue, policy makers need to 'replace their place-based way of thinking with a focus on connectivity, performance and flow'.

Conclusions

All of this then clearly begs the question as to why the discourse of competitiveness is so dominant, particularly with respect to policy? Several reasons can be provided. First, it is reasonable comprehensible by the business community given its resonance with existing business discourse as well as clearly predicating the importance of business influence in policy determination. Second, as Krugman (1994) noted, competitive images are exciting and are reflective of the rise of the neo-liberal economy as well as the neo-liberal consensus with respect to public–private relationships and 'Third Way' politics. However, he also noted that they are wrong. Indeed, he argued that many of the theorists of competitiveness 'make seemingly sophisticated arguments, most of which are supported by careless arithmetic and sloppy research. Competitiveness is a seductive idea, promising easy answers to complex problems. But the result of this obsession is misallocated resources, trade frictions and bad domestic economic policies'.

Third, the regional-competitiveness discourse suggests that regional policy makers can actually strongly influence their own futures and that interventions, of a particular kind, will bring results. Indeed, it should be noted that some forms of competitive strategies, those we associate with the high road (Malecki, 2004), can be economically and social beneficial.

> Competitiveness reached through territorial quality and public service effi-
> ciency brings benefits to all local economic and social activities. Competi-
> tiveness attained by creating local synergies among local actors, or integrating
> external firms in the local relational web, exploits spillovers and increasing
> returns that are at the very base of economic development, in its positive-sum,
> 'generative' sense (Malecki, 2004, p. 1114).

Fourth, the competitiveness discourse, based as it is upon neoclassical economic assump-tions, is resonant with the increased managerialism of public-policy institutions in the developed world that 'is founded upon economistic and rationalistic assumptions which include an emphasis upon measuring performance in the context of a planning system driven by objectives and targets' (Bristow, 2005, p. 297). This is not to suggest that benchmarking and indicators are not warranted or useful. Environmental scanning, continual monitoring and benchmarking are what intelligent cities and regions do. But they do it intelligently realizing the pitfalls of such analysis as well as ensuring that they understand the difficulties in measuring soft infrastructure (Malecki, 2004). Finally, and perhaps most fundamentally,

Bristow (2005) argues that it is interests rather than the intrinsic merits of ideas that shape policy making. Here, the interests are primarily political and business. However, what Bristow does not indicate, except perhaps obliquely, is that academic interests are also significant, particularly to which academic knowledge is also produced, framed, disseminated and received in relation to certain 'economic' knowledges. This last point is significant because academic research and knowledge transfer is an integral component of the soft infrastructure of place competitiveness.

Although there is an understanding of the importance of scientific and technological knowledge transfer and agglomeration externalities there is little overt analysis of the policy role that academic creativity plays in regional-economic development. Nor, just as significantly as to how the credibility of such research is mobilized (Gibson & Klocker, 2004), for example through publisher's promotional campaigns or more likely through the self use of indices that rank the journals you publish in or the number of articles you publish.

Issues associated with academic and institutional competitiveness within the contemporary neo-liberal agenda are capable of the same critique as that associated with regional-competitiveness discourse. Indeed, the two are inseparably related as they are inherently a component of the circuits of cultural capital that are part of economic development policy. Research and publishing which is regarded as credible and 'detached' is undertaken within dominant discourses. For example, Gibson and Klocker (2004) noted that research on the supposed creative city is being undertaken within a creative industry and is inherently a part of the discourse that it is trying to understand. 'Such research is now complicit within its own subject — a pursuit of creative information production' (2004, p. 424). Something that is perhaps analogous with the low-road path of innovation as serial reproduction rather than being genuinely entrepreneurial and innovative in problem solving. Indeed, within the dominant regional-competitiveness discourse the credibility of the academic celebrity and perhaps the discourse itself is embedded in the machinations of the academic fashion cycle, 'which plays out through a particular industrial actor-network of academic knowledge production, circulation and reception' (Gibson & Klocker, 2004, p. 425); within which 'favoured academic personalities' are:

> Swept up into international circuits of academic celebrity, a move that is dependent less upon internal disciplinary modes of evaluation than on the shifting imperatives of knowledge dissemination… Dedicated followers of fashion hurry to buy the new…book, an act of discernment and discrimination that starkly reveals the truism that identity is constructed in and through the consumption of commodities (Barnett, 1998, p. 388).

This chapter has clearly argued that the seemingly hegemonic discourse of regional and place competitiveness needs greater interrogation and reflexivity than what has often been the case by policy makers and academic alike. Yet it has also suggested that within such an analysis concerns need also be raised about the positionality of those who contribute towards such discourses and the institutions and interests that enable the credibility of some research to become mobilized and not others. This chapter therefore shares with other recent writing (Rose, 1997; Sidaway, 2000; Gibson & Klocker, 2004, 2005; Paasi, 2005), of the need to end the denial of the need for reflexivity, particularly by those who might seek to evade the subjectivity and situatedness of their own theories and standing. This also means dealing with the denial enacted by many academics and policy makers in 'semiperipheral margins of academic knowledge production' (Gibson & Klocker, 2004, p. 433). For Gibson and Klocker, this is Australia. For me this is not just a place, though I also see the cultural cringe of many policy makers and academics in other locations as well, but it is also the field of tourism.

Acknowledgement

This chapter is a revised version of the oral presentation 'Cutting Away at Tourism: Thin Policies of Competitive Destinations and Competitive Institutions Within the Hard Outcomes of Neoliberalism' presented at the Cutting Edge in Tourism conference held at the University of Surrey, 2006.

References

Barnett, C. (1998). The cultural turn: Fashion or progress in human geography? *Antipode, 30*, 379–394.

Boyer, C. (1988). The return of aesthetics to city planning. *Society, 25*(4), 49–56.

Brenner, N. (1998). Global cities, global states: Global city formation and state territorial restructuring in contemporary Europe. *Review of International Political Economy, 5*, 1–37.

Bristow, G. (2005). Everyone's a 'winner': Problematising the discourse of regional competitiveness. *Journal of Economic Geography, 5*, 285–304.

Buhalis, D. (1999). Tourism on the Greek Islands: Issues of peripherality, competitiveness and development. *International Journal of Tourism Research, 1*(5), 341–358.

Buhalis, D. (2000). Marketing the competitive destination of the future. *Tourism Management, 21*, 97–116.

Coles, T., Hall, C. M., & Duval, D. (2005). Mobilising tourism: A post-disciplinary critique. *Tourism Recreation Research, 30*(2), 31–41.

Cooke, P. (2002). *Knowledge economies: Clusters, learning and cooperative advantage.* London: Routledge.

Crouch, G. I., & Ritchie, J. R. B. (1999). Tourism, competitiveness, and societal prosperity — 1996/2006. *Journal of Business Research, 44*(3), 137–152.

Deas, I., & Giordano, B. (2001). Conceptualising and measuring urban competitiveness in major English cities: An exploratory approach. *Environment and Planning A, 33*, 1411–1429.

Doel, M. A., & Hubbard, P. J. (2002). Taking world cities literally: marketing the city in a global space of flows. *City, 6*, 351–368.

Dwyer, L., & Kim, C. (2003). Destination competitiveness: Determinants and indicators. *Current issues in Tourism, 6*(5), 369–414.

Dwyer, L., Mellor, R., Liviac, Z., Edwards, D., & Kim, C. (2004). Attributes of destination competitiveness: A factor analysis. *Tourism Analysis, 9*(1–2), 91–101.

Enright, M. J., & Newton, J. (2005). Determinants of tourism destination competitiveness in Asia Pacific: Comprehensiveness and universality. *Journal of Travel Research, 43*(4), 339–350.

Faulkner, B., Oppermann, M., & Fredline, E. (1999). Destination competitiveness: An exploratory examination of South Australia's core attractions. *Journal of Vacation Marketing, 5*(2), 125–139.

Friedman, M. (1953). The methodology of positive economics. In: M. Friedman (Ed.), *Essays in positive economics* (pp. 3–43). Chicago: University of Chicago Press.

Gibson, C., & Klocker, N. (2004). Academic publishing as 'creative' industry, and recent discourse of 'creative economies': Some critical reflections. *Area, 36*(4), 423–434.

Gibson, C., & Klocker, N. (2005). The 'cultural turn' in Australian regional development discourse: Neoliberalising creativity? *Geographical Research, 43*(1), 93–102.

Go, F., & Govers, R. (2000). Integrated quality management for tourist destinations: A European perspective on achieving competitiveness. *Tourism Management, 21*(1), 79–88.

Gooroochurn, N., & Sugiyarto, G. (2004). *Measuring competitiveness in the travel and tourism industry 2004/7*. Nottingham: Tourism and Travel Research Institute, University of Nottingham.

Grabher, G. (Ed.), (1993). *The embedded firm: On the socioeconomics of embedded networks*. London: Routledge.

Hall, C. M. (1997). Geography, marketing and the selling of places. *Journal of Travel and Tourism Marketing, 6*(3/4), 61–84.

Hall, C. M. (2004). Sports tourism and urban regeneration. In: B. Ritchie, & D. Adair (Eds.), *Sports tourism: Interrelationships, impacts and issues*. Clevedon: Channelview Publications.

Hall, C. M. (2005). Reconsidering the geography of tourism and contemporary mobility. *Geographical Research, 43*(2), 125–139.

Hall, C. M. & Müller, D. (Eds.) (2004). *Tourism, recreation and second homes*, Clevedon: Channelview.

Harvey, D. (1989). From managerialism to entrepreneurialism: The transformation in urban governance in late capitalism. *Geografiska Annaler, 71B*, 3–17.

Harvey, D. (1990). Between space and time: Reflection on the geographic information. *Annals Association of American Geographers, 80*, 418–434.

Hassan, S. S. (2000). Determinants of market competitiveness in an environmentally sustainable tourism industry. *Journal of Travel Research, 38*(3), 239–245.

Hawkins, D. (2004). Sustainable tourism competitiveness clusters: Application to World heritage sites network development in Indonesia. *Asia Pacific Journal of Tourism Research, 9*(3), 293–307.

Hewison, R. (1991). Commerce and culture. In: J. Corner, & S. Harvey (Eds.), *Enterprise and heritage: Crosscurrents of national culture* (pp. 162–177). London: Routledge.

Huggins, R. (2003). Creating a UK competitiveness index: Regional and local benchmarking. *Regional Studies, 37*, 89–96.

Jessop, B. (2002). Liberalism, neoliberalism, and urban governance: A state-theoretical perspective. *Antipode, 34*, 452–472.

Judd, D. R. (2003). Building the tourist city: Editor's introduction. In: D. R. Judd (Ed.), *The infrastructure of play: Building the tourist city* (pp. 3–16). Armonk: M.E. Sharpe.

Kotler, P., Haider, D. H., & Rein, I. (1993). *Marketing places: Attracting investment, industry, and tourism to cities, states, and nations*. New York: Free Press.

Kozak, M., & Rimmington, M. (1999). Measuring tourist destination competitiveness: Conceptual considerations and empirical findings. *International Journal of Hospitality Management, 18*(3), 273–283.

Krugman, P. (1994). Competitiveness: A dangerous obsession. *Foreign Affairs, 73*(2), 28–44.

Leitner, H., & Garner, M. (1993). The limits of local initiatives: A reassessment of urban entrepreneurialism for urban development. *Urban Geography, 14*, 57–77.

Leitner, H., & Sheppard, E. (1998). Economic uncertainty, interurban competition and the efficacy of entrepreneurialism. In: T. Hall & P. Hubbard (Eds.), *The entrepreneurial city: Geographies of politics, regimes and representation* (pp. 285–307). Chichester: Wiley.

Lovering, J. (1995). Creating discourses rather than jobs: The crisis in the cities and the transition fantasies of intellectuals and policy makers. In P. Healey, S. Cameron, S. Davoudi, S. Graham, & Madani-Poura. (Eds.) *Managing cities: The new urban context*, (pp. 109–126). Chichester: Wiley.

Lovering, J. (1999). Theory led by policy: the inadequacies of the 'New Regionalism" (illustrated from the case of Wales). *International Journal of Urban and Regional Research, 23*, 379–396.

Lowes, M. (2004). Neoliberal power politics and the controversial siting of the Australian Grand Prix Motorsport event in an urban park. *Society and Leisure, 27*(1), 69–88.

Maillat, D. (1995). Territorial dynamic, innovative milieus and regional development. *Entrepreneurship and Regional Development, 7*, 157–165.

Malecki, E. J. (2002). Hard and soft networks for urban competitiveness. *Urban Studies, 39*, 929–945.

Malecki, E. J. (2004). Jockeying for position: What it means and why it matters to regional development policy when places compete. *Regional Studies, 38*(9), 1101–1120.

Markusen, A. (1999). Fuzzy concepts, scanty evidence, policy distance: The case for rigour and policy relevance in critical regional studies. *Regional Studies, 33*(9), 869–884.

Martin, R., & Sunley, P. (2003). Deconstructing clusters: chaotic concept or policy panacea? *Journal of Economic Geography, 3*, 5–35.

Mathiason, N. (2006). Olympics budget 'must rise by £2bn'. *The Observer* 2 April.

Mihalic, T. (2000). Environmental management of a tourist destination — A factor of tourism competitiveness. *Tourism Management, 21*(2), 65–74.

Owen, K. A. (2002). The Sydney 2000 Olympics and urban entrepreneurialism: Local variations in urban governance. *Australian Geographical Studies, 40*, 323–336.

Paasi, A. (2005). Globalisation, academic capitalism, and the uneven geographies of international journal publishing spaces. *Environment and Planning A, 37*, 769–789.

Peck, J. (2001). Neoliberalizing states: Thin policies/hard outcomes. *Progress in Human Geography, 25*(3), 445–455.

Peck, J. (2005). Struggling with the creative class. *International Journal of Urban and Regional Research, 29*(4), 740–770.

Peck, J., & Tickell, A. (2002). Neoliberalizing space. *Antipode, 34*, 380–403.

Porter, M. E. (1985). *Competitive advantage*. New York: Free Press.

Porter, M. E. (1990). *The competitive advantage of nations*. London: Macmillan.

Porter, M. E. (2002). *Regional foundations of competitiveness: Issues for Wales*. Paper presented at Future Competitiveness of Wales: Innovation, Entrepreneurship, and Technological Change. Wales, April 3. Available http://www.isc.hbs.edu/archive-speeches.htm

Ritchie, J. R. B., & Crouch, G. I. (2000). The competitive destination: A sustainability perspective. *Tourism Management, 21*(1), 1–7.

Ritchie, J. R. B., & Crouch, G. I. (2003). *The competitive destination: A sustainable tourism perspective*. Walllingford: CABI Publishing.

Rose, G. (1997). Situated knowledges: Positionality, reflexivities and other tactics. *Progress in Human Geography, 21*, 305–320.

Schoenberger, E. (1998). Discourse and practice in human geography. *Progress in Human Geography, 22*, 1–14.

Sheppard, E. (2000). Competition in space and between places. In: E. Sheppard & T. Barnes (Eds.), *A companion to economic geography*. Oxford: Blackwell.

Sidaway, J. (2000). Recontextualizing positionality: Geographical research and academic fields of power. *Antipode, 32*, 260–270.

Sternberg, R., & Arndt, O. (2001). The firm or the region: What determines the innovation behaviour of European firms? *Economic Geography, 77*, 364–382.

Storper, M. (1997). *The regional world*. New York: Guilford Press.

Swyngedouw, E. A. (1992). The mammon quest. 'Glocalisation', interspatial competition and the new monetary order: The construction of new scales. In: M. Dunford, & G. Kaflakas (Eds.), *Cities and regions in the New Europe*, London: Belhaven.

Todtling, F., & Kaufman, A. (2001). The role of the region for innovation activities of SMEs. *European Urban and Regional Studies, 8,* 203–215.

Turner, A. (2001). *Just capital: The liberal economy.* London: MacMillan.

Webb, D., & Collis, C. (2000). Regional development agencies and the 'new regionalism' in England. *Regional Studies, 34,* 857–873.

Williams, R. (1977). *Marxism and literature,* Oxford: Oxford University Press.

World Economic Forum Global Competitiveness Network http://www.weforum.org/site/homepublic.nsf/Content/Global+Competitiveness+Programme

SECTION 4:

AN AGENDA FOR TOURISM RESEARCH

Chapter 16

An Agenda for Cutting-Edge Research in Tourism

Donna Chambers

The surest way to corrupt a young man is to teach him to esteem more highly those who think alike than those who think differently.

(Friedrich Nietzsche)

While many might wish to challenge the above quotation from Nietzsche for its patriarchy, the key point that should be highlighted here is the idea that difference is something to be celebrated and not derided. Throughout history it has been demonstrated that it is through difference that a number of ideas, many of which have revolutionised the way we think about social, economic, cultural and political phenomena, have emerged. Of course in order for one to accept and embrace difference, one must have a particular philosophical perspective or world view which recognises the 'validity' of difference. Against this background, in this chapter it will be argued that 'cutting-edge' research is about valorising different approaches to tourism research and necessarily, tourism practice. 'Cutting-edge' research is importantly, about the interrogation of established ways of seeing, being and knowing *in* tourism. In order to illustrate this point, the chapter will first, reflect on those key ideas that have emerged within the discourse of tourism and which, it is argued, have transformed the way we think about this phenomena. Second, the discussion will turn to ongoing research that is being conducted on gay tourism in Jamaica, which draws on postcolonial perspectives and which, it is suggested, presents a different way to think about this issue. Third, and finally, an agenda for tourism research that is 'cutting edge' will be proposed.

Reflections on Cutting-Edge Research in Tourism

When one thinks about the term 'cutting edge' certain words like *avant-garde*, groundbreaking, vanguard and forefront come to mind. And in this context, cutting-edge

Developments in Tourism Research
Copyright © 2007 by Elsevier Ltd.
All rights of reproduction in any form reserved.
ISBN: 978-0-080-45328-6

research in tourism can be understood as involving four separate though interrelated elements:

(a) Research that propounds novel *methodological* approaches to understanding the phenomena that is tourism
(b) Research that puts forward novel *methods* of undertaking tourism research
(c) Research that proposes novel ways of *practicing* the business of tourism and
(d) Research that offers novel *pedagogical* approaches to tourism education and training

Broadly speaking then, cutting-edge research in tourism embraces new *discourses* and *practices* of tourism. However, it is important to note that there are three main issues with the notion of 'cutting edge'. The first is that the term is necessarily culturally contingent. The concept of cultural contingency means that what is cutting edge in one cultural context might not be similarly acclaimed in a different cultural context. And in this regard culture is understood at both a macro level in the sense of *societal culture* and at a more micro institutional level as in *organizational culture*. The point here is that there is no universalism or essentialism in the concept of cutting edge. The second issue with cutting edge is that it is historically contingent. Historical contingency suggests that what is deemed to be cutting edge in a particular historical period is often subject to a degree of displacement when new understandings and realities come to light. In other words, cutting edge is not eternal or immutable. That is not to say however that one cannot discern continuities from one historical period to another. The third and possibly the most important issue with the concept of cutting edge, and which underpins both the cultural and historical contingency of the term is the question of power. For when one thinks about cutting-edge research one must distinguish it from research that is not cutting edge. And in making this determination, it is clear that some research will be included while others will be excluded. So there is an inherent problem in the notion of cutting edge, that is, in a particular culture and at a particular historical moment, who determines what is *avant-garde* or groundbreaking in research? Further, on what criteria are inclusions and exclusions based?

These ruminations on the contingency of the concept of cutting edge and questions of power have been inspired respectively, by Kuhn's (1970) notion of paradigms which challenged the objectivism of the dominant positivist approach and the Foucauldian (Foucault, 1972, 1979) notion of discourse which was subsequently further elucidated by Laclau and Mouffe (1985) in their concept of antagonisms. For Kuhn, paradigms are 'universally accepted scientific achievements that for a time provide model problems and solutions to a community of practitioners' (Kuhn, 1970, p. viii). While one can challenge Kuhn's use of the word 'universal' in this statement, there are two key issues that should be highlighted in this statement. The first is the argument that a paradigm is always subject to critique because it cannot 'explain all the facts with which it can be confronted' (Kuhn, 1970, pp. 17–18). In other words, inherent in every paradigm are discrepancies or anomalies that cannot be explained by that paradigm. This leads to the second key issue and that is the admission by Kuhn of the historical contingency of paradigms. Paradigms are historically contingent because of their inherent anomalies which might lead to the questioning of the very foundations on which the paradigm is based. In this case, Kuhn argues, a 'scientific revolution' takes place and a new paradigm emerges. However, this does not imply that the presence of anomalies inevitably leads to a scientific revolution. Indeed, a scientific revolution represents the most drastic form of paradigm change. More often what happens is that what might at first appear to be an anomaly can turn out to be solvable through adjustment and modification without the need to totally abandon the existing paradigm. That is, a new paradigm can, and often does, bear traces of the old paradigm.

Unfortunately, Kuhn did not provide satisfactory clarification of what he meant by paradigm and has been criticised for his multiple and ambiguous use of the term. However, if one were to interpret paradigm to mean a way of seeing or knowing about particular phenomena, it can be argued that there have been a number of cutting-edge paradigms in tourism since the 1960s which have defined the way that we think and know about tourism. In another sense, a paradigm can be seen as a discourse, which according to Foucault (1972) defines the limits of the sayable. Indeed, a discourse is a powerful political formulation, which for a time can define the way we think and know about tourism. Discourses are powerful because they establish boundaries between what can be included and what can be excluded, what can be said about tourism and what must remain silent. However, for Laclau and Mouffe (1985), the issue with discourses is that they can never totally dominate ways of seeing, being and knowing as there are antagonisms, which exist outside of the discourse that can challenge and destabilise it. Within tourism, many of the cutting-edge paradigms or discourses that have dominated tourism thinking and knowledge have subsequently been challenged, although one could argue that they have not been entirely displaced.

In this context, this author has identified what she believes to be five cutting-edge paradigms, which have had a significant impact on the way in which we think about tourism. However, while all of these paradigms have been subsequently critiqued, they nevertheless form the basis of much of the work that is still being done today in tourism research and are often included as fundamental aspects of most introductory tourism programmes at university level. It is recognised that by identifying just five key paradigms others have necessarily been excluded. In fact it is certain that for every 'cutting-edge' paradigm that is identified in this chapter others will be able to cite several more (or indeed might even disagree with the ones that have been selected!). However, this chapter is in no way seeking universality or claiming comprehensiveness. Rather, on the contrary, what the chapter is seeking to do is to develop an argument — that is, that within tourism studies there are cutting-edge paradigms, which have defined the way we think and know about tourism. Further, many of these paradigms have been subject to a degree of displacement, which while often not leading to a scientific revolution in Kuhn's sense, nevertheless have introduced new ways of seeing, being and knowing *in* tourism.

The first cutting-edge paradigm that will be discussed is that of authenticity. While admittedly, authenticity is not a concept that was coined or even originally discussed within the context of tourism (note, e.g., the work of Heidegger (1962) in *Being and Time* which philosophised on the meaning of authenticity), the concept nevertheless gained currency in tourism studies largely through the work of Dean McCannell (1973, 1976) who can, arguably be said to have inaugurated the polemic on authenticity within tourism studies. Of course, McCannell, in his discussion of authenticity, was himself influenced by the earlier works of scholars like Boorstin (1964) who raged against mass tourism as being comprised of *pseudo*-events which lacked authenticity and in which the tourist sought after the contrived rather than the original. While McCannell disagreed with Boorstin's singling out of the mass tourist as the only grouping seeking the 'inauthentic', McCannell nevertheless assumed that there is some objective way of determining what is contrived and what is original and further, that both notions (i.e., original and contrived) are binary oppositions.

McCannell argued that what motivates the modern tourist is a search for authenticity which is apparently absent in the tourists' day-to-day life experiences. Borrowing from Goffman's (1959) distinction between a front region and a back region, McCannell argued that the tourist's search for authenticity (the back region) cannot ever be realised and what the tourist consumes therefore is a 'staged authenticity' (a front region). The implication in McCannell's argument is that a distinction can be made between a front and a back region, the former staged authenticity and the latter its opposite, i.e., the 'reality' of the toured cultures. However, McCannell's thesis, which essentially reflected an objectivist paradigmatic approach, was subsequently challenged by constructivists who believed that this approach was too simplistic and failed to provide an adequate explanation of tourism objects and experiences. For constructivists there is no single reality or single authentic product or experience. Rather, authenticity and reality are plural and result from social constructions. Hobsbawm and Ranger (1983) refer to the invention of tradition where society constructs traditions from the past to meet the needs of the present (one such need being the quest for identity). Another influential theorist within this genre is Bruner who argues that

> *No longer is authenticity a property inherent in an object, forever fixed in time; it is seen as a struggle, a social process, in which competing interests argue for their own interpretation of history* (Bruner, 1994, p. 408).

Wang (1999) presents a cogent summary of the constructivist challenge to McCannell's more objectivist approach to authenticity thus:

> *For constructivists, tourists are indeed in search of authenticity: however, what they quest for is not objective authenticity (i.e., authenticity as originals) but* **symbolic** *authenticity which is the result of social construction. The toured objects or others are experienced as authentic not because they are originals or reality, but because they are perceived as the signs or symbols of authenticity. Symbolic authenticity has little to do with reality out there* (Wang, 1999, p. 356).

Further challenges emerged from postmodernist understandings of authenticity, which, while similar to the constructivist perspective, were much more radical as they questioned the existence of the 'real' itself. In this sense it is believed that there is no essential reality 'out there' waiting to be discovered. Indeed postmodernists believe that 'reality' is itself a construct and is often reflective of the interests of those in positions of power. Thus 'reality' becomes politically charged and what is deemed authentic often ignores and negates the voices of the powerless. Issues of concern then become what and whose authenticity is being presented to the tourist. In a postmodernist context, authenticity is always negotiated and what is presented to the tourist is the result of this process of negotiation. Waitt (2000, p. 846) notes that postmodernists redefine authenticity 'in existential or self-oriented terms, rather than by measurement against some stable autonomous reality'. Silver (1993) indicates that in much of the tourism of the Third World, what is marketed to the tourist is a notion of authenticity constructed by powerful players such as tour operators and their agents and therefore what is consumed by the tourist is not an 'authentic' culture but a marketed representation of that culture. This discussion thus renders McCannell's dichotomy between front stage and back stage irrelevant. Indeed, in the tourism literature another influential scholar on the concept of authenticity, Eric Cohen (1988), has argued that rather than searching for some nebulous objective authenticity, the postmodern tourist seeks playful enjoyment and is fully aware of the constructed nature of the toured cultures and objects. This argument is supported by Urry (1995, p. 140) who notes that the 'post-tourist finds pleasure in the multitude of games that can be played and knows that there is no authentic tourist experience'.

Today objectivist approaches to authenticity (like that of McCannell) which dominated the thinking on authenticity within tourism studies have been displaced and it is now generally accepted that authenticity means different things to different people and indeed, is historically, culturally, politically and even personally determined. There has therefore been a paradigmatic shift in approaches to authenticity and a plethora of journal articles have been written based on new understandings of authenticity, which reflect its plural meanings. Indeed, it cannot be denied that today the issue of authenticity 'runs as an obligato through tourism studies' (Hughes, 1997, cited in Apostolakis, 2003, p. 801) and is still of paramount importance in tourism discourse and practice, the latter particularly relevant to the operations of tourism establishments that promote culture, heritage and history.

The second cutting-edge paradigm in tourism that will be discussed is that of the 'tourist gaze', conceptualised by John Urry (1990) from the Foucauldian adaptation of the notion of *le regard* or the disciplinary gaze. Urry sought to explain the way in which the tourist 'gazes' or views the different scenes, landscapes, peoples, histories and cultures encountered on visits to foreign lands. It was Urry who, through his research, made the notion of the gaze central to tourism when he set out to determine how:

> *In different societies and especially within different social groups in diverse historical periods the tourist gaze has changed and developed...[how] the gaze is constructed and reinforced...who or what authorises it, what its consequences are for the 'places' which are its object, and how it interrelates with a variety of other social practices* (1990, p. 1).

Urry sought to discern how the tourist gaze was created and developed and came to be authorised and authenticated by different discourses, including education (as in the Grand Tour), health (as in restorative tourism), enlightenment (as in cultural tourism), group solidarity (as in several Japanese tourist practices) and play (with regard to the post-tourist) (1990, p. 135). He went on to note that at minimum, what produces a distinctive tourist gaze, a distinctive way of seeing, is the binary opposition between the ordinary/everyday and the extraordinary. That is, potential objects of the tourist gaze must be different in some way or other (1990, p. 11). It is important to note however, that Urry claimed that there is no single tourist gaze but several gazes. There is thus, in a Nietzschean/Foucauldian sense no 'essence' to the tourist gaze. Instead, there are several gazes, several objects of the gaze and several discourses lending authenticity to these gazes. Postmodernity, Urry contended, has opened up or democratised the tourist gaze and this meant that 'almost all spaces, histories and social activities can be materially and symbolically remade for the endlessly devouring gaze' (1990, p. 156).

Urry, through his application of Foucauldian discourse, thus brought the concept of surveillance and its consequent issues of power, firmly under the spotlight within tourism studies. This point was emphasised by Hollinshead (1999) who argued that while Urry's thesis did not explicitly recognise its indebtedness to Foucauldian analyses on the 'eye of power' or panopticism, it has nevertheless allowed for personal reflections on the nature of the relationships created between the tourist and the toured. Indeed Hollinshead states that Urry:

> *Thereby advocates for all of us in tourism (as in other domains) that we should undertake exploration not to **distant** lands but to **proximate** (but as yet uninspected) **mental territories**.* (Hollinshead, 1999, p. 15).

Since Urry's seminal thesis was published, it has been criticised on a number of fronts. One of the more insightful critiques of Urry's cutting-edge approach is that it is ocularcentric and does not take into account the physical and corporeal nature of travel and the role of the body within this context. Veijola and Jokinnen (1994), in their seminal article, indicated that the concept of the tourist gaze failed to take into account the gendered nature of the gaze (white male). Indeed it is evident that the concept of embodiment has served to destabilise the 'tyranny of the visual' thereby demonstrating the importance of the body and performance within tourism studies. Urry himself, in a second edition of his text published in 2002, acknowledged this omission by adding a chapter titled *Globalising the Gaze*, which dealt somewhat with issues of embodiment.

The third cutting-edge paradigm to be discussed is that of the host/guest which was inaugurated in tourism studies through the seminal work of Valene Smith (1977, 1989) in her edited text *Hosts and Guests* (first published in 1977 with a second edition in 1989). This text presented primarily anthropological analyses of the impact of tourism particularly on those societies visited. While there are some differences between the first and second editions of this volume, it is hereby suggested that in both volumes tourism is represented largely as being complicit in the perpetuation of the exploitative relationship between the West and the rest, that is, between the tourist guests (usually from wealthy Western, industrialised nations) and the local hosts (largely from poor, developing societies). However, while the book focuses on the negative consequences of tourism for the cultures of host societies, it is also recognised that the hosts also benefit from tourism although primarily in an economic, rather than a cultural context (this positive contribution of tourism is especially evident in the second edition). The dilemma that some of the chapters in the book present (whether explicitly or implicitly) is the extent to which the economic benefits derived from tourism is worth the loss of traditional cultural values and practices within the host communities.

This text, at the time of its emergence, was arguably, one of the first to marry anthropology so firmly with tourism and stimulated new thinking on the nature of the relationships created between tourists and locals resulting from increasingly vast movements of people across the globe. It thus stimulated a plethora of case studies, which examined this host–guest relationship.

However, in more recent years, the usefulness of this host–guest paradigm has been challenged. Specifically, Aramberri (2001) has argued that this paradigm should be discarded because 'it does not meet the challenges of explaining mass tourism, nor does it fully address the complex interactions between modern societies and pre-modern communities' (p. 738).

For Aramberri the host–guest paradigm might, arguably, be more applicable to traditional societies but it fails to explain the host–guest interactions in more mature tourism destination, which are today in the vast majority. Nor, he claims, does the paradigm explain domestic tourism. He explicitly denounces the anti-cultural commoditization of anthropological lobbyists thus:

> *Culture should not be sold by the pound; traditions must remain faithful to their sacred history (even when they are openly divisive and exclusionary?). Over and over their attempts to ignore the key forces of the present mass societies appear as a call to cultural immobility and intellectual helplessness. These are not the best tools to brush up one's theoretical discussions about tourism* (p. 758).

Notably, by the time Smith published a third edition of the book in 2001, it was evident that there was some departure from this host–guest dichotomy. Instead, this third edition presented an eclectic mix of papers including a discussion of tourism in the 21st century.

The fourth cutting-edge paradigm is that of the Tourism Area Life Cycle (TALC) which Richard Butler (1980) brought into the study of tourism. While Butler's concept of the tourism area life cycle has generated much subsequent criticism it is still seen as a useful conceptual tool for the explanation of the evolution of tourism development in destination areas (see, e.g., Agarwal, 1997). The major criticisms surrounding Butler's model include the fact that it does not address exogenous and endogenous factors that might affect the destination's development; the fact that it does not suggest the tourist numbers and time periods associated with each stage; and that it seems to suggest a certain inevitability and unilinearity of the various stages (Oppermann, 1998). Yet the tourism area life cycle has dominated the thinking on the development of tourism destinations and is still used today for its theoretical value particularly in terms of case study research where researchers' aim to either validate or refute the model. Butler has revisited the TALC model in the most recent editions of his work.

The fifth and final cutting-edge paradigm that will be discussed is that of the old tourist–new tourist dichotomy propounded by Auliana Poon (1993) in her seminal thesis titled *Tourism, Technology and Competitive Strategies.* According to Poon,

> *The standardized mass tourism of the 1960s and 1970s is being superseded by a 'new' tourism driven by advances in technology, greater sensitivity in consumer tastes and deregulation and concentration in the industry. Such tourism offers an opportunity both for increasing the sustainability of the product and for the creation of wealth in previously vulnerable destinations* (Poon 1994, p. 91).

Poon argued that in order to succeed in what was a new tourism context, organisations would need to focus on developing appropriate and effective competitive strategies. Poon's thesis, published in 1993, has formed the basis for subsequent discussions of tourist motivation and behaviour and several authors have put forward suggestions for organisations in how to develop strategies to deal with the 'new tourist'. Still, Poon's research has also been criticised on a number of fronts, most importantly on the fact that new tourism has not totally displaced old tourism but both are coexisting. Indeed, there has also emerged a kind of hybrid tourist who displays some characteristics of the new tourist and some of the old tourist. Further old tourism is still flourishing (in the form of the packaged tour) more than ten years after Poon predicted its demise.

So far in this chapter five paradigms within tourism research deemed to be 'cutting edge' have been discussed. These have been identified as cutting edge because at the time of their emergence they defined the thinking in tourism studies and came to dominate much of the research in tourism. However, their historical contingency has also been demonstrated in the sense that many of their normative assumptions about tourism have subsequently been challenged. However, it is here suggested that what has occurred is not a scientific revolution in the Kuhnian sense, but a modification and an adjustment of the mentioned cutting-edge paradigms. Indeed, new ways of thinking about tourism often bear traces of these dominant cutting-edge paradigms. It is important to note also that the cutting-edge paradigms discussed here are the result of interdisciplinary research in the sense that theories, concepts and methodologies from other disciplines like philosophy, anthropology, geography and sociology have been utilised to explain tourism phenomena. Indeed, Tribe's (1997) article on the *Indiscipline of Tourism*, which argued against seeing tourism as a discipline, still remains relevant. Indeed, one wonders whether the multifaceted nature of tourism will ever lend itself to the strictures required for disciplinary status. So that cutting-edge paradigms in tourism, it is suggested, will necessarily draw on other disciplines in order to present new ways of seeing, being and knowing *in* tourism. And in this regard the chapter will proceed to discuss ongoing research that is being conducting on gay tourism in Jamaica.

Tourism and Homosexuality in Jamaica

The research project that is to be discussed here does, it is believed, present a different way of thinking about homosexuality and tourism. This is because it emerges from a particularly Caribbean perspective and draws upon postcolonial theory to understand the attitudes of Caribbean people toward homosexuality and how this might be inconsistent with the development of a gay tourism product in the region. So far there has been a dearth of studies on homosexuality and tourism and those that have been done focus either on the gay tourist in terms of motivations and identity formation (Hughes, 1997; Clift & Forrest, 1999) or in terms of the importance of gay space and place for the gay consumer (Pritchard, Morgan, & Sedgely, 1998) or even in the context of issues of embodiment within tourism studies (Johnston, 2001). Undoubtedly, the discussion of gay tourism represents a new way of thinking about gender, sexuality, embodiment and identity within tourism studies.

However, so far there have been no studies within the tourism academy, which seek to understand the views of host societies in the developing world on gay tourism and the way in which these views are grounded in the particular cultural, religious and legal systems of these host societies. Further, there is a dearth of studies, which seek to understand how these cultural, religious and legal systems are related to the historical location of these societies as distinctly postcolonial. The particular focus of this chapter will be on the island of Jamaica, which has, arguably the oldest tourism industry in the region and is the largest English speaking island both in terms of size and population. In addition, the author is herself a Jamaican and consequently is well placed to speak about this issue.

Tourism in Jamaica, as in several countries within the Caribbean, has traditionally been considered a heterosexual phenomenon. Indeed, many of Jamaica's ubiquitous all-inclusive hotels have accepted only heterosexual couples and this is in fact consistent with the legal, cultural and religious context of the island in which attitudes to homosexuality range from a qualified tolerance to outright hostility. With regard to the legal context, the *Offences Against the Person Act*, Section 76 provides for a prison term not exceeding 10 years for 'whosoever shall be convicted of the abominable crime of buggery, committed either with mankind or with any animal' while Section 79 describes it as 'outrages on decency' the commission 'by any male person of…any act of gross indecency with another male person' (Offences Against the Person Act, 1969).

In religious terms, Jamaica is predominantly a Christian society with one of the highest densities of churches per square kilometre than anywhere else in the world and in this context homosexuality is seen as being contrary to biblical tenets. Specifically, Jamaicans still point to the following biblical passages as support for the 'sinfulness' of homosexuality. The first is the instructions given to Adam and Eve in Genesis 1:28 which mandate them to 'Be fruitful and increase in number'. The second is the story of Sodom and Gomorrah in Genesis 19, which was allegedly a city largely inhabited by homosexuals and thus destroyed by God for this iniquity. The third passage is Leviticus 20:13 which in the New International Version (NIV) of the Bible states that 'If a man lies with a man as one lies with a woman, both of them have done what is detestable. They must be put to death: their blood will be on their own heads'.

Culturally, as indicated before, attitudes range from a qualified tolerance to outright hostility. An example of the former is in this statement by a prominent Jamaican newspaper columnist:

> *Like the vast majority of Jamaicans, I in no way condone violence against homosexuals or even discrimination against them… Am I ready to cheer as gay parades with some of the more unusual looking human beings go prancing by? Not Yet!* (Abrahams-Clivio, 2004).

An example of the latter is contained in this letter to the editor of the main newspaper in Jamaica:

> *Regardless who is the spokesperson for homosexuality it cannot be right, it is a detestable act with shame and dire consequences to those who practice it* (Stennett, 2002).

However, some of the most vitriolic condemnations of homosexuality are evident in Jamaican dancehall music, which is an expression of Jamaican popular culture. Dancehall music blossomed in Jamaica during the pre-independence 1950s in Kingston's inner cities characterised by colonial legacies of poverty, overcrowding and violence amongst a largely black 'underclass'. Within the context of this kind of deprivation, dancehall music, which was largely the province of young black males, was used as a medium to express an exaggerated masculinity in the face of the emasculation of the black male (see, e.g., Cooper, 1993).

In a popular dancehall song by dancehall artiste Elephant Man (in which gay men are referred to derogatively as *chi chi* men), the artiste seemingly advocates violence against homosexuals. The artiste claims that support for his views that stem from the people of Jamaica (yuh nuh see seh a dis ya dance di people dem want? Or Don't you see that this is the dance that the people want?) and from religion (God a me backative or God supports me). For this artiste music is the tool (*music a mi tool*) available to him to express and propagate this anti-gay message. According to Stanley-Niaah (2004, p. 103) dancehall music:

> *tells the story of a people's survival and the need for a celebration of that survival against forces of imperialism and systems of exclusion. Dancehall's story is ultimately the choreographing of an identity that critiques aspects of Western domination.*

In fact, in Jamaica homosexuality is often perceived as a sexual deviance, which has been imported and imposed from the West thus representing a way of life that is non-indigenous to the island. This view of Western imposition is also expressed by the former Prime Minister of Jamaica, P.J. Patterson — in an interview with the Guardian (UK newspaper) on January 5, 2005 — when pressed to review the laws which made homosexuality illegal:

> *Let me make it very clear, the laws of Jamaica must be determined by the Parliament of Jamaica, and that right we will maintain. We will never, never, compromise.*
>
> (Aitkenhead, 2005)

However, as the forces of globalisation become more powerful and insidious, Jamaica is increasingly being criticised for its failure to conform to recent advances within the developed world, which are moving toward the legitimisation of homosexuality. In this context, the island's tourism industry, which has been the main foreign exchange earner since the 1980s and which is heavily dependent on tourist flows from the developed countries of North America and Europe is, it is proposed, being used as one of the tools to bring the country in line with current developed world thinking on homosexuality. In this context, a major Caribbean all-inclusive chain — Sandals Resorts — which is based in Jamaica but with resorts all over the Caribbean and traditionally a heterosexual couples' only resort, was banned from placing its advertisements on the London Underground in 2004 due to its unwelcoming attitudes toward homosexuals. Threats were also made that its ads would be banned from London taxis, and in the face of this economic pressure, Sandals was forced to formally withdraw its anti-gay policy (Hencke, 2004).

Against this background, the current research presents an exploratory argument, grounded in a postcolonial theoretical context and drawing on evidence from an eclectic mix of secondary sources including newspaper articles, journals, magazines and the internet, which makes two main contentions: The first is the suggestion that the negative attitudes of many Jamaicans toward homosexuality can be seen as a reflection of a wider postcolonial political struggle. The second is the argument that the pressure exerted on the island to conform to the more 'liberal', 'enlightened' attitudes of the developed, capitalist world toward homosexuality can be viewed as a form of postcolonial imperialism which is increasingly being played out in and through tourism. Indeed, recent attempts by the UK to bring Jamaica in-line with developed world thinking on homosexuality can be perceived as a form of colonial discourse in which the [former] colonised are constructed as primitive and barbaric with the aim of the imperial project being to ensure cultural and moral improvement.

Conclusion

To conclude, it is necessary to return to the title of this chapter, which is *'An Agenda for Cutting-Edge Research in Tourism'*. Based on the previous discussion, it is clear that the concept of cutting edge is historically and culturally contingent and is also underpinned by issues of power. In other words, there are some ways of thinking and knowing in and of tourism which have, for a time, dominated the study of tourism and thus have necessarily precluded other ways of seeing, being and knowing *in* tourism. However, it has also been demonstrated that these dominant paradigms or discourses have been challenged and now there are new ways of thinking and knowing about the phenomena that is tourism. Still these new ways of thinking have not entirely displaced the older paradigms although they have demonstrated their lack of fixity. It might be also that these new ways of thinking about tourism will themselves assume dominance and so on in an endless iterative process.

How then can anyone, in this context, seek to put forward an agenda for cutting-edge research? The only response to this is that while one cannot put forward any normative or universal agenda for cutting-edge research, what can be propounded are the author's own thoughts on what she believes cutting-edge research should entail. First, it is suggested that cutting-edge research in tourism should embrace novel methodologies, methods, practices and pedagogies in and of tourism which will inspire new ways of seeing, being and knowing. Many of these new perspectives will necessarily be interdisciplinary as the multifaceted nature of tourism precludes it from developing its own unique methodological and theoretical perspectives. Second, cutting-edge research should be about embracing difference, not for its own sake, but in so far as difference can open up our understanding to the multifarious discourses and practices of tourism. Finally an agenda for cutting-edge research in tourism should be self-reflective in declaring and indeed in critiquing its own paradigmatic assumptions. However, one of the challenges to developing cutting-edge research in tourism and which might inspire some apprehension and indeed fear in tourism researchers is encapsulated in a quote that has been attributed to Zalman Stern who noted that *the problem with the cutting edge is that someone has to bleed...*

References

Abrahams-Clivio, T. (2004). Homosexuality can seem shocking, hard to understand. *Jamaica Observer*, June 24, 2004.

Agarwal, S. (1997). The resort cycle and seaside tourism: An assessment of its applicability and validity. *Tourism Management, 18*(2), 65–73.

Aitkenhead, D. (2005). Their homophobia is our fault. *The Guardian*, January 5, 2005.

Apostolakis, A. (2003). The convergence process in heritage tourism. *Annals of Tourism Research, 30*(4), 795–812.

Aramberri, J. (2001). The host should get lost: Paradigms in the tourism theory. *Annals of Tourism Research, 28*(3), 738–761.

Boorstin, D. J. (1964). *The image: A guide to pseudo-events in America*. New York: Atheneum.

Bruner, E. (1994). Abraham Lincoln as authentic reproduction: A critique of postmodernism. *American Anthropologist, 96*(2), 397–415.

Butler, R. (1980). The concept of a tourism area life cycle of evolution. *Canadian Geographer, 24*, 5–12.

Clift, S., & Forrest, S. (1999). Gay men and tourism: Destinations and holiday motivations. *Tourism Management, 20*(5), 615–625.

Cohen, E. (1988). Authenticity and commoditization in tourism. *Annals of Tourism Research, 15*(3), 371–386.

Cooper, C. (1993). *Noises in the blood: Orality, gender and the 'vulgar' body of Jamaican popular culture*. London: MacMillan Caribbean.

Foucault, M. (1972). *The archaeology of knowledge*. London: Tavistock.

Foucault, M. (1979). *Discipline and punish: The birth of the prison*. London: Peregrine Books.

Goffman, E. (1959). *The presentation of self in everyday life*. Harmondsworth: Penguin.

Heidegger, M. (1962). *Being and time*. London: SCM Press.

Hencke, D. (2004). Holiday firm ends ban on gay couples. *The Guardian*, October 12.

Hobsbawm, E., & Ranger, T. (1983). *The Invention of Tradition*. Cambridge: Cambridge University Press.

Hollinshead, K. (1999). Surveillance of the worlds of tourism: Foucault and the eye-of-power. *Tourism Management, 20*(1), 7–23.

Hughes, H. (1997). Holidays and homosexual identity. *Tourism Management, 18*(1), 3–7.

Johnston, L. (2001). (Other) bodies and tourism studies. *Annals of Tourism Research, 28*(1), 180–201.

Kuhn, T. (1970). *The structure of scientific revolutions* (2nd ed.). Chicago: University of Chicago Press.

Laclau, E., & Mouffe, C. (1985). Hegemony and socialist strategy: Towards a radical democratic politics. London: Verso.

McCannell, D. (1973). Staged authenticity: Arrangements of social space in tourist settings. *American Journal of Sociology, 79*, 589–603.

McCannell, D. (1976). *The tourist: A new theory of the leisure class*. New York: Schocken Books.

Offences Against the Person Act. (1969). Kingston: Government of Jamaica.

Oppermann, M. (1998). What is new with the resort cycle? *Tourism Management, 19*(2), 179–180.

Poon, A. (1993). *Tourism, technology and competitive strategies*. Wallingford: CAB International.

Poon, A. (1994). The 'new tourism' revolution. *Tourism Management, 15*(2), 91–92.

Pritchard, A., Morgan, N., & Sedgely, D. (1998). Reaching out to the gay tourist: Opportunities and threats in an emerging market segment. *Tourism Management, 19*(3), 273–282.

Silver, I. (1993). Marketing authenticity in third world countries. *Annals of Tourism Research, 20*(2), 302–318.

Smith, V. (Ed.) (1977). *Hosts and guests: The anthropology of tourism*. Philadelphia: University of Pennsylvania Press.

Smith, V. (Ed.) (1989). *Hosts and guests: The anthropology of tourism* (2nd ed.). Philadelphia: University of Pennsylvania Press.

Smith, V., & Brent, M. (Eds.) (2001). *Hosts and guests revisited: Tourism issues of the 21st century*. New York: Cognizant Communications.

Stanley-Niaah, S. (2004). Kingston's dancehall: A story of space and celebration. *Space and Culture,* 7(1), 102–118.

Stennett, R. (2002). On gay rights vs my rights. *Jamaica Gleaner*, August 5, 2002.

Tribe, J. (1997). The indiscipline of tourism. Annals of Tourism Research, 24(3), 638–657.

Urry, J. (1990). *The tourist gaze: Leisure and travel in contemporary societies*. London: SAGE.

Urry, J. (1995). *Consuming places*. London: Routledge.

Urry, J. (2002). *The tourist gaze* (2nd ed.). London: SAGE.

Veijola, S., & Jokinnen, E. (1994). The body in tourism. *Theory, Culture and Society, 6*, 125–151.

Waitt, G. (2000). Consuming heritage: Perceived historical authenticity. *Annals of Tourism Research,* 27(4), 835–862.

Wang, N. (1999). Rethinking authenticity in tourism experience. *Annals of Tourism Research, 26*(2), 349–370.

Subject Index